LONDON'S SECRETS:
PUBS & BARS

by
Graeme Chesters

Survival Books • Bath • England

First published 2013

All rights reserved. No part of this publication
may be reproduced, stored in a retrieval system or
recorded by any means, without prior written
permission from the publisher.

Copyright © Survival Books 2013
Cover design: Di Bruce-Kidman
Cover photo: © londoniscallingus.wordpress.com
Maps © Jim Watson

Survival Books Limited
Office 169, 3 Edgar Buildings
George Street, Bath BA1 2FJ, United Kingdom
☎ +44 (0)1935-700060
✉ info@survivalbooks.net
🖥 www.survivalbooks.net

Also available as a Kindle eBook

British Library Cataloguing in Publication Data
A CIP record for this book is available
from the British Library.

ISBN: 978-1-907339-93-6

Printed in China by International Press Softcom Limited

Acknowledgements

I have been the fortunate recipient of much help, support and enthusiasm in researching and writing this book. First of all thanks are due to Peter Read for editing and proofing; Robbi Atilgan for further editing; David Woodworth for final proof reading; Di Bruce-Kidman for DTP, photo selection and cover design; Jim Watson for making my *Blue Peter*-like maps look splendid; and to the many who helped with information and provided photographs, notably Jayne Nelson at Young's, John Humphreys at Shepherd Neame, Kristel Valaydon at KV Communications and Nadia El-Kholti at Paramount. Finally, thanks to all the unnamed photographers whose beautiful images help bring the pubs and bars to life.

As ever, special thanks to my wife Louise for continuing with the pretence that writing is a proper job.

YOUR CHOICE?

Not everyone will agree with the choice of places listed in this book and many will wonder why their favourite watering hole was omitted. Well, first of all there isn't enough space to include every place, and secondly, we (reluctantly) have to admit that we don't know ALL the pubs and bars in London!

Drop us a line and let us know about your favourites and we'll try to include them in the next edition.

Information Boxes

The notes below refer to the general information provided for each pub and bar.

◆ **Address:** Includes the phone number and website (if applicable). You can enter the postcode to see a map of the location on Google (and other map sites).

◆ **Opening hours:** It's advisable to confirm the opening hours, particularly if you're travelling a long distance. Pubs near markets have special licensing hours and may open as early as 6 or 7am, while some places have no official closing time or just say 'until late' (presumably after midnight or when the last customer falls off their bar stool!). It's traditional for pubs to close later on Fri-Sat and close earlier on Sundays. Some are closed at weekends – particularly pubs located in the City of London – or on Sundays and/or Mondays.

◆ **Transport:** The nearest tube or rail station(s) is listed, although in some cases it may involve a lengthy walk. You can also travel to most venues by bus. Some pubs and bars are best reached by car, although parking may be difficult or impossible (not many central London pubs have car parks), and you'll need a sober driver to get home or to take a taxi.

◆ **Go for:** All pubs and bars included in this book have particular attractions – even if it's simply that they're traditional pubs (devoid of any frills) serving good beer and hearty pub grub – as noted.

CAMRA

The Campaign for Real Ale (CAMRA, 🖳 camra.org.uk) is an independent, voluntary organisation that campaigns for real ale, community pubs and consumer rights.

Formed in 1971 in protest against the bland processed beers produced by the big-name breweries, its aim was to encourage the production of traditional, flavoursome real ale using traditional ingredients, which are allowed to mature in the cask through a process called secondary fermentation.

CAMRA has been (and remains) hugely influential – revitalising beer brewing and drinking in the UK, where it now has over 200 branches – and has been described as the most successful consumer campaign in Europe.

Contents

Chapter 2: City & East London 110

Chapter 3: North London — 168

Chapter 4: West London   208

Chapter 5: Southwest London   242

Chapter 6: Southeast London   272

DISABLED ACCESS & FACILITIES

Many pubs and bars are accessible to disabled people,
although few make special provisions such as providing
'disabled' toilets. However, landlords are required to make
their premises accessible for people who use a wheelchair,
e.g. by providing a ramp. If you have special requirements,
contact the venue in advance.

Author's Notes

♦ **Bookings:** Many pubs/bars allow you to book a table, particularly gastropubs, although this isn't always the case. For example, most hotel bars don't accept bookings and you may have to queue for a table at busy times.

♦ **Cost:** An indication of prices is given, both for drinks and food, but generally cocktail, hotel and destination bars are the most expensive, and specialist beer and brew pubs are usually more expensive than heritage and traditional pubs. (Beer costs anything from £2.50 to £5 a pint, depending on the establishment and the pedigree of the beer.) You may also pay extra for drinks when entertainment (comedy, music, theatre, TV sports, etc.) or a late licence is provided. Some bars charge a 'members' entrance fee after a certain time – usually after most pubs have closed – or may have a minimum spend (to deter those inclined to nurse one drink all evening!). Most pubs and bars accept Visa and Mastercard, but may not accept all cards – and some pubs don't accept payments by card at all!

♦ **Families & children:** The legal age for drinking alcohol in pubs and bars in the UK is 18 (proof of age may be requested). Under-14s are only allowed into gardens, separate family rooms and the restaurant areas of pubs and wine bars, unless the premises have a special 'children's certificate', in which case children must be accompanied by an adult. Children aged 14-17 can enter a bar but may only consume soft drinks.

♦ **Food:** Most pubs and bars serve 'bar' snacks and many also serve full meals, often in a separate dining room or restaurant. Many pubs – particularly gastropubs offering fine dining – are foodie destinations in their own right, and some even have Michelin stars. Many pubs show menus and prices – for both drinks and food – on their websites, along with food serving times.

♦ **Smoking:** Since 2007, smoking has been banned in pubs and bars (and other indoor public spaces), for which there's a maximum fine of £200. Some pubs provide a heated, sheltered outdoor area for smokers, although it's more likely that you'll have to enjoy your ciggy on the pavement in the cold and rain!

The Ale House Door, Henry Singleton (c. 1790)

Introduction

B ritish pubs and bars are world famous for their unique
atmosphere, bonhomie and fine ales, while increasing numbers
are also noted for the excellence of their cuisine. Nowhere is this
diversity and quality more evident than in London, which has a
bewildering number of watering holes of all shapes and sizes: classic
historic boozers and trend-setting bars; traditional riverside inns and
luxurious cocktail lounges; welcoming wine bars and cosy brew pubs;
mouth-watering gastropubs and brasseries; sophisticated hotel bars
and raucous music venues.

The number and variety of London venues presents an obvious
challenge: which to choose? This book seeks to help, selecting the
most lauded pubs and bars of various types and in different price
bands, split over six geographical areas: central, City and East End,
north, west, southwest and southeast. Different areas tend to favour
different types of hostelry. For example, the swisher parts of west and
north London have more than their fair share of gastropubs, while the
southeast is a happy hunting ground for fans of craft beer joints. And
if you need to get suited and booted to impress a date or client with
high-end cocktails at a designer bar, the W1 postcode provides more
opportunities than most.

The venues in this book were chosen gradually and pensively,
over the course of the four years I spent criss-crossing London while
researching a series of books about the city. Indeed, a number of the
places became regular stops, where I rested, sought refuge from the
rain, made notes and reviewed photographs. They were invaluable for
their atmosphere, drinks, food and, not least, bathroom facilities; the
spectacular gents' loos at The Princess Louise, a classic Victorian gin
palace on High Holborn, deserve a special mention.

Despite having lived in the capital for decades – in northwest,
central and southeast London – and being a regular patron of its pubs
and bars, I was surprised and heartened by the choice and quality I
found. The number of innovative cocktail lounges, glamorous hotel
bars and venues with magisterial views was particularly notable, as,
indeed, was my worrying familiarity with a large number of London's
drinking dens!

So, whether you're seeking somewhere for a pint of real ale, a
glass of 'organic' wine, a designer cocktail or a delicious meal, a place
to meet and have fun with your mates or just somewhere to relax and
chill out, you're bound to find your perfect venue in London – with the
help of the insider 'secrets' in this book!

Bottoms Up!

Graeme Chesters

June 2013

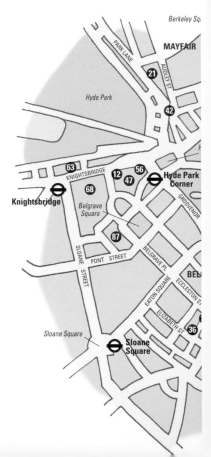

CHAPTER 1

CENTRAL LONDON

See overleaf for more maps.

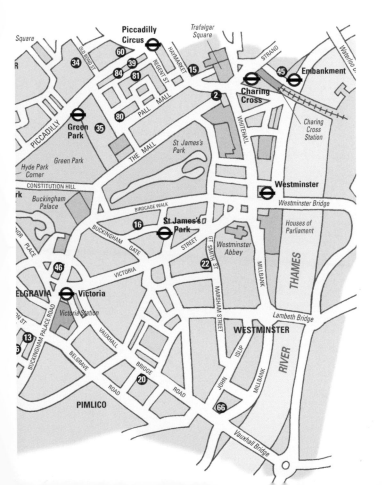

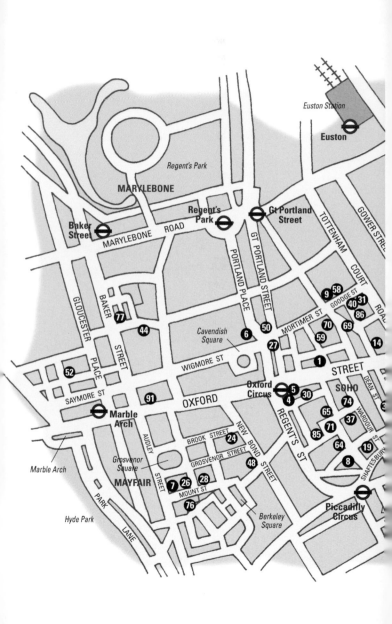

See page 14 for key.

THE ADAM & EVE

Address: 77A Wells Street, W1T 3QQ (☎ 020-7636 0717,
🖳 geronimo-inns.co.uk/theadamandeve).
Opening hours: Mon-Fri, 11am to 11pm; Sat, noon to 11pm; Sun, noon to 6pm. See website for kitchen opening times.
Transport: Oxford Circus or Tottenham Court Road tube.
Go for: The beer, wine and food – it does them all well!

This gastropub – or 'food pub' as it styles itself – is owned by Geronimo Inns, which has around 30 pubs in London. This one in Fitzrovia (or Noho, as they like to call it) has an airy, modern interior which 'pays homage to English icons', with colourful cushions, shelves full of knick-knacks, and arty prints on the walls; there are a number of outdoor tables for when the weather behaves.

The Adam & Eve offers a wide choice of British and international beer (it's a freehouse), and a regularly changing wine list chosen by John Clevely, a Master of Wine – most are available by the glass in two sizes, costing from £4 per glass and £15.50 a bottle. It also serves decent food so, in short, it has something for everyone.

Booking is recommended if you want to eat, which many do, and its 'rations' include such iconic treats as Eggs Benedict and Cumberland sausage and mash. Bar snacks are available and the service is friendly. A great all-rounder, and somewhere to escape the hubbub of Oxford Street.

THE ALBANNACH

Address: 66 Trafalgar Square, WC2N 5DS (☎ 020-7930 0066,
🖥 albannach.co.uk).
Opening hours: Mon-Sat, noon to 1am; Sun, noon to 7pm (and as below).
Transport: Charing Cross tube/rail.
Go for: Terrific choice of malt whisky in a sophisticated environment.

The Albannach is an outpost of
'Scottishness' deep in the heart of
enemy territory, close to Trafalgar
Square, generally regarded as the
geographical heart of the Sassenach
capital. It dubs itself the 'The
Albannach Restaurant and Whisky
Bar', and is split into various drinking
and eating areas.

It's a slick place – there's a smart-
casual dress code – with an emphasis on Scotch whisky, but you can
also try Irish and Japanese examples as well as bourbon; there are
over 120 in total. The Albannach also serves cocktails, not all of which
are whisky based, in its vaulted cocktail bar – the 'A Lounge' (open
Thu-Sat, 7pm-1 or 3am, Sun-Wed, special events only) – which has a
minimum spend policy of £15 per head on some nights.

19

You can also eat well at The Albannach, mainly Scottish
specialities, including haggis and fish dishes. Standards are high
throughout. This isn't a budget destination, as you might assume
from its prime location, but given the quality of the décor, service,
drinks and food, it isn't a particularly expensive one either. Booking is
recommended.

THE AMERICAN BAR

Address: Savoy Hotel, 100 Strand, WC2R 0EU (☎ 020-7836 4343,
🖥 fairmont.com/savoy-london/dining/americanbar).
Opening hours: Mon-Sat, 11.30am to midnight; Sun, noon to 11pm.
Transport: Charing Cross tube/rail.
Go for: An evocative, if expensive, treat at the spiritual home of the cocktail.

The American Bar on the Savoy Hotel's first floor evokes an atmosphere of the '20s, the so-called golden era of cocktails. It's an impressive venue, with understated Art Deco styling, elegant curves, a white ceiling and Terry O'Neill photographic portraits on the walls, while a tuxedoed pianist plays American jazz to add to the ambience.

20

It's attracted celebrities for many years and is still a smart, sophisticated place to enjoy a cocktail from the extensive, pricey list (around £14 and upwards). Bear in mind that *The Savoy Cocktail Book*, published by Savoy barman Harry Craddock in the '30s, remains the cocktail mixologist's bible, and the position of head bartender at the American Bar is still regarded as one of the hospitality trade's most prestigious. Dress the part – smart-casual or better and definitely no sportswear – and be prepared to queue as there's a no reservations policy.

It you desire an alternative to the American Bar's timeless elegance, the Savoy also houses the newer, equally glamorous **Beaufort Bar** (see page 27).

AQUA SPIRIT

Address: 240 Regent Street, W1F 7EB – entrance at 30 Argyll Street – (☏ 020-7478 0540, ▭ aqua-london.com).
Opening hours: Mon-Sat, noon to 1am; closed Sun.
Transport: Oxford Circus tube.
Go for: Cocktails and champagne served with glamour and great views.

This bar and restaurant complex at the top of what used to be Dickens and Jones department store comprises Aqua Nueva, a Spanish restaurant; Aqua Kyoto, a Japanese restaurant; and Aqua Spirit, a glamorous cocktail bar. The latter's roof terrace makes it one of London's most desirable places to enjoy a drink on a warm summer evening.

21

The inside space is chic and sleek with a round bar, while the terrace has a wooden floor, comfortable chairs and great views. Bookings aren't accepted for the terrace, so arrive early if you want a seat. Views vary depending on where you sit, and can include the BT Tower, Liberty and the London Eye, among other landmarks.

As for drinks, there's a list of around 30 cocktails, priced at £9.50-15. Champagne costs from £14.50 per glass and £72.50 a bottle, while there's a choice of seven wines from £7 per glass and £28 a bottle. In addition to a couple of beer choices, there's a wide selection of spirits, notably rum and tequila. All this is enjoyed by a well-groomed (and well-off) clientele at this effortlessly upmarket spot.

THE ARGYLL ARMS

Address: 18 Argyll Street, W1F 7TP (☎ 020-7734 6117, 🖳 nicholsonspubs.
co.uk/theargyllarmsoxfordcircuslondon).
Opening hours: Mon-Thu, 10am to 11.30pm; Fri-Sat, 10am to midnight;
Sun, 10am to 11pm.
Transport: Oxford Circus tube.
Go for: Wonderful Victorian décor and excellent ale.

There's been a pub here since 1742,
when Argyll Street was built, but the
current establishment dates from
1869 and was remodelled in the
1890s. It's a large, Grade II listed,
Nicholson's establishment, with lots
of original Victorian fittings, including
etched glass, mahogany, mirrors and an ornate plaster ceiling. It
also has screened-off drinking areas known as 'snugs' and designed
to separate the social classes (something the status-conscious
Victorians were keen on).

The Argyll Arms might be sited at one of London's busiest
pedestrian hubs, but it's relaxed inside and has a 'beer menu' with
a wide range of well-kept British and international brews. You can
taste before ordering, with a 'sip before you sup' approach, while the
upstairs bar has table service for the traditional pub grub on offer.

As you'd expect from its central location, the pub attracts a varied
international crowd, which is younger and livelier on Fri-Sat nights. So
go at other times if you want a contemplative pint in one of London's
best late Victorian pub interiors.

THE ARTESIAN

Address: Langham Hotel, 1C Portland Place, Regent Street, W1B 1JA
(☎ 020-7636 1000, 🖥 artesian-bar.co.uk).
Opening hours: Mon-Sat, noon to 2am; Sun, noon to midnight.
Transport: Oxford Circus tube.
Go for: Great design, fine cocktails – somewhere to really spoil someone.

One of London's most attractive bars in one of its grandest hotels, the Artesian is a triumph of classic-meets-contemporary design. Recently updated by the noted David Collins Studio, it blends the Victorian – marble bar, embroidered napkins and mirrors – with the modern: purple, leather-effect upholstery, ornate wood panelling and an extravagant 'Chinese Chippendale' centrepiece, as the pagoda-like back bar is called.

Rum is a speciality here, with around 50 on offer, which the Artesian claims is London's largest selection. There's an extensive champagne list and an excellent choice of cocktails – it was winner of Tales of the Cocktail's 'World's Best Cocktail Menu' in 2011. The Artesian also prides itself on its 'gourmet bar food', and has faultless (yet friendly) service.

The dress code is smart-casual and the location, opposite Broadcasting House, means you might see or hear the odd familiar face or voice. It isn't the place for a cheap date, but neither is it ruinously expensive, considering the Artesian was voted the 'World's Best Bar' by Drinks International in 2012.

23

THE AUDLEY

Address: 41-43 Mount Street, W1K 2RX (☎ 020-7499 1843,
🖳 taylor-walker.co.uk/pub/audley-mayfair/c3003).
Opening hours: Mon-Sat, 11am to 11pm; Sun, noon to 10.30pm.
Transport: Bond Street or Green Park tube.
Go for: One of London's finest Victorian pub interiors.

A Taylor Walker pub, this is a grand, showy Victorian establishment spread over three floors in a building that used to be a hotel. The exterior is clad with attractive pale pink terracotta tiles and the large arched windows are decorated with flower-filled window boxes.

As befits its location in prestigious Mayfair, the interior resembles a gentlemen's club, with gilded and polished wood, original crystal chandeliers, a fine mahogany clock and a red ceiling, giving a warm, welcoming ambience for the locals and tourists who patronise the Audley. It's smart, certainly, as you'd expect in this part of town, but also relaxed and civilised with good service, and offers drinkers a range of beer – and an extensive wine list. It also serves reasonable pub grub and has a dining room and an outdoor terrace. They must be doing something right, at least in the eyes of our American friends at the nearby US Embassy on Grosvenor Square: Michelle Obama brought her children here for fish and chips in 2009, suggesting that it provides an authentic English experience.

24

BAR AMÉRICAIN AT BRASSERIE ZEDEL

Address: 20 Sherwood Street, W1F 7ED (☏ 020-7734 4888,
🖥 brasseriezedel.com/bar-americain).
Opening hours: Daily, 4.30pm to midnight.
Transport: Piccadilly Circus tube.
Go for: Opulent decor, classic cocktails and an authentic speakeasy style.

London has a number of bars modelled on the Prohibition era
theme and this is one of the best conceived and executed. It's in the
basement of the former Regent Palace Hotel, which was Europe's
largest hotel when it was built in 1915, and is next door to the classic
Parisian Brasserie Zédel.

The plush bar has enticing Art Deco decor, with gold-panelled
rooms, dark wood panelling, tiger print carpets and elegant lamps.
It provides the ambience of being aboard an ocean liner during the
golden era of transatlantic travel.

Cocktails and champagne are the drinks of choice. There's
a succinct list of six classic cocktails and six house cocktails, all
good quality, costing £9.75 and served with nibbles. Of the eight
champagnes, six are available by the glass as well as the bottle;
glasses cost from £12.30, bottles from £67.50. There's also a
selection of cognacs and American whiskeys, and list of around 20
wines, some of which can be bought by the glass (prices start from
£5.90 a glass and £32 a bottle). Great service, drinks and décor
combine to make this an ideal venue for an important date.

BARRICA

> **Address:** 62 Goodge Street, W1T 4NE (☎ 020-7436 9448, 🖳 barrica.co.uk).
> **Opening hours:** Mon-Fri, noon to 11.30pm; Sat, 1-11.30pm; closed Sun.
> **Transport:** Goodge Street or Tottenham Court Road tube.
> **Go for:** The great choice of Spanish wine and sherry.

This Iberian outpost in Fitzrovia draws the punters with its choice of Spanish wine and sherry, and enjoyable, reasonably-priced food. It's a bright, modern bar, with yellow walls, a black and white tiled floor and plenty of tables. The 'homeland' is celebrated with Iberico hams suspended from the ceiling and Spanish-themed posters on the walls.

There are over 20 sherries to sample, and more than 100 white, red, rose and sparkling wines, including some rather good offerings and a fair smattering of rare ones. They take wine storage seriously here, with the reds stored in a temperature-controlled cabinet. Helpful tasting notes are provided for the wines, along with suggestions of food matches from the selection of artfully-presented, good-quality tapas.

Barrica is popular, both with the area's media workers and those from further afield. It appeals to those after a quick beer or fino and plate of almonds, as well as to wine geeks and foodies looking to settle in for the evening, and booking is recommended for this friendly and professional venue.

26

THE BEAUFORT BAR

Address: Savoy Hotel, 100 Strand, WC2R 0EW (☎ 020-7836 4343,
🖥 fairmont.com/savoy-london/dining/beaufortbar).
Opening hours: Mon-Sat, 5pm to 1am; Sun, 2.30-6.30pm for the Art
Decadent Tea.
Transport: Charing Cross tube/rail.
Go for: Art Deco glamour, champagne – and a super-indulgent afternoon tea.

The Beaufort is the Savoy's newcomer on the bar front, and while it's less feted than the **American Bar** (see page 20), it's arguably more atmospheric and plush. It's quite the glamour puss, in fact, with a stunning interior – a riot of gold leaf and black velvet – sleek service and fine drinks.

It specialises in 'champagne, cocktails and cabaret', and offers one of London's better choices of champagne by the glass, from around £16 upwards. Cocktail aficionados should choose the American Bar, however, as the Beaufort's list is less extensive. Its USP is its Art Decadent Tea served on Sunday afternoons – an

alcohol-infused afternoon tea which includes champagne and 'Tipsy Tea' cocktails alongside the sandwiches and scones.

Like its counterpart, this is a place to dress up for – smart-casual at the very least – and, similarly, you may have to queue to gain entry, as there's a no reservations policy. Last, but not least, don't forget to fill your wallet or have somebody else pay. This is a glamorous, high-end venue, as shown by the £62.50 per head price tag for the Art Decadent Tea.

BEDFORD & STRAND

Address: 1A Bedford Street, WC2E 9HH (☎ 020-7836 3033,
🖳 bedford-strand.com).
Opening hours: Mon-Fri, noon to midnight; Sat, 5pm to midnight; closed Sun.
Transport: Covent Garden tube or Charing Cross tube/rail.
Go for: A tasty bistro with a broad wine list and good-value eats.

This basement venue in Covent Garden stands out from the tourist traps and bland restaurant chains that rather dominate this area. The name is an American-style play on its location, which is the corner of Bedford Street and the Strand, and it bills itself (accurately) as a bistro, wine bar and delicatessen, with seasonal French and British cooking.

28

The extensive, reasonably priced selection of wines is the draw for many punters, with a mix of Old and New World offerings. A couple of dozen are available by the glass or carafe, as well as by the bottle, and some sherries and champagnes are also sold by the glass. The bar area is partitioned from the white-tableclothed dining room, which offers bistro fare of good quality, while a separate deli counter serves charcuterie and finger foods to those wishing to snack on something lighter.

Bedford & Strand has become popular with discerning local workers who like the clean décor, relaxed atmosphere and attractive quality and prices, and it also draws passing tourists, therefore booking is recommended.

THE BLUE BAR

Address: Berkeley Hotel, Wilton Place, SW1X 7RL (☎ 020-7235 6000, ⌨ the-berkeley.co.uk/knightsbridge-bars/blue-bar).
Opening hours: Mon-Sat, 9am to 1am; Sun, 9am to 11pm.
Transport: Hyde Park Corner tube.
Go for: Excellent cocktails and wines at one of London's smartest hotel bars.

Designed by the celebrated David Collins, this bar lives up to its name, with a 'Lutyens Blue' colour scheme that encompasses its chairs, plasterwork and leather menus. These are set against a white onyx bar and black crocodile print leather floor, the Rococo and Art Deco detailing twinned with oversized armchairs (big enough for the largest of bottoms), red lampshades and soft lighting.

Staff are professional and understated, and there's none of the snootiness you sometimes find in these venues; everyone is treated the same. It's an intimate space, with a capacity of around 60 people, so it doesn't feel soulless like some larger hotel bars. The drinks are as classy as the environment: cocktails are excellent, and there are also some high-end wines (a number available by the glass) and whiskies (over 50), as well as tapas-type snacks.

It isn't cheap, of course, but then this is an prestige, treat-yourself, people-spotting establishment, with the usual smart-casual dress code, and is regarded by many to be one of London's finest bars.

29

BOISDALE OF BELGRAVIA

Address: 15 Eccleston Street, SW1W 9LX (☎ 020-7730 6922, 🖳 boisdale.co.uk/belgravia).
Opening hours: Mon-Fri, noon to 1am; Sat, 6pm to 1am; closed Sun.
Transport: Victoria tube/rail.
Go for: A vast range of whisky, wine and cigars, accompanied by excellent jazz.

A Scottish-themed Belgravia bar and restaurant (with a City outlet at 202 Bishopsgate and one at Canary Wharf on Cabot Place), the Boisdale's décor is an interesting blend of tacky and upscale, and not a place to go if you loathe tartan.

But it's club-like and comfortable, with a lively atmosphere and smart-casual dress code. Admission is £5 up to 10pm, £12 after, usually well justified by the quality of the jazz that's invariably playing here. You can eat and the food is excellent, if pricey – Boisdale is famous for its steaks – but for many, the drinks are the main attraction.

As might be expected in a place that celebrates all things Scots, there's a huge choice of malt whisky (more than 250) and also a vast wine list (400 plus), particularly strong on claret (the red wine of Bordeaux); the drinks list contains detailed tasting notes. Boisdale also has a wide range of cigars, and smoking is allowed on the bookable covered and heated terrace. In short, a place for old-school indulgence, but don't forget your platinum credit card.

BRADLEY'S SPANISH BAR

Address: 42-4 Hanway Street, W1T 1UT (☎ 020-7636 0359, 🖥 bradleysspanishbar.co.uk).
Opening hours: Mon-Thu, noon to 11.30pm; Fri-Sat, noon to midnight; Sun, 3-10.30pm.
Transport: Tottenham Court Road tube.
Go for: Nicely tatty, bohemian charm.

Inauspiciously situated in an alley near Tottenham Court Road tube station, Bradley's has been around for over 50 years, so it's obviously doing something right. It's a dark, two-floor affair, with a tiny bar at street level and a larger one below, and plenty of nooks and crannies for drinkers.

It's hard to put your finger on the appeal of this popular bar, as it's slightly tatty with some cheesy Spanish decor, famously bad loos and a fairly limited (international) drinks selection. You can enjoy some Spanish beers, such as Mahou; there's a small wine list, starting at around £12.50 a bottle, and a wide choice of spirits, including tequila.

31

Part of the attraction is the jukebox, one of the few to still spin vinyl and well stocked with classic rock. And Bradley's doesn't have any pretensions as a foodie joint: there are no tapas, unless you count crisps, nuts and pork scratchings. Best of all is the bohemian, congenial atmosphere. It's hard to pin down, but the place has a quirky *no sé qué* (*je ne sais quoi*) that keeps punters coming back for more.

THE BRUMUS BAR

Address: Haymarket Hotel, 1 Suffolk Place, SW1Y 4BP (☎ 020-7470 4000, 🖳 firmdalehotels.com/london/haymarket-hotel).
Opening hours: Mon-Sat, 7am to midnight; Sun, 8am to 11pm.
Transport: Piccadilly Circus tube.
Go for: A relaxed cocktail or two in Theatreland.

The Haymarket Hotel is situated in the heart of London's theatre district and its Brumus Bar is a convenient place to rest your feet and revive your equilibrium before or after visiting one of the West End's attractions. The décor is bright and lively, with lots of pinks and reds, and a wooden board floor. The backs of the bar stools and some of the armchairs have striking silhouettes of dogs.

Cocktails are a speciality here, with a mix of classic and designer mixes, priced from around £11 which is about par for an upmarket hotel bar. There's also a good wine list, with many wines available by the glass. Prices are quite high – there aren't many bottles under £30 and bubbly starts from £56. Glasses of wine start at £7.50, with champagne from £12.25.

You can eat in the restaurant and there's also bar food, including tapas-type snacks (£3.50-5) and sharing platters (£16.50-18.50). The pre-post theatre meal is good value at £19.95 for three courses. As for atmosphere, there's no pomposity here, and the relaxed ambience extends to both staff and clientele.

THE BUCKINGHAM ARMS

Address: 62 Petty France, SW1H 9EU (☎ 020-7222 3386,
🖥 youngs.co.uk/pub-detail.asp?pubid=365).
Opening hours: Mon-Fri, 11am to 11pm; Sat-Sun, 11am to 6pm.
Transport: St James's Park tube.
Go for: Decent ale in an attractive, traditional pub.

The Buckingham Arms and **The Star Tavern** (see page 104) have
the distinction of being the only two London pubs to appear in every
edition of the CAMRA (Campaign for Real Ale) *Good Beer Guide*.
The Buckingham is located in Petty France (the name comes from
Petit France, as it once had a community of Huguenots, members of
the Protestant Reformed Church of France), in front of the Wellington
barracks and just down the road from the Ministry of Justice.

It's an attractive Victorian pub dating from the early 19th century,
with leather armchairs and a nice mirrored back bar. There's an
interesting side corridor which has an elbow ledge for drinkers and the
pub will appeal to fans of traditional, non-pretentious venues serving
well-kept ale.

As well as Wells and Young's beer, there are two guest ales, often   33

including something from
Sambrook's, the Battersea-
based brewer. In view of the
pub's location, its clientele
is made up of civil servants,
soldiers and tourists who've
wandered slightly off the
beaten track.

CAFÉ DES AMIS

Address: 11-14 Hanover Place, WC2E 9JP (☎ 020-7379 3444,
📧 cafedesamis.co.uk).
Opening hours: Mon-Sat, noon to 11.30pm; Sun, noon to 8pm.
Transport: Covent Garden tube.
Go for: A cosy, comfortable place to enjoy wine.

This well-established Gallic bolthole in Covent Garden is, like **Bedford
& Strand** (see page 28), a haven of civilisation in a sometimes fraught
and chaotic part of London. It's both a restaurant, serving solid, tasty
brasserie fare in a space with cosy corners and chandeliers (the set
menus are especially good value), and a bar.

Located in the cellar, the bar is modern and understated with nicely
subdued lighting. Its wine list isn't extensive but is of sound quality, not
just French but international – from around £16.50 a bottle or £4.45 a
glass. Brief tasting notes are provided, which is useful for non-experts.
The bar also has a food menu, including French classics, baguettes
and platters of charcuterie and cheese for sharing.

The atmosphere at Café des Amis is friendly, the service
professional, prices competitive
and it's in a central location:
a sure recipe for success. As
a result, it's popular with local
workers – including actors,
ballet dancers and opera
singers from the nearby cultural
spots – therefore booking is
recommended.

THE CALTHORPE ARMS

Address: 252 Gray's Inn Road, WC1X 8JR (☎ 020-7278 4732,
🖥 youngs.co.uk/pub-detail.asp?pubid=265).
Opening hours: Mon-Sat, 11am to 11.30pm; Sun, noon to 10.30pm.
Transport: King's Cross tube/rail.
Go for: A quiet pint in a traditional local.

Dating from the early Victorian period, this Grade II listed establishment is situated where Bloomsbury meets Clerkenwell and Holborn, which isn't generally regarded as a hotbed of fine drinking dens. Indeed, the Calthorpe Arms is something of rarity in central London: a friendly, traditional corner pub.

35

The interior is brown and cream, with a cosy and nicely 'lived-in' ambience. It's a Young's establishment and stocks their usual range of beer and, sometimes, guest ales too. They're well cared for, as a number of CAMRA (Campaign for Real Ale) awards testify, and the pub is a long-term entrant in the *Good Beer Guide*.

Prices are reasonable and hearty, traditional food is available, too, including a good Sunday lunch – there are no gastro pretensions or prices here. In short, this is an old-school, local boozer, a good place for a pensive pint and a plate of filling pub grub. Some might find it rather plain and quiet, while others will love it for the same reason.

EL CAMION

Address: 25-7 Brewer Street, W1F 0RR (☎ 020-7734 7711, 🖳 elcamion.co.uk).
Opening hours: Mon-Sat, noon to 3am; Sun, noon to 11pm. The Pink Chihuahua Cocktail Bar opens Mon-Sat, 6pm to 3am.
Transport: Piccadilly Circus tube.
Go for: Tequila, margaritas and a plate of nachos to soak it up.

El Camion's restaurant and its basement cocktail bar The Pink Chihuahua share a gaudy skulls-and-sombreros décor which recalls Mexico's *Dia de los Muertos* (Day of the Dead). It may sound morbid, but the restaurant is authentic and the bar is fun, especially after 10pm when it begins to fill up.

The Soho branch is El Camion's second outlet – the original is on Portobello Road – and aims to 'bring a little bit of Baja California to London'. It serves good drinks and Mexican-style food (burritos, nachos, tacos, etc.) via an efficient, friendly table service. Not surprisingly, it's strong on tequila, with a decent range of *blanco* (white), *reposado* (rested) and *anejo* (aged) examples to try; aficionados sip the better ones neat. Individual shots cost from around £2.75 to £7, depending on their age and quality.

El Camion also serves good margaritas (£6.50 and £7.50) and a few other cocktails, and has a range of bottled Mexican beers as well as a short wine list, including a Mexican Chardonnay! Its affability, affordability and late licence have made it popular, therefore it's a good idea to book.

THE CASK PUB & KITCHEN

Address: 6 Charlwood Street, SW1V 2EE (☎ 020-7630 7225,
🖥 caskpubandkitchen.com).
Opening hours: Mon-Sat, noon to 11pm; Sun, noon to 10.30pm.
Transport: Pimlico tube.
Go for: A tremendous choice of ale in a beer lovers' den.

Although slightly off the
beaten track – in Pimlico
– and only in existence
since 2009, the Cask is
already winning awards and
now has a sister venue in
Clerkenwell, the **Craft Beer
Company** (see page 126).
It's part of the new(ish) type
of drinking establishment – a
cross between a pub, a bar
and a restaurant – which
aims to combine the best

37

British real ale with fine international keg and bottled beer, to offer
clients both quality and choice.

It's easy to overlook the Cask Pub & Kitchen, as it's unimpressive
from the outside and located on an ugly '70s council estate. But the
bar's interior is rather better, large and airy, though not the cosiest
of environments. Staff are friendly and there's an interesting mix of
clientele: locals, office workers, tourists and CAMRA types. Food is
good, too.

As for the all-important beer, there are around nine real ales on
tap, with BrewDog, Dark Star and Thornbridge featuring regularly.
There's also a huge bottled selection, including craft beers from such
far-away places as Japan and New Zealand, and all beers, including
draught ales, are available to take away.

CHINA TANG

> **Address:** The Dorchester, 53 Park Lane, W1K 1QA (☎ 020-7629 8888, 🖥 thedorchester.com/china-tang).
>
> **Opening hours:** Mon-Fri, 11am to 3.30pm (4pm Sat-Sun) and 5.30pm to midnight daily.
>
> **Transport:** Hyde Park Corner tube.
>
> **Go for:** Cocktails, glamour and atmosphere with an Oriental twist.

The brainchild of Hong Kong businessman and socialite Sir David Tang, this is a luxurious cocktail bar in '30s Art Deco style, that's redolent of Shanghai between the world wars. Situated in the Dorchester's basement, China Tang is certainly swish, with a hint of the cinematic. One of London's most opulent destinations, it's probably better than the hotel's own bars and not as crushingly busy as you might expect.

It's an intimate space, decorated with antiques and birdcages hanging from the ceiling, a fine venue to sip classic cocktails and snack from the dim sum menu. (The associated restaurant serves upscale Cantonese food, which is expensive and receives mixed reviews.) Fans of single malt whisky and wine are also catered for.

The bar attracts its fair share of celebrities and has a lively, fun atmosphere, with obliging staff. As you might expect, it's a high-end, pricey destination, so be prepared to dress up and get into the spirit of things – and try to not to choke on your spring roll when you receive the bill!

THE CINNAMON CLUB

Address: 30-32 Great Smith Street, SW1P 3BU (☎ 020-7222 2555, 🖥 cinnamonclub.com).
Opening hours: Library Bar: Mon-Sat, 11am to 11.45pm; closed Sun.
Club Bar: Mon-Sat, 4-11.45pm; closed Sun.
Transport: St James's Park or Westminster tube.
Go for: Cocktails, wine, sleek service and excellent Indian food.

The area around Westminster Abbey was traditionally a wasteland for those in search of a drink, so this Grade II listed former library's current incarnation as a prestigious Indian restaurant and bar (since 2001) has been welcome.

There are, in fact, two bars, very different in style and atmosphere: the Library Bar on the ground floor, which was originally the library's reading room and which retains that relaxed ambience, with shelves displaying books alongside bottles of wine; and the Cinnamon Club Bar, which is much funkier and has a contemporary minimalist decor, including projection screens, leather walls and cosy seating alcoves.

Cocktails are taken seriously here and there's an impressive wine list. Indeed, the Cinnamon Club restaurant holds 'Wine and Spice' events at which Individual dishes and wines are matched, while its other food 'specials' are light years away from the high street curry house experience. Service is sleek and professional, the dress code is smart-casual and prices are accordingly high. Not surprisingly, the colonial, club-like atmosphere draws some of the area's political power brokers – but don't let that put you off!

THE CITTIE OF YORK

Address: 22 High Holborn, WC1V 6BN (☎ 020-7242 7670).
Opening hours: Mon-Sat, noon to 11pm; closed Sun.
Transport: Chancery Lane or Holborn tube.
Go for: History, atmosphere and keenly-priced beer.

This Sam Smith's establishment looks as if it could be one of London's oldest pubs and a sign outside states that there's been a tavern here since 1430. There has, but the current one is a rebuild dating from only 1924 – although it's claimed that some of the original 15th-century material was used – and the pub has only been known by its current Olde English-sounding name since 1979.

Despite the somewhat faux antiquity, the Cittie of York is Grade II listed, and is an impressive space, a large, warren-like pub with more than a hint of baronial hall. There's a vaulted ceiling, a notably long bar and numerous side booths, originally designed for lawyers to have undisturbed chats and refreshments with their clients – this part of town is London's legal heartland. Overhead, and slightly alarmingly, huge wine butts are suspended from the ceiling.

As for drinks, there's a limited choice of beer, including the usual keenly-priced Sam Smith's offerings. This is a pub for an atmospheric, inexpensive night out in an unusual environment – not the sort of place that grows on trees in central London.

CLARIDGE'S BAR

Address: 49 Brook Street, W1K 4HR (☎ 020-7629 8860, 💻 claridges.co.uk/
mayfair-bars/claridges-bar).
Opening hours: Mon-Sat, noon to 1am; Sun, noon to midnight.
Transport: Bond Street tube.
Go for: Cocktails and champagne in an uber-glamorous environment.

41

One of London's finest hotels has, appropriately, one of its finest
cocktail bars. Designed by the noted David Collins, this is a sleek,
opulent venue in Art Deco style. There's a silver-leafed ceiling, green
glass chandelier and red leather banquettes, while the round tables
are decorated with a single dark red rose. But it isn't an intimidating
place and the staff are unstuffy and pleasant, attentive but discreet.

The atmosphere is both buzzy and sophisticated, and you should
dress up to fit in; 'elegant smart-casual' is the minimum required. It's
deservedly popular, regarded as one of London's best spots for a
cocktail or glass of champagne, with a wide choice of the latter. It isn't
the place for a cheap date, of
course; expect to pay from
around £25 for a couple of
drinks (or a lot more, if you
choose).

Claridges is a small
bar, with a capacity of no
more than around 70. This,
combined with the no-
reservations policy, means
that you might have to
queue to get in.

THE COACH & HORSES

Address: 29 Greek Street, W1D 5DH (☎ 020-7437 5920,
🖥 coachandhorsessoho.co.uk).
Opening hours: Mon-Thu, 11am to 11.30pm; Fri-Sat, 11am to midnight; Sun,
noon to 10.30pm.
Transport: Leicester Square or Piccadilly Circus tube.
Go for: Bonhomie, location, nostalgia – and veggie food.

42 Not just a Soho institution, the Coach and Horses on Greek Street is one of London's most famous pubs. Much of this is down to former landlord Norman Balon, who retired in 2006. He was famously rude and foul-mouthed (although reputed to have a heart of gold) and punters used to queue up to be insulted or barred by him.

The pub also has a long history of attracting London's famously thirsty journalists, particularly the infamous *Spectator* columnist Jeffrey Bernard, who wrote the magazine's *Lowlife* column, mainly about his own dissolute, drunken adventures. *Private Eye* also has a long association with the Coach, holding its fortnightly lunch upstairs.

It's a slightly shabby place, but attracts a (large) friendly, mixed crowd, many of whom drink outside, as it's a good spot from which to observe Soho going about its business. There's also a selection of good beer, although availability can be a bit mixed. A piano is the source of regular sing-alongs, while the pub's food menu claims it to be 'London's first vegetarian pub', serving such culinary treats as tofu and chips. Jeffrey Bernard would surely disapprove!

THE COBURG BAR

Address: The Connaught, Carlos Place, W1K 2AL (☎ 020-7499 7070, 🖥 the-connaught.co.uk/mayfair-bars/coburg_bar).
Opening hours: Sun-Mon, 8am to 11pm; Tue-Sat, 8am to 1am.
Transport: Bond Street or Green Park tube.
Go for: Cocktails, whisky and discreet luxury.

This is one of two bars at this renowned Mayfair hotel (see **The Connaught Bar** on page 45), the less well-known of the pair (for now). It's a stylish, Parisian-designed establishment, with luxurious wingback chairs in velvet and leather, and black glass tables. The Coburg is sophisticated, certainly, as well as discreet and elegant, but it isn't intimidating, which can't be said for all such bars; the staff manage to be friendly and slightly formal at the same time.

It's noted for its cocktails and whisky – its drinks menu reads like a chronological history of the cocktail and also lists around 75 different whiskies – and also has a fine wine list, specialising in French wines. Good quality nibbles are free and cocktails come with a palate-cleansing sliver of iced fruit, served on a silver dish.

These touches all help to justify and soften the blow of the prices, which are high. But this is an exceptional hotel bar, somewhere to treat yourself and/or impress others. So fill your wallet, dress up the part and enter into the spirit of things.

43

THE COCK TAVERN

Address: 27 Great Portland Street, W1W 8QG (☎ 020-7631 5002).
Opening hours: Mon-Sat, 11am to 11pm; Sun, noon to 10.30pm.
Transport: Oxford Circus tube.
Go for: Fine Victorian décor and fairly-priced beer.

This Sam Smith's pub is an attractive Victorian pile full of original features, including ornate cornicing, patterned tiled floors and decorative frosted-glass snob screens. These last could be opened or closed, and shielded gentlemen from customers in the other bars and/or the bar staff. This was important to the status-conscious Victorians, who liked to keep their identity, business and drinking habits to themselves. How times change.

As well as the nicely ornate interior, four huge glass lanterns decorate the outside of the pub. It also has a beautiful terracotta frieze above the first floor windows and a corner turret extending to roof level in the Victorian 'look at me' fashion; the corner position is no coincidence, as it maximises visibility.

44

It's a popular place, with a mixture of locals and tourists, drawn by the typically inexpensive Sam Smith's range of beer and the opportunity to escape the chaos of nearby Oxford Street. The Cock Tavern isn't a particularly large pub, so arrive early if you want to bag a seat.

THE CONNAUGHT BAR

Address: The Connaught, Carlos Place, W1K 2AL (☏ 020-7499 7070,
🖥 the-connaught.co.uk/mayfair-bars/connaught-bar).
Opening hours: Mon-Sat, 4pm to 1am; closed Sun.
Transport: Bond Street or Green Park tube.
Go for: The house martini, in understated, elegant surroundings.

This is the more famous of this noted Mayfair hotel's two bars (see
The Coburg Bar on page 43) and is an ultra-stylish drinking den, its
look inspired (rather obscurely) by English Cubist and Irish '20s art.
It's another David Collins design, with a pastel palette of lilac, pink,
pistachio and silver. The Art Deco styling is in leather, marble and metal.

45

Voted the World's Best Hotel Bar 2010, the Connaught Bar is cosy
and understated, with subtle lighting and excellent service. Drinks
are of good quality and there's some pleasing pizzazz about the way
they're served. Complimentary nibbles help to stave off hunger and
if you want something more substantial, there's good food from the
hotel's noted chef, Helene Darroze. Cocktails are a speciality here
and the hotel is especially renowned for its perfect martinis, which
are quietly stirred, never shaken (sorry, Mr Bond). There's also a wide
choice of fine wine and
champagne.

This excellent bar
is expensive, but it
effortlessly manages to
combine 21st-century
style with considerable
Old World charm, the
type of place where
you're made to feel
special by the friendly,
professional staff.

THE CORK & BOTTLE

Address: 44-6 Cranbourn Street, WC2H 7AN (☎ 020-7734 7807,
🖳 thecorkandbottle.co.uk).
Opening hours: Mon-Sat, 11am to 11.30pm; Sun, noon to 10.30pm.
Transport: Leicester Square tube.
Go for: A vast choice of wine and a convivial atmosphere.

This is something of a beacon of civilisation in the messy chaos
surrounding Leicester Square, which is depressingly dominated by bland,
high-street chain bars and restaurants. The Cork & Bottle has been here
since 1971, the brainchild of a Kiwi, Don Hewitson, who wanted to offer
people a decent glass of wine and something good to eat with it.

It's a basement establishment, reached via a narrow, spiral
staircase; at ground level, it's just a doorway with an awning above,
so keep your eyes peeled. The cosy wine bar below has a large,
interesting and varied wine list running to more than 300 wines; it's
worth taking the time to peruse it (perhaps on the website, before
you go). The bar isn't cheap, but considering that it's just around the
corner from Leicester Square tube, it isn't particularly expensive either.

Many choose to eat as well as imbibe and there's good-quality,
robust wine bar food on offer, such as its legendary raised ham
and cheese pie. The Cork & Bottle attracts a loyal clientele and can
become busy at lunchtimes and evenings, so if you wish to guarantee
a table you'll need to book.

THE COURTHOUSE HOTEL BAR

Address: 19-21 Great Marlborough Street, W1F 7HL (☏ 020-7297 5555,
💻 courthouse-hotel.com/bars/the_bar).
Opening hours: Mon-Sat, 11 to 1.30am; Sun, 11am to 11pm.
Transport: Oxford Circus tube.
Go for: A genuine lock-in experience.

47

The Courthouse Hotel is located in a Grade II listed former magistrate's court and retains many of the historical features from its former incarnation. The hotel's cocktail bar makes the most of this good fortune by employing three of the original cells as 'cosy VIP rooms', with the heavy, barred cell doors remaining, which some people find slightly unnerving – those with guilty consciences, perhaps?

'VIP rooms' is an appropriate term to use, as the cells once held Oscar Wilde and Sir Mick Jagger, before those esteemed gentlemen appeared in court. The three rooms can be reserved in advance or are available on a first-come-first-served basis, and can hold up to around eight people – a cosy novelty. The décor of the rest of the bar is sleek, stylish and stone-clad.

Cocktails are the speciality here, with all the classics available, as well as signature cocktails with legal themes. Spirits, beer and wine are also served, as well as bar snacks. Prices are typical for a central London hotel bar, from around £10 for a cocktail.

THE CRAZY BEAR

Address: 26-8 Whitfield Street, W1T 2RG (☎ 020-7631 0088,
🖳 crazybeargroup.co.uk).
Opening hours: Mon-Wed, noon to midnight; Thu-Sat, noon to 1am; Sun,
noon to 11.30pm.
Transport: Goodge Street tube.
Go for: Cocktails, plush luxury and exotic loos.

48

It's obvious that plenty of money was lavished on the design of this sumptuous, dimly-lit cocktail bar, which sits beneath a restaurant serving modern Chinese, Japanese and Thai cuisine. It's the Fitzrovia location of the Crazy Bear Group, which has three other outlets – in Beaconsfield, Covent Garden and Stadhampton (Oxfordshire) – as well as its own farm in Oxfordshire to supply its eateries; that's attention to detail.

This bar is most definitely plush – even the loos are extravagantly done, replete with crystal and mirrors aplenty. But it isn't all about show. The friendly bar staff mix an excellent cocktail, albeit a pricey one: you can pay around £30 for a couple of drinks. It's popular, too, and becomes busy and noisy – a lot of diners from the restaurant seem to begin and end their evening in the bar – so book if you wish to ensure somewhere to sit. You can eat here too, dim sum and sushi from the well-regarded upstairs restaurant.

This is a showy place, therefore dress smartish casual to fit in with the moneyed local media types who frequent it (if that doesn't deter you from going!).

DE HEMS

Address: 11 Macclesfield Street, W1D 5BW (☎ 020-7437 2494,
🖥 nicholsonspubs.co.uk/dehemsdutchcafebarsoholondon).
Opening hours: Mon-Thu, 10am to midnight; Fri-Sat, 10am to 12.30am;
Sun, 10am to 11pm.
Transport: Leicester Square tube.
Go for: Its range of Dutch and Belgian beer.

Located on the edge of Chinatown (the road sign is in Chinese as well as English), London's only Dutch bar is part of the Nicholson's group and is named after the seaman who bought it in 1890. The pub's origins go back to the 17th century, but in its current form it began life as a home-from-home for Dutch sailors and was later a rallying point for the Dutch Resistance in the Second World War. It was a music industry haunt in the '60s and now draws aficionados in search of fine Low Countries' brews.

It's surprisingly modern inside – bland even – given the ornate, traditional exterior, but that isn't the draw: the wide selection of beer is what brings in the punters. You can also fortify yourself with a range of Dutch snacks and nibbles served by friendly, knowledgeable staff, many of whom seem to have a proper Dutch accent (rather than a Steve McClaren one).

De Hems is a large bar but justifiably popular, so get there early if you wish to bag a seat, many of which are at shared tables.

THE DOG AND DUCK

Address: 18 Bateman Street, W1D 3AJ (☎ 020-7494 0697,
🖳 nicholsonspubs.co.uk/thedogandducksoholondon).
Opening hours: 10am to 11pm.
Transport: Tottenham Court Road tube.
Go for: The decorative interior, jovial atmosphere and good range of beer.

This small, attractive corner pub is another Nicholson's establishment.
It has a notable artistic and literary heritage: John Constable, Dante
Gabriel Rossetti and George Orwell used to slake their thirsts here,
while ageing diva Madonna famously recommended it for its Timothy
Taylor Landlord (a beer, to the uninitiated) in a 2005 interview.

The Dog and Duck has a lovely, authentic interior, with etched
mirrors, mahogany and beautiful, glazed wall tiles, in a building that
dates from 1897, although there's been a tavern on the site for much
longer. The name is a hunting reference, a nod to Soho's former life
as a royal hunting ground (indeed, the name Soho is said to come
from a hunting cry, *So-ho*).

As if the artistic and aesthetic heritage weren't enough, the pub also
has a constantly changing selection of good ales. These attractions
conspire to make the Dog and Duck popular and it's often packed,
with punters spilling outside to drink on the pavement in all weathers.

50

THE DONOVAN BAR

Address: Brown's Hotel, 33-4 Albemarle Street, W1S 4BP (☎ 020-7493 6020, ⌨ brownshotel.com/dining/the-donovan-bar).
Opening hours: Mon-Sat, 11am to 1am; Sun, noon to midnight.
Transport: Green Park tube.
Go for: Rum, whisky and fabulous photographs.

51

One of London's older hotels, Brown's dates from 1837 and is renowned for being among the capital's most elegant and discreet destinations. Like the hotel, the Donovan Bar is a fine blend of old and new, and succeeds in being both glamorous and laid-back at the same time.

The bar pays homage to the late Terence Donovan, world-renowned photographer – hence the name – and is decorated with around 50 of his black and white prints. It's worth visiting to see this gallery which portrays an earlier age of elegance – and also to enjoy the drinks. The well-constructed wine list offers many choices by the glass as well as the bottle; there are also cocktails, but spirit drinkers are probably best served here, particularly those fond of rum and single malt whisky. Bar nibbles are available.

As for the décor, imagine a chic redesign of an Edwardian lounge, incorporating a striking stained glass window of St George. The Donovan Bar is an intimate space, therefore you might have to wait at the bar before securing a table, but it's worth it, especially if you aren't picking up the tab.

DUKES HOTEL BAR

Address: 35 St James's Place, SW1A 1NY (☎ 020-7491 4840,
🖥 dukeshotel.com/foodanddrink-dukesbar.php).
Opening hours: Mon-Thu, from 2pm; Fri-Sat, from noon; Sun, from 4pm
(closes around 11pm).
Transport: Green Park tube.
Go for: Martinis – as James Bond likes them.

Dukes is a small, comfortable bar at an exclusive hotel in a classy part of London, known for its gentlemen's clubs and high-end wine merchants. It resembles a smart, period sitting room and has a tranquil, soothing atmosphere, discreet, elegant and exclusive.

The martinis here are well regarded (and reassuringly strong), to such an extent that some people rate them as the best in the world. The James Bond author Ian Fleming used to drink here and the bar is said to have inspired 007's preference for 'shaken, not stirred'. And if that isn't sufficient inducement to order a martini here (no more than two, given their strength), what possibly could be?

If you're looking for old-school charm, discretion and traditional decor, Dukes does the job perfectly. It isn't cheap, of course, and there's a smart-casual dress code and a no reservations policy. Arrive early to bag a perch at this small haven – your reward will be one of the capital's more elegant drinking experiences.

THE EBURY RESTAURANT & WINE BAR

Address: 139 Ebury Street, SW1U 9QU (☎ 020-7730 5447,
🖳 eburyrestaurant.co.uk).
Opening hours: Mon-Sat, 11am to 11pm; Sun, noon to 10.30pm.
Transport: Sloane Square tube or Victoria tube/rail.
Go for: The extensive but reasonably priced wine list.

This bow-fronted wine bar and bistro is a long-established
Belgravia favourite and has been serving the locals in this well-
to-do part of London for over half a century, as well as drawing
local workers and tourists. There's a small front bar with a dining
room behind, the latter in dark
greenish wood and with a striking
fresco, specialising in French and
Mediterranean dishes (it's included
in the 2012 *Michelin Guide*).

53

The interesting, varied wine list is
an attraction for many, with offerings
from the Old and New Worlds; around
30 are available by the glass as well
as bottle. Pleasingly, the wines are
keenly priced, unusual in London
wine bars, particularly those with
prestigious postcodes. Those wanting
to eat don't need to repair to the
restaurant, as there's a bar menu of
lighter dishes from noon to 10.15pm.

The Ebury is a refined venue in
a civilised area, serving up decent
wine and old-fashioned charm. No
reservations are taken for the bar
area, only the restaurant (for groups
of seven or more people a £10 per
person deposit is required).

THE ENDURANCE

Address: 90 Berwick Street, W1F 0QB (☎ 020-7437 2944,
🖥 theendurance.co.uk).
Opening hours: Drinks: Mon-Sat, noon to 11pm; Sun, noon to 10.30pm.
Food: hours vary – see website.
Transport: Leicester Square or Oxford Circus tube.
Go for: Soho ambience, jukebox sounds and a chance to top up your tan.

Once called the King of Corsica, this traditional Victorian pub is on
Soho's nicely seedy Berwick Street, the location of a noted fruit and
vegetable market. This is reflected in the pub's clientele, which is a
mixture of market traders, the ubiquitous Soho media workers and
the odd celebrity. They combine well to create an atmosphere that's
laid-back and fun.

Music lovers are drawn here by the jukebox (which is appropriate,
as Berwick Street used to be known for its independent record shops),
on which punk and indie sounds predominate, so you might wish to go
elsewhere if you're a disco diva or soul fan. The pub has also become
quite food-oriented, offering solid British and European dishes. As for
the drinks, there's a reasonable range of decent beer and wine.

The Endurance manages to be a successful blend of the old school
and the trendy, while, appealingly, the 'outdoor seating is on the sunny
side of the street, ideal for a pint and a tan' – as ever, it's the small
things that count.

THE EXPERIMENTAL COCKTAIL CLUB

Address: 13A Gerrard Street, W1D 5PS (☎ 020-7434 3559,
🖥 chinatownecc.com).
Opening hours: Mon-Sat, 6pm to 3am; Sun, 6pm to midnight.
Transport: Leicester Square tube.
Go for: Great cocktails, atmosphere and decor.

This London outpost of Paris's Experimental Cocktail Club is a two-floor, speakeasy-style bar with a colonial feel and hints of the Orient: think antiques shop blended with '30s Shanghai, so the location in Chinatown is apt.

Half of the capacity is for walk-in customers, the rest for reservations (which are by email only – ✉ reservation@chinatownecc.com – with the reservation desk open Tue-Sat until 5pm; they don't take bookings for large groups at weekends). You should dress up in order to gain entry past a bouncer and through the tatty door, and there's a £5 cover charge after 11pm.

Cocktails are, of course, the thing to drink here, although there's also a good wine list. The cocktails cover the classics as well as more off-the-wall mixes, highly appropriate given the venue's name, and they're invariably brilliantly creative, served by friendly, knowledgeable staff. Prices go from the not unreasonable (£10-12) to the wallet-busting (£150). Its popularity means that the ECC can become very crowded, with standing room only.

55

5TH VIEW

Address: Waterstone's, 203-5 Piccadilly, W1J 9HA (☎ 020-7851 2433, 🖳 5thview.co.uk).
Opening hours: Mon-Sat, 9am to 10pm; Sun, noon to 5pm.
Transport: Piccadilly Circus tube.
Go for: A cocktail with a view!

This lounge bar and restaurant's views over Piccadilly used to be something of a secret, enjoyed only by those who ventured upstairs after browsing Waterstone's considerable expanse of bookshelves (it's Europe's largest bookshop). But now the genie's out of the bottle, so it can become crowded; as a result, service is sometimes slow.

56

But it's a comfortable place with a good atmosphere and a civilised spot to have a drink while taking in the views, which are good rather than stunning (it isn't really high enough for the latter). There are around a dozen well-made cocktails, three of which are 'virgin' – all priced at around £10, and half price during Tuesday and Wednesday's happy hour (5-7pm) – some bottled beers and a modest wine selection from £19.95 a bottle, some of which are also available by the glass.

As for food, there's a bar as well as restaurant menu, so you can graze on chunky chips, Scotch eggs and calamari with your drinks as you watch the sun set over the surrounding rooftops.

THE FITZROY TAVERN

Address: 16 Charlotte Street, W1T 2NA (☎ 020-7580 3714).
Opening hours: Mon-Sat, 11am to 11pm; Sun, noon to 10.30pm.
Transport: Goodge Street tube.
Go for: Atmosphere and history.

According to some, this Fitzrovia stalwart is London's finest Sam Smith's establishment. Originally a coffee house, it became a pub in 1887 and developed a bohemian reputation, as the photographs decorating the walls demonstrate. It also gave the area its name.

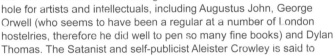

The Fitzroy Tavern became famous/infamous from around the '20s to the '50s as a watering hole for artists and intellectuals, including Augustus John, George Orwell (who seems to have been a regular at a number of London hostelries, therefore he did well to pen so many fine books) and Dylan Thomas. The Satanist and self-publicist Aleister Crowley is said to

57

have designed a cocktail for the pub – I wouldn't like to speculate on what was in it!

Unlike some of the area's other pubs, it has a friendly, unpretentious atmosphere and still carries a whiff of its racy past, although today you're more likely to be supping your keenly-priced Sam Smith's brew next to one of the area's media professionals, rather than a poet or hell-raiser. The odd famous face can, however, still be spotted.

THE FRENCH HOUSE

Address: 49 Dean Street, W1 5BG (☎ 020-7437 2477,
🖳 frenchhousesoho.com).
Opening hours: Mon-Sat, noon to 11pm; Sun, noon to 10.30pm.
Transport: Leicester Square or Piccadilly Circus tube.
Go for: History, conviviality and a slightly raffish air.

This Soho institution is small, atmospheric and usually packed,
including the cramped, roped-in outside area which is invariably
wreathed in a fug of smoke. During the Second World War, the French
House was a favourite haunt of Charles de Gaulle and the Free
French, and it still retains its French air. It serves a choice of wine and
champagne – 30 are available by the glass as well as the bottle –
cider and beer (in halves only, no vulgar British pints).

In the '50s, writers such as Brendan Behan and Dylan Thomas
were regulars, and although it's no longer a bohemian hangout it
retains a pleasing air of old school, literary booziness. And the French
House's rule of banning noise from music, machines, television and
mobile phones is welcome in this age of media bombardment and
information overload.

If you wish to stave off the effects of the alcohol, the upstairs dining
room has developed a sound reputation for its food, which includes
such Gallic treats as onion soup and pork rillettes.

GALVIN AT WINDOWS

Address: Park Lane Hilton, 22 Park Lane, W1K 1BE (☎ 020-7208 4021,
🖥 galvinatwindows.com).
Opening hours: Mon-Wed, 11 to 1am; Thu-Sat, 11 to 3am; Sun, 11am to
10.30pm.
Transport: Hyde Park Corner tube.
Go for: Sipping cocktails while peering into the Queen's back garden.

As you might expect with a 28th-floor location, the Galvin at Windows bar and adjacent restaurant enjoy mightily impressive, panoramic views, including the grounds of Buckingham Palace. They're probably among London's best vistas and go some of the way to explain the high prices at this venue, which is part of the stable of the Michelin-starred chef brothers Chris and Jeff Galvin.

As for the drinks, good cocktails are served – from around £13.50 – and there's an extensive wine list, French-oriented, with prices ranging from affordable to sky high; it includes a selection of 'natural' wine made using organic and/or biodynamic principles.

If you don't want to eat at the high-end, but well-regarded restaurant, you can sustain yourself with good-quality but pricey bar food, including Scotch eggs, which is clearly a plus point. The caviar selection starts at £75, further evidence (if needed) that this isn't a budget destination – but it's a memorable one; somewhere for a celebration or a treat for someone you love. Do dress accordingly, smart-casual or just smart.

GARLIC & SHOTS

Address: 14 Frith Street, W1D 4RD (☎ 020-7734 9505, ⌨ garlicandshots.com).
Opening hours: Mon-Wed, 5pm to midnight; Thu-Sat, 6pm to 1am; Sun, 5-11.30pm.
Transport: Leicester Square tube.
Go for: Vodka, garlic, a quirky attitude and a heavy metal soundtrack.

The original of this Soho oddity is in Stockholm and there's also a branch in Palma, Majorca. The name derives from the fact that all the food in the upstairs restaurant is laced with garlic, the ice cream included. A small pot of parsley is provided on each table – when chewed, the herb apparently ameliorates garlic breath.

The 'shots' part of the name comes from the downstairs bar's speciality: vodka. There are 101 shots available, many vodka-based, in a wide range of flavours (including garlic!) and at reasonable prices for Soho. The other speciality is rock music, notably the heavy metallic kind, making this venue much favoured by rockers and Goths – and the staff can be a bit rock-and-roll in attitude. But it's open to all and you won't be made to feel unwanted if you aren't covered in tats and don't resemble a member of Cradle of Filth.

As you might expect, the bar isn't luxurious, with dim lighting, a few tables and thumping music. So it's a love-it-or-hate it sort of place, but it's certainly unique.

THE GEORGE BAR

Address: Durrants Hotel, 26-32 George Street, W1H 5BJ (☏ 020-7935 8131, 🖥 durrantshotel.co.uk/food-drink/george-bar).
Opening hours: Mon-Fri, 11am to 11pm; Sat-Sun, 11am to 10.30pm.
Transport: Bond Street tube.
Go for: Understated gentlemen's club style.

61

This very English hotel in Marylebone first opened in 1790 and its current owners, the Millers, have been at the helm since 1921. It's a 92-bedroom, Georgian townhouse affair and a rarity in London, being a private, family-run hotel. The George Bar reflects its traits of history and continuity, with a relaxing, traditional decor; like the hotel, it's an oasis of calm and civilisation.

The bar's décor and atmosphere have more than a hint of an exclusive gentlemen's club, with panelled walls, leather seating and a welcoming coal fire when the weather is cold. It's a cosy yet sophisticated place to enjoy a drink and relax after a demanding stint of Bond Street shopping or before heading to the theatre.

Prices are reasonable for a classy London hotel bar and you'll need to dress smartly to blend in with the business types and ladies who lunch who'll be your fellow tipplers. The hotel is known for its extensive wine list and a clientele discerning enough to appreciate it.

GORDON'S

Address: 47 Villiers Street, WC2N 6NE (☎ 020-7930 1408,
🖥 gordonswinebar.com).
Opening hours: Mon-Sat, 11am to 11pm; Sun, noon to 10pm.
Transport: Embankment tube or Charing Cross tube/rail.
Go for: Fortified wine and atmosphere in the capital's oldest wine bar.

Established in 1890, Gordon's is London's oldest wine bar and one
of its drinking institutions – a must-visit-at-least-once destination. A
fairly anonymous doorway between Charing Cross and Embankment
stations opens onto narrow, rickety stairs leading down to this lively,
convivial basement bar, housed in cramped, atmospheric cellars.

The ambience is decidedly 1940s, candlelit, romantic and slightly
tatty. It's also often very crowded; standing room only if you don't
arrive early enough to bag a table. Gordon's offers a solid range of
wine (nothing else), including sherry, port and Madeira by the glass,
drawn from sizeable casks by efficient staff who are used to dealing
with large volumes of punters. Drinks aren't unreasonable, but the
robust hot and cold food is quite pricey.

Upstairs and running along the side of Gordon's and behind
Embankment Gardens, is a line of much-prized outdoor tables, which
constitute a civilised
drinking terrace. Many
a happy afternoon has
been whiled away here
by people who should
probably be somewhere
else, notably the office.

THE GORING HOTEL

Address: 15 Beeston Place, SW1 0JW (☎ 020-7396 9000, 💻 thegoring.com).
Opening hours: Daily, 7am to 11pm.
Transport: Victoria tube and rail.
Go for: A tremendous wine list in sumptuous surroundings.

This hotel has been owned by the Goring family for around a century and is tranquil, traditional and sophisticated. It appeared in the headlines when the Middleton family stayed here before the royal wedding – a sound indication that this isn't a cheap venue.

The hotel's bar is comfortable and sumptuous, with a rich décor of dark wood panelling, high-backed bar stools, and armchairs of leather and brown wood. It isn't just another hotel bar, however, describing itself as 'really about the people and the ambience'. But it's also about the wine, with an exceptional list that has its own separate page on the website. The Gorings have laid down wines over four generations and the cellars carry over half a million pounds' worth, including some very fine vintages.

There are over 500 bins, with claret (Bordeaux red) and Burgundy forming the backbone. Wine is priced from £27 a bottle, champagne from £60. And this is a civilised, professionally-run place in which to enjoy them, relaxed and with an interesting mix of clientele. You're requested to switch off your mobile phone and not to use laptops and tablets, so you can enjoy your surroundings in peace and quiet.

63

THE GRENADIER

Address: Old Barrack Yard, 18 Wilton Row, SW1X 7NR (☎ 020-7235 3074, 🖥 taylor-walker.co.uk/pub/grenadier-belgrave-square/c0800).
Opening hours: Daily, noon to 11pm.
Transport: Hyde Park Corner tube.
Go for: Its haunted history, Bloody Marys and sausages on sticks.

Reputedly built originally as the Duke of Wellington's officers' mess (in 1720), this popular mews pub near Belgrave Square became a tavern in 1818. It apparently inherited the ghost of an army officer caught cheating at cards and rather over-enthusiastically flogged to death as a result. The haunting is supposed to peak in September.

A Taylor Walker establishment, the Grenadier is a small, dark and cosy pub, festooned with military memorabilia and with an original pewter bar. There's also a modestly-sized restaurant, serving traditional English food. Weather-permitting, punters spill outside on to Wilton Row, which thankfully eases the crowding inside. The pub is in a number of tourist guides, which contributes to its popularity, and it can be rather Hooray Henry-filled at times (this is, after all, one of their stomping grounds), but it's still engaging.

The pub's specialities add to its slight air of quirkiness: Bloody Marys (made to a secret recipe) and sausages on sticks served with a lick of ketchup and mustard, surely the food of officers and gentlemen.

THE GUINEA

Address: 30 Bruton Place, W1J 6NL (☎ 020-7409 1728, 🖥 theguinea.co.uk).
Opening hours: Mon-Fri, 11.30am to 10.30pm; Sat, noon to 11pm; closed Sun.
Transport: Bond Street or Oxford Circus tube.
Go for: A pint and a steak and kidney pie.

As might be expected (and hoped for) given its location in an attractive Mayfair mews, this is a thoroughbred in the stable of Young's pubs. Originally established in 1675 (although there's said to have been a tavern here since the 15th century), it was first called the Guinea in 1755 and was a popular spot with the rich and famous in the '50s, even drawing international stars.

It has a small bar and a larger restaurant, the latter well regarded but rather expensive. However, you can eat splendidly in the bar (Mon-Fri), as the Guinea is famous for its award-winning steak and kidney pies.

65

As for the ambience, the pub retains a cosy, pleasant '50s feel. It's quite plain, with dark wood and low lighting – perfect for convivial supping. The Guinea can become crowded during the week, including its small outside space, but is sometimes quieter on Saturday evenings, when a fair few of its regulars have cleared off to the countryside to lay waste to the wildlife.

THE HARP

Address: 47 Chandos Place, WC2N 4HS (☎ 020-7836 0291, 🖥 harpcoventgarden.com).
Opening hours: Mon, 10.30am to 11pm; Tue-Sat, 10.30am to 11.30pm; Sun, noon to 10.30pm.
Transport: Charing Cross tube/rail.
Go for: A great choice of real ale and cider; excellent sausages, too.

Built in the 1830s (and originally called the Welsh Harp), this centrally located freehouse has an attractive stained glass front and what's reputed to be the West End's best choice of real ale. It's an ever-changing selection, with regulars including Dark Star, Harveys, Sambrook's and Twickenham Ales.

The surrounds of the long, narrow bar counter are decorated with a large collection of beer mats, which is appropriate for a pub that was the first London boozer to win CAMRA's (Campaign for Real Ale) 'National Pub of the Year' award (in 2010). Some wine is also sold, as is cider and perry (pear cider) – indeed, the Harp was 'London Cider Pub of the Year' in 2011. Home-cooked sausages are a popular way to line stomachs and tend to sell out quickly.

The pub's many attractions combine to mean that it's invariably busy, inside and out. Its position, a mere stone's throw from Charing Cross station, is also a draw for commuters needing to fortify themselves before braving Britain's infamously stressful rail network.

THE HEIGHTS BAR

Address: St George's Hotel, Langham Place, Regent Street, W1B 2QS
(☎ 020-7580 0111, ▭ saintgeorgeshotel.com).
Opening hours: Mon-Sat, 7am to midnight; Sun, 7am to 11pm.
Transport: Oxford Circus tube.
Go for: Capital views and BBC radio stars.

The views from this 15th-floor lounge bar and restaurant at the (less than glamorous) St George's Hotel are the main draw. Its position near Broadcasting House, home of BBC radio, means that you might also see and/or hear a familiar voice.

The London Eye's popularity has shown how much people enjoy aerial views of London and from the Heights Bar you can gaze down on Oxford Street, Regent Street, Hyde Park and more; if you're lucky, on a clear day you might even see Canary Wharf, Hampstead Heath or Wembley Stadium.

Aside from the views, it's a fairly standard hotel bar: leatherette, brass trim, patterned carpet et al. But the vistas make it an unusual place in which to enjoy a cocktail or beer and while prices are (typically for a hotel bar) above average, they aren't excessive and are partly justified by the table service. This is a much cheaper alternative to certain other London bars with notable views, such as **Galvin at Windows** (see page 59) and **Vertigo 42** (see page 159).

67

THE HOLBORN WHIPPET

Address: 25-29 Sicilian Avenue, WC1A 2QH (☎ 020-3137 9937,
🖳 holbornwhippet.com).
Opening hours: Mon-Thu and Sat, noon to midnight; Fri, noon to 1am;
closed Sun.
Transport: Holborn tube.
Go for: A great range of craft beer.

A recent arrival, the
Holborn Whippet is a
strangely-shaped corner
bar in Sicilian Avenue, a
small, stylish Edwardian
shopping arcade. It's so
named because 'the folk of
Bloomsbury and Holborn
parishes relaxed with a spot
of whippet racing well into
the 1800s'.

The décor has hints
of the '50s, with wooden
floorboards, brown tiles,
cream walls and pictures of dogs on the walls. Large windows provide
fine views of the arcade, while there are outside tables where you can
drink in more clement weather.

But the beer is the big draw here. While there's a constantly
changing wine list and good sandwiches, posh burgers and pizza,
craft beer is the main attraction, as it's bound to be when you discover
that the place is part-owned by the people behind the **Euston Tap**
(see page 182). There are always at least 15 beers on tap; the range
is constantly changing and includes ales from Adnams, Arbor, Bristol
Beer Factory, Camden Town, Dark Star, Ilkley, Magic Rock, Meantime
and Redemption, among others.

HUNTER 486

Address: Arch London, 50 Great Cumberland Place, W1H 7FD (☎ 020-7724 0486, ⌨ thearchlondon.com/hunter-486-brasserie).
Opening hours: Daily, 6am to 10.30pm.
Transport: Marble Arch tube.
Go for: Cocktails, champagne, designer furniture and an arty atmosphere.

The obscure name of this bar and restaurant in the boutique Arch hotel comes from Marylebone's pre-war telephone code. It's a smart but relaxed place, strong on design features: the stylish bar has a striking pewter top, there's a pressed tin ceiling and the bar stools are by international design icon Philippe Starck. So you should dress accordingly, smart-casual certainly, but probably with a bit of pizzazz, too, if you can manage it.

As for the drinks, cocktails are a speciality (from around £9, which isn't unreasonable by smart hotel standards) and there's an extensive choice of good wine and champagne, beginning at around £25 a bottle (like most boutique hotels, this isn't a cheap destination). It's a popular place and booking is recommended, certainly on Fridays and Saturdays.

69

For those wanting to celebrate, there's also Le Salon de Champagne, an area within the bar which unsurprisingly specialises in champagne and has 'an arty social vibe'. The designer look is continued here with chairs by Tom Dixon, who's apparently rather good at that sort of thing.

LAB

Address: 12 Old Compton Street, W1D 4TQ (☎ 020-7437 7820, 🖥 labbaruk.com).
Opening hours: Mon-Sat, 4pm to midnight; Sun, 4-10.30pm.
Transport: Tottenham Court Road tube.
Go for: Cocktails and a party vibe.

LAB stands for the London Academy of Bartenders, which is quite a grand claim. Not surprisingly, they're serious about mixing drinks at this Soho spot and state that they've been 'at the forefront of exceptional cocktails for over ten years', another demonstration of self-confidence.

They back this up with an impressive list of high-quality cocktails, the drinks menu running to around 120 choices and at reasonable prices for this part of London (from around £7). And the staff aren't at

70

all sniffy if you want a simple classic mix – you don't have to go for designer or experimental drinks.

LAB's décor wouldn't claim to be ground-breaking or prize-winning (it has a whiff of the '70s about it), but it doesn't need to be, as it's a friendly, popular place with a good atmosphere and can get packed. DJs on Thu-Sat add to the party atmosphere, while various areas of the bar can be reserved (see website for details). In short, it's is one of those places where it's difficult not to have a good time.

THE LAMB

Address: 94 Lamb's Conduit Street, WC1N 3LZ (☎ 020-7405 0713,
🖥 youngs.co.uk/pub-detail.asp?pubid=421).
Opening hours: Mon-Wed, noon to 11pm; Thu-Sat, noon to midnight; Sun,
noon to 10.30pm.
Transport: Holborn or Russell Square tube.
Go for: The fine Victorian interior, interesting history and lively conversation.

This Grade II listed Young's
pub was built in 1729 but later
remodelled and what we see
today is Victorian. It's named
after William Lamb, who in 1577
renovated an existing conduit to
bring clean water from Holborn,
an act of charity to benefit the
neighbourhood; this was so
laudable that the street was
named after him also!

71

The interior is a fine example
of Victorian design, including
etched glass, a central horseshoe bar and snob screens to protect
drinkers' privacy (and conceal how much they were drinking). It dates
from a time when actors and music hall stars were regulars; today,
pictures of them adorn the walls. Charles Dickens also used to drink
here when he lived in nearby Doughty Street (in a house that's now
the Charles Dickens Museum).

But as well as the heritage and aesthetic appeal, the Lamb is a
living local boozer in this civilised, artistic part of town. It's an inviting
place to sample a pint of Young's brew and the traditional pub grub on
offer, and promises 'no TV or music, just lively conversation'.

THE LAMB & FLAG

Address: 33 Rose Street, WC2E 9EB (☎ 020-7497 9504,
🖥 lambandflagcoventgarden.co.uk).
Opening hours: Mon-Sat, 11am-11pm; Sun, noon-10.30pm.
Transport: Covent Garden tube.
Go for: Characterful, historic (if touristy) pub with good beer.

The Lamb & Flag is an atmospheric Fuller's pub in Covent Garden
and is one of the area's drinking institutions. It dates from the late 17th
century, with the current premises built in 1772. At one time it was
nicknamed the Bucket of Blood, as it hosted bare-knuckle fights in the
back room. Later, Charles Dickens was a frequent customer; this is one
of a number of London pubs where he was a regular (famously, Dickens
was a great walker, sometimes covering up to 20 miles at a time).

Today it's popular with those wishing to sample its selection of
quality cask ales and to soak up the convivial atmosphere, often in
the small courtyard at the front, which frequently fills with drinkers
(unless it's raining). Traditional pub fare is served in the back room
and upstairs.

72

The Lamb & Flag is
invariably packed, as its
genuine sense of history
and its convenient central
location have seen it
listed in a number of
tourist guides. The only
drawback is that getting
served promptly can be a
challenge.

THE LIBRARY BAR

Address: Lanesborough Hotel, 1 Lanesborough Place, Hyde Park Corner, SW1X 7TA (☎ 020-7259 5599, 🖥 lanesborough.com/en/lanesborough-library-bar).
Opening hours: Mon-Sat, 11am to 1am; Sun, noon to 10.30pm.
Transport: Hyde Park Corner tube.
Go for: Cognac, cocktails and luxurious elegance.

The Lanesborough Hotel is in a building dating from 1828, which used to be a hospital. Its Library Bar, however, was designed with the rich and sumptuous Regency era in mind: high ceilings, dim lighting, leather wing chairs, shelves full of leather-bound books and a roaring fire in winter. It's a comfortable and welcoming environment, the service professional and understated.

The bar's speciality is what it calls a collection of 'liquid history', this being one of London's widest selections of vintage cognacs. Unsurprisingly, these tend to be very expensive, with some costing several hundred pounds for a single measure! Cocktail drinkers are also well served, with good quality mixes – at around £15 they aren't cheap either.

But this is a five-star hotel in Knightsbridge, therefore it's to be expected. It's a place for the most special of special occasions, when you want to enjoy an atmosphere redolent of a private gentlemen's club, so you should dress to impress, take your gold card and try to avoid wincing when the bill arrives.

THE LOBBY BAR

Address: One Aldwych, WC2B 4BZ (☎ 020-7300 1000, 🖥 onealdwych.com/food-drink/lobby-bar.aspx.
Opening hours: Mon-Fri, 8am to midnight; Sat, 9am to midnight; Sun, 9am to 10.30pm.
Transport: Covent Garden or Temple tube.
Go for: A wow factor interior and well-made cocktails.

74

This hotel bar is apparently situated in the part of London 'where the City meets the West End', therefore attracts both financial and creative types. It's definitely a place to take somebody if you wish to impress them: an ultra-stylish lobby bar with pillars, ceiling-high windows, original contemporary sculptures (check out the mighty Oarsman), huge flower displays on perspex plinths and a polished limestone floor, while candles manage to add some intimacy to the large space.

The bespoke furniture includes high-backed armchairs and sofas, while the service is by friendly, attentive uniformed staff. There's a wide choice of drinks, with well-made cocktails (around £12.50) and an extensive choice of champagne, wine and beer, as well as an interesting bar menu, including sharing platters – so there's something for everyone.

The *Sunday Telegraph* named it as one of their top five hotel bars in the world, which might be pushing things a bit, but it's definitely one of London's more glamorous drinking spots, with a buzzy atmosphere and well turned-out clientele.

THE LONDON COCKTAIL CLUB

Address: 61 Goodge Street, W1T 1TL (☎ 020-7580 1960,
🖥 www.londoncocktailclub.co.uk).
Opening hours: Mon-Fri, 4.30pm to midnight; Sat, 5pm to midnight; Sun,
private bookings only.
Transport: Goodge Street tube.
Go for: Well-made, well-priced cocktails in a cosy environment.

The owners (one of the directors is the renowned chef Raymond
Blanc) describe this venue as 'our famous gin palace on Goodge
Street' and it's one of the capital's most inviting cocktail bars. It's a
smallish, cosy, L-shaped space, with a long bar, wooden floors, warm
lighting and comfortable sofas.

Most cocktails are keenly priced in the £7.50-9 band and grouped
under four categories: classics, contemporaries, gastro mixology and
gin favourites. They also have a Cocktail School here, which provides
lessons in how to make cocktails like a pro, but despite this and the
venue's name, it isn't a pompous, mixology-obsessed place; rather,
it's relaxed and doesn't take itself too seriously.

There's food too, including sliders (baby burgers) at £6, deli boards
for £12, charcuterie, cheeses and more. The dress code is smart-
casual and the bar gets busy, notably Thu-Sat when booking is
recommended. The formula obviously works, as the London Cocktail
Club team have a similar outlet at 224 Shaftesbury Avenue, which
they call an 'underground rum bar'.

75

THE LONG BAR

Address: Sanderson Hotel, 50 Berners Street W1T 3NG (☎ 020-7300 5588, 🖥 sandersonlondon.com).
Opening hours: Mon-Sat, 11am to 3am; Sun, noon to midnight.
Transport: Tottenham Court Road or Oxford Circus tube.
Go for: Cocktails and sophistication, from lunchtime till late.

The bar at this designer hotel is aptly named, being of impressive length: around 80 feet (24m) of glowing onyx, with stools lining both sides. It's an impressive location for a drink, if not quite as cutting-edge and chic as it once was. According to the hotel's blurb, the bar 'is light, white and airy, and radiates freshness and cleanliness'. There's also an outdoor area, the Courtyard, which is atmospherically candlelit at night.

Drinkers of cocktails and spirits are well served by a huge selection, plus a short wine list. Prices are highish (wine from £7.50 per glass, champagne from £12.50 per glass, cocktails from around £12), as they invariably are in hotels with the adjective 'designer' attached, but it isn't punishingly expensive.

The atmosphere is buzzy and friendly, and although the Long Bar isn't quite as celebrity-packed as it was a few years ago (an advantage, some will say), it still attracts a sophisticated clientele and is a renowned people-watching spot.

LONGITUDE 0°8'

Address: Le Meridien Hotel, 21 Piccadilly, W1J 0BH (☎ 020-7734 8000, 🖥 longitude08.co.uk).
Opening hours: Mon-Sat, 2pm to 1am; Sun, 4pm to midnight.
Transport: Piccadilly Circus tube.
Go for: Coffee, aperitifs and cocktails in a super-chic setting.

What used to be the Burlington Bar has been redesigned and is now Longitude 0°8', which claims to provide 'three very different experiences during the course of the day, defined by music, lighting and service'. In daytime it specialises in fine coffee, with artisan chocolates and pastries; after work it becomes a sophisticated venue for pre-dinner drinks; post-dinner it's a chic cocktail bar, with a specially crafted range of drinks.

It's certainly strikingly designed, slick and stylish, a mixture of modern and classic elements. This really comes into its own after dark: you pass through an entrance portal into a space of mirrored surfaces and shimmering light, with plenty of intimate nooks and crannies, and comfortable seating. Rather than tables, there are 'glowing cubes of light'.

There's a good choice of spirits, while the cocktails are popular although not inexpensive at £12.50-14.50 a drink. There are tapas-type snacks for the peckish and live entertainment, all in a friendly atmosphere.

THE LORD JOHN RUSSELL

Address: 91-3 Marchmont Street, WC1N 1AL (☎ 020-7388 0500).
Opening hours: Mon-Sat, 11.30am to 11pm; Sun, noon to 10.30pm.
Transport: Russell Square tube.
Go for: A wide, well-kept choice of beer and a convivial atmosphere.

LORD JOHN RUSSELL

This might be the dingier, less-cultured part of Bloomsbury, but the Lord John Russell is a great traditional pub and one of the area's better hostelries. It's named after a two-time 19th-century Prime Minister, a descendant of the family that developed Bloomsbury and grandfather of the philosopher, humanist and philanderer Bertrand Russell, who (Lord John, not Bertrand Russell) received a dedication from Charles Dickens in *A Tale of Two Cities*.

78

But this isn't a blowsy, glitzy Victorian gin palace. It started not as a pub but as a whisky merchant, and the interior is smallish and quite spartan, with floorboards, plain tables and wooden seats. In fact, the décor resembles a gastropub, although the food available is much more pasty-and-chips than pan-seared bass with lemongrass whatnots.

The wide choice of well-kept beer and real ale (up to around 15)

draws in the punters, as do the Sunday roasts and big rugby matches, which are watched with enthusiasm on large-screen TV in a convivial, friendly atmosphere. There's also a reasonable amount of outside seating for when the weather isn't too awful.

LOWLANDER

Address: 36 Drury Lane, WC2B 5RR (☎ 020-7379 7446, ⌨ lowlander.com).
Opening hours: Mon-Wed, 11.30am to 11pm; Thu-Sat, 11.30am to 11.30pm; Sun, noon to 10.30pm.
Transport: Covent Garden or Holborn tube.
Go for: A splendid selection of Belgian and Dutch beer.

This dubs itself 'London's premier Belgian bar and brasserie', although competition for the title is admittedly somewhat limited. Be that or not, Lowlander is an elegant spot in Covent Garden, modelled after a Belgian café, with seating at long tables and waiter service.

79

It offers an enticing selection of Belgian and Dutch beer, around 15 on tap and 50 by the bottle, including dark beers, fruit beers, golden ales, micro-brews, pilsners, Trappist ales and wheat beers. However, be aware that some of these are notably high in alcohol, up to 12 per cent which is more than some wines! The wine list has a choice of around 20, many available by the glass as well as the bottle.

There's also an extensive food menu, including *moules frites* (mussels and chips), which is all but compulsory for a Belgian joint, as well as light snacks, sharing platters and what are described as 'beer cuisine specialities'. Lowlander is a friendly, popular place and although it charges Covent Garden 'tourist' prices, is well worth a visit.

THE MANDARIN BAR

Address: Mandarin Oriental Hyde Park Hotel, 66 Knightsbridge, SW1X 7LA
(☎ 020-7201 3724, 🖥 mandarinoriental.com/london/fine-dining).
Opening hours: Mon-Sat, 10.30am to 1.30am; Sun, 10.30am to 12.30am.
Transport: Knightsbridge tube.
Go for: Showy, exclusive elegance and large cocktails.

This fine cocktail bar is decidedly swish and showy, which is appropriate in an impressive, marble-decked Knightsbridge hotel. The bar is certainly eye-catching, the walls lined with beige silk and the décor a mix of marble, mirrors, mohair, wood and leather armchairs.

It's been said that 'this bar has theatre', perhaps because the bottles are stored and the drinks are mixed by staff behind frosted, back-lit glass walls – so you get an impression of them rather than a full view – while showcases display handmade cocktail glasses and ornamental barware. In this era of austerity, the bar's shiny ostentation is something of a throwback to a time when money was no object (which it still isn't to the hotel's clientele). Cocktails are the speciality here and efficient, professional staff dispense good quality examples, notable for their large size.

The Mandarin Bar's style and substance draw in the punters and it can become very busy. It isn't cheap, of course, but this is a destination venue that knows how to provide customers with a memorable, stylish time.

MARK'S BAR

Address: 66-70 Brewer Street, W1F 9UP (☎ 020-7292 3518, ⌨ marksbar.co.uk).
Opening hours: Mon-Sat, noon to 1am; Sun, 11am to 11pm.
Transport: Piccadilly Circus tube.
Go for: A great selection of drinks and food in a stylish environment.

Part of the stable of the entrepreneurial chef Mark Hix (with one of his restaurants on the ground floor), this is a stylish, speakeasy-like downstairs venue. A zinc bar, tin ceiling and Chesterfield sofas make for a striking yet comfortable environment.

Some thought has obviously gone into the selection of drinks. There's an impressive cocktail list, including a number of old classics – most are priced between £10.50 and £12.75 – and a well-chosen selection of wine, champagne, sherry, port and dessert wine, with champagne from £8 per glass and wine from £6.95 per glass (£26.25 a bottle). Beer drinkers are also well catered for (not always the case at upmarket venues), with a variety of styles, including some of Mark Hix's own brews such as an IPA and an Oyster Ale.

81

There's a no reservations policy and the licence dictates that drinkers have to order some food. This includes great bar snacks such as pork crackling (£3.95), baked bone marrow with toast (£4.95) and fish fingers (£5), and you can also choose from the restaurant menu.

MILK & HONEY

Address: 61 Poland Street, W1F 7NU (☎ 020-7065 6841, 🖳 mlkhny.com).
Opening hours: Open to members: Mon-Fri, 6pm to 3am; Sat, 7pm to 3am; closed Sun. Open to non-members: Mon-Sat, 6-11pm, but reservations are required and in practice entry is restricted to the earlier part of the week. (The membership fee is around £400.)
Transport: Oxford Circus tube.
Go for: Great cocktails at one of London's most lauded bars.

This renowned cocktail bar and members' club has bars on three floors, and since it opened in 2002 has managed to earn and retain a reputation as one of the hippest places in town (but this could change, of course, as is the nature of these things).

Lying behind a deliberately anonymous doorway (to suggest that it's a secret and exclusive destination), the interior is modelled after a '40s American jazz joint, with hints of Art Deco and moody low lighting. There are scores of inviting booths, nooks, crannies and larger areas in which to park yourself. As for drinks, you can order excellent cocktails (around £9 – less than you might expect for a noted West End venue), champagne, wine and whisky.

The problem is that non-members must make an effort to visit Milk and Honey (see above) but, while it can be posey and pretentious, it's also a great experience. So it's worth taking the time to book, dress smartly (and slightly edgily if you can – black and white shoes with spats, perhaps?) and arrive on time to visit this multi-award-winning venue.

THE MORPETH ARMS

Address: 58 Millbank, SW1P 4RW (☎ 020-7834 6442, ☐ morpetharms.com).
Opening hours: Mon-Sat, 11am to 11pm; Sun, noon to 11pm.
Transport: Pimlico tube.
Go for: A civilised riverside pint.

83

Built in 1845 on the site of the old Millbank penitentiary, the Morpeth Arms is an elegant, Grade II listed, Young's pub – and one with a fascinating history. Beneath the pub is a corridor of holding cells which are rumoured to be haunted by the prisoners of Millbank, who were kept in cells prior to being transported to Australia aboard prison ships.

Named after Viscount Morpeth, who was responsible for developing this part of London, the pub has a classy, spacious and well-conceived interior over two floors, with leather sofas, wooden tables and comfortable chairs. There are also a number of sought-after outdoor tables, good spots from which to observe the Thames. Upstairs is The Spying Room, themed around the first world war alleged spy Mata Hari, which enjoys views across the river to the south bank and the eye-catching, monolithic MI6 building.

As for drinks, the Morpeth Arms serves Young's and Wells beer, and is something of a haven in an area lacking good pubs. It's close to Tate Britain and can become crowded with tourists when the gallery is open.

THE MUSEUM TAVERN

Address: 49 Great Russell Street, WC1B 3BA (☏ 020-3603 1354, 🖳 taylor-walker.co.uk/pub/museum-tavern-bloomsbury/c0747).
Opening hours: Mon-Thu, 11am to 11.30pm; Fri-Sat, 11am to midnight; Sun, noon to 10pm.
Transport: Tottenham Court Road tube.
Go for: Good beer in an attractive Victorian pub.

Dating from the early 18th century, when it was the Dog and Duck, the Museum Tavern was renamed when the British Museum pitched up across the road. It underwent a major refit in 1855 and retains a number of original Victorian fittings, including attractive etched glass and mirrors, panelled ceilings and the

84

gilt-mirrored, heavy wooden back bar. There are also some pavement tables – good spots from which to observe goings-on in this busy corner of Bloomsbury

Now a Taylor Walker pub, the interior is small, cosy and busy, as its position opposite a major attraction provides plenty of trade. Past customers included JB Priestley, Sir Arthur Conan Doyle and Karl Marx, but today the friendly staff are well used to dealing with

bewildered foreigners struggling to understand Britain's strange beer offerings.

The Museum Tavern is a solid choice for real ale fans, with around seven on tap, regular guest brews and a couple of annual beer festivals. You can sample the likes of Adnams, BrewDog, Fuller's, Greene King, Harveys, Sharp's, St Austell, Theakston Old Peculiar, Timothy Taylor and Young's, while stomachs are lined with standard pub fare.

THE NAG'S HEAD

Address: 53 Kinnerton Street, SW1X 8ED (☎ 020-7235 1135).
Opening hours: Mon-Sat, 11am to 11pm; Sun, noon to 10.30pm.
Transport: Hyde Park Corner or Knightsbridge tube.
Go for: An atmospheric boozer where mobile phones are banned.

Dating from the late 18th or early 19th century, this small freehouse on a back lane in Belgravia is in a tranquil spot, despite being close to manic Hyde Park Corner. It's unspoiled, nicely higgledy-piggledy and decorated with all sorts of ephemera, memorabilia, old arcade games and cartoons. The wood panels, low ceilings and real fires give it a Dickensian atmosphere, while drinkers spill outdoors in balmy weather.

The choice of drinks and food is reasonable rather than remarkable – including Adnams beer – but atmosphere and quirkiness are the attractions here. The Nag's Head has one of the lowest bar tops in London owing to the sunken serving area and as a result has notably small bar stools. Mobiles aren't allowed and the landlord has been known to eject those who flout the rule.

This unexpectedly individual pub isn't cheap – we are in Knightsbridge, after all – but it's friendly, historic and atmospheric, the antithesis of a homogenised pub chain establishment, and definitely an enjoyable place to while away an afternoon.

THE NEWMAN ARMS

Address: 23 Rathbone Street, W1T 1NG (☎ 020-7636 1127,
🖥 newmanarms.co.uk).
Opening hours: Mon-Fri, noon to midnight.
Transport: Goodge Street or Tottenham Court Road tube.
Go for: A pie and a pint in a proper pub.

This Fitzrovia freehouse dubs
itself 'a proper little boozer in
the West End' and that sums
it up well, distinguishing it from
some of the area's anodyne and/or fancy venues. It's in a building
that dates from 1730 which has had many functions over the years,
including ironmonger, picture framer and brothel, becoming a pub
in 1860. It's the area's only family-run boozer and sometimes three
generations of the Bird family work here together.

George Orwell and Dylan Thomas (again – they got around) used
to be regulars and the pub has often been used as a location by
film and television crews, appearing in the *Ali G Show*, *The Bill* and
Minder.

There isn't a wide selection of drinks, but you can sup the likes of
beer drinkers' favourites London Pride and Seafarers, and there's a
sound wine list. Food is a major draw here. The upstairs restaurant is
called The Pie Room and serves popular Newman's home-baked pies
and savoury suet puddings, which are the perfect accompaniment to a
pint or glass of red.

NORDIC

> **Address:** 25 Newman Street, W1T 1PN (☎ 020-7631 3174, 🖥 nordicbar.com).
> **Opening hours:** Mon-Wed, 5pm to midnight; Thu, noon to midnight; Fri, noon to 2am; Sat, 5pm to midnight; closed Sun.
> **Transport:** Tottenham Court Road tube.
> **Go for:** Scandinavian cocktails, beer, vodka and nibbles.

Nordic is an understated, Scandinavian basement bar near the Telecom Tower in Fitzrovia. It isn't particularly smart or trendy, but it's friendly, welcoming and fun, with dark furniture and dimmed lighting. And it has a wide choice of drinks, as might be expected from our famously alcohol-loving Scandi friends: beer, lager, cocktails, vodka and wine.

Nordic's speciality is cocktails based on Scandinavian mixes and ingredients, including fruits and berries. They're competitively priced, too. During happy hour (5-7pm), cocktails are £5 and house wine is £10 a bottle – these are among the lowest prices listed in this book (or available in London).

87

Given the strength of some of the drinks, it's a good idea to eat as well; you can choose from a selection of typical Scandinavian savouries such *gravad lax*, herrings, hotdogs and meatballs, available separately or as part of a smorgasbord.

In 2012, Nordic introduced The Tuborg Bar, which is the first of its kind in Britain for the Danish brewer, where you can try new Tuborg offerings before they're launched elsewhere.

THE OLD COFFEE HOUSE

Address: 49 Beak Street, W1F 9SF (☎ 020-7437 2197).
Opening hours: Mon-Sat, 11am to 11pm; Sun, noon to 10.30pm.
Transport: Oxford Circus or Piccadilly Circus tube.
Go for: Good beer meets cosy conviviality.

This isn't a purveyor of overpriced caffeinated beverages, as the name suggests, but a fine, traditional corner pub, regarded by some punters as one of Soho's best; this is quite an accolade in an area with several decent boozers.

The building, which dates from the 1850s, was originally a Temperance movement coffee house, run by an organisation that thought alcohol was the Devil's milk – so its popularity as a pub is nicely ironic. It's a smallish single bar, eccentrically decorated with memorabilia, stuffed birds and more, and has a cosy and relaxed atmosphere, although it can become crowded.

There's a fair range of beer, cider and lager (reasonably priced for the area), pub grub of the jacket spud and pie sort – but tasty with generous portions – and a nicely mixed clientele. The Old Coffee

House is a Brodie's pub, promoting the East London microbrewery's ales, plus a rotating London guest beer.

THE PARAMOUNT

Address: Centre Point, 101-103 New Oxford Street, WC1A 1DD (☎ 020-7420 2900, 🖳 paramount.uk.net/level-32/bar).
Opening hours: Mon-Wed, 8pm to 1.30am; Thu-Fri, 8pm to 2.30am; Sat, noon to 2.30am; Sun, noon to 4pm.
Transport: Tottenham Court Road tube.
Go for: Cocktails, wine and 360 degree views of London.

You must book in advance, dress formally (smart-casual at the very least) and check in with staff on the ground floor before taking the lift 385 feet (117m) up to the 32nd floor of the starkly ugly Centre Point building at the eastern end of Oxford Street. Here, you're greeted by a striking, custom-made copper bar, designed by Tom Dixon, which occupies the centre of this bar in the sky.

The rest of the décor is under- rather than over-stated, so as not to distract from the views. They're suitably impressive, 360 degree vistas over the heart of London, making this a great place to watch the sun set.

As for drinks, many opt for the well-made, inventive cocktails, with champagne cocktails at £14, others at £11. There's also an interesting list of wine and champagne, including some high-end examples. You can graze on items from the bar menu and for those wanting something more substantial there's a restaurant. One floor up is the Viewing Gallery bar, but despite its more elevated position the atmosphere is less buzzy.

THE PEARL BAR & RESTAURANT

Address: Chancery Court Hotel, 252 High Holborn, WC1V 7EN (☎ 020-7829 7000, 🖥 pearl-restaurant.com).
Opening hours: Mon-Fri, 11am to 11pm; Sat, 6-11pm; closed Sun.
Transport: Holborn tube.
Go for: Cocktails, champagne or wine – and a special occasion.

The Pearl Bar & Restaurant is housed in the Chancery Court Hotel, an impressive, nicely blowsy building which was once the head office of Pearl Assurance. The Pearl, which is a combined Asian-accented French restaurant (run by TV heart-throb chef Jun Tanaka) and cocktail bar, takes this association one step further with its spectacular décor, consisting of lighting in the form of pearl chandeliers and strands of hand-strung pearls.

As for the drinks, there's a choice of interesting, imaginative cocktails (from around £10.50), while the wine list is large – over 200 – and time-consuming to navigate (a taster is available online). A few wines are available by the glass as well as the bottle, and not many bottles are priced under £40. There's plenty of champagne on the list, which is also strong on US vintages, presumably to please the hotel's American guests.

This is a smart, stylish, prestigious destination, with a smart-casual dress code and best saved for a special occasion. Take a thick wad and/or your bank manager.

THE PLAYER

Address: 8 Broadwick Street, W1F 8HN (☎ 020-7065 6841, 🖳 thplyr.com).
Opening hours: Tue-Thu, noon to 1am; Fri, noon to 2am; Sat, 6pm to 2am.
Members only after 11pm.
Transport: Oxford Circus or Tottenham Court Road tube.
Go for: Fine cocktails, DJ sounds and a touch of retro cool.

91

Part of the Match chain, this small bar is one of those door-in-the-wall Soho establishments which like to suggest that they're something of a secret, a venue for those in the know. It's no longer quite the glamorous, place-to-see-and-be-seen destination that it was in the early noughties, but it's still a sexy, fun, late-night basement bar with something of a '70s disco vibe.

The Player offers excellent cocktails, as well as beer and wine. Service is slick and you're recommended to pre-book a table. Snacks are available (but aren't the bar's strong point) and prices are far from unreasonable for the area and type of venue, e.g. £7 for a glass of prosecco, cocktails from £7.50 upwards and £20 for a bottle of house wine.

As it's in Soho, the Player attracts a smattering of Soho types, with fashion, film and music people in evidence letting their hair down. There are regular DJ nights, for which modest entrance fees are charged – see website for details.

THE PRINCESS LOUISE

Address: 208 High Holborn, WC1V 7BW (☎ 020-7405 8816).
Opening hours: Mon-Fri, 11.30am to 11pm; Sat, noon to 11pm; Sun, noon to 10.30pm.
Transport: Holborn tube.
Go for: The stunning, rare, must-see interior.

Built in 1872 and named after a daughter of Queen Victoria, this Sam Smith's establishment is one of London's best preserved Victorian pubs. Unremarkable from the outside, the interior is spectacular, a Grade II listed gin palace of the best sort; even the loos are opulent, which can be something of a distraction.

The pub's design is a riot of mosaic tiles, etched glass, moulded ceilings, mirrors and carved wood, a fine tribute to Victorian craftsmanship. Such ostentation was once common in English pub interiors, perhaps a reflection of the confidence and wealth of a country that controlled the world's largest empire.

Screens separate a number of different areas in the pub, a throwback to the days when drinkers were segregated by social class. Today, a number of Princess Louise regulars come from nearby Bloomsbury's educational and cultural establishments, and the pub also attracts a steady stream of tourists, its glorious glitz having earned it a place in many guidebooks. As for the beer, there's the usual range of solid, well-priced Sam Smith's offerings.

THE PUNCHBOWL

Address: 41 Farm Street, W1J 5RP (☎ 020-7493 6841,
🖥 punchbowllondon.com).
Opening hours: Mon-Sat, noon to 11pm; Sun, noon to 5pm.
Transport: Green Park tube.
Go for: The chance to drink with Guy Ritchie and his celebrity friends.

93

Dating from 1750, this is Mayfair's second-oldest pub, situated on a mainly residential street in this quietly upmarket part of London. The Grade II listed Georgian building has been altered over the years but retains a number of attractive, original features, including a dog-leg staircase, dado panelling and cornicing.

Part of the pub's appeal is the possibility of supping alongside famous faces, as it's co-owned by film director Guy Ritchie (he gained Madonna's share as part of the divorce settlement). It's also an attractive space, understated and classy, with dark wood, warm lighting, wooden tables and chairs, and large, framed portraits, including one of Winston Churchill. Good food is served in the warm, cosy dining area behind the main bar.

Drinks are of good quality, with a reasonable choice of wine and whisky, as well as a solid choice of beer, including Deuchars IPA, Shepherd Neame Spitfire and Wells Bombardier. None of this comes cheap, but then you wouldn't expect it to in a celebrity-owned bar in a posh part of London.

PURL

Address: 50/54 Blandford Street, W1U 7HX (☎ 020-7935 0835,
🖥 purl-london.com).
Opening hours: Mon-Thu, 5-11.30pm; Fri-Sat, 5pm to midnight; closed Sun.
Transport: Bond Street tube.
Go for: Inventive cocktails with a theatrical flourish.

Located in the basement of a Georgian house, this Marylebone bar is a relaxed and unfussy place, with plenty of individual seating areas, leather furniture, brick walls and a low, vaulted ceiling. As for the name, purl is a dangerously potent, old English drink made of warm ale, gin, spices and wormwood, which provides a clue to some of the dramatic drinks on offer.

Beer and wine are available, but it's the well-made, inventive cocktails and the associated theatre of making and serving them that's the main draw. As the website puts it, Purl serves drinks 'that satisfy on a multi-sensory level, using aroma, fogs, airs, foam, food, bespoke service-wear and liquid nitrogen to bring the drink to life and transport the guest to another place or time'.

Cocktail prices vary enormously, from around £9 to as much as £65!

Purl provides table service, all customers must be seated and it's full on most nights, therefore you need to book. Tables are allocated for two hours only, so if you wish to stay longer, book a second table for two hours later. Note, however, that only snacks are served.

THE QUEEN'S HEAD

Address: 66 Acton Street, WC1X 9NB (☎ 020-7713 5772,
⌨ queensheadlondon.com).
Opening hours: Mon, 4-11pm; Tue-Sat, noon to midnight; Sun, noon to 11pm.
Closing times are flexible, with the addendum 'later if we fancy'.
Transport: King's Cross tube/rail.
Go for: Interesting beer and an enjoyable all-round pub experience.

This attractive, friendly
Victorian pub in King's Cross
is a great little neighbourhood
boozer. Recently revamped,
it isn't a glittering 19th-
century gin palace, but has
an understated interior with
wooden floors, red leather
sofas, nicely worn tiles,
wooden tables and chairs,
original cornicing and stained-
glass windows.

95

Punters are drawn by the imaginatively-chosen beer, lager, porter,
stout and cider, and there's also a selection of whisky and a wine
list, all served by knowledgeable staff. The food is also good – solid
well-priced fare – designed to complement the drinks: cheeseboards
(£7.50), pies (£6), meat boards (£8.50) and more.

The Queen's Head describes itself as 'a great place to eat, drink
and laugh', which is probably many people's definition of a good pub.
There's often entertainment, including open mic comedy, acoustic folk
sessions, blues nights, quizzes and sing-alongs around the piano.
They also hold beer events and festivals. Use Facebook and Twitter to

keep up with the latest
news on these various
offerings – or see the
website.

THE QUEEN'S LARDER

Address: 1 Queen Square, WC1N 3AR (☎ 020-7837 5627,
🖳 queenslarder.co.uk).
Opening hours: Mon-Sat, 11.30am to 11pm; Sun, noon to 10.30pm.
Transport: Russell Square tube.
Go for: Good beer in a traditional pub with royal connections.

The Queen's Larder is a small, traditional, corner pub in a secluded,
tranquil part of Bloomsbury, and dates from 1720. For once with a
boozer, the royal name is actually justified: Queen Charlotte, wife
of the supposedly 'mad' King George III (who reigned 1760-1820),
stored special food and medicines in a small cellar beneath the pub
with which to help treat the afflicted, misunderstood monarch (who
was seeing a doctor at a house on the square).

There's another medical connection: Great Ormond Street Hospital
for Children is nearby and its staff are some of the pub's regulars.
They come for the enjoyable, well-priced food and solid selection of
beer, often quaffed in the large outdoor seating area, which overlooks
leafy Queen Square and is one of Bloomsbury's better people-
watching spots.

The Queen's Larder is probably the area's best pub, with a convivial
atmosphere created by the mixture of locals, professionals and
tourists. It tends to be busier on weekdays – often very busy – and
quieter at weekends.

THE RED LION (CROWN PASSAGE)

Address: 23 Crown Passage, off Pall Mall, SW1Y 6PP (☎ 020-7930 4141).
Opening hours: Mon-Sat, 11.30am to 11pm; closed Sun.
Transport: Green Park or St James's Park tube.
Go for: Atmosphere, history and old-fashioned charm.

Crown Passage has a Dickensian aura, with its small shops and cafés. There's been a tavern here for over 300 years, although this building is late Georgian. It looks the part – old and traditional – with a frontage of black timber and leaded windows, while the small, cosy interior has dark wood panels, red upholstery and low lighting. It's rumoured to have once been a brothel.

The licence at this St James's venue is claimed to be around 350 years old, making it one of the West End's oldest. As it's down a narrow alley, it mainly attracts local workers, but some tourists find their way here also, making for an interesting, friendly mix of punters, including doormen and waiters from the nearby gentlemen's clubs, some of the gentlemen themselves and wine merchants from the area's distinguished grape juice retailers.

97

They gather together to drink beers such as Adnams, St Austell Tribute and Stella, while there's also a wide choice of whisky and good sandwiches. The Red Lion can become busy at night, but this adds to the hospitable atmosphere.

THE RED LION (DUKE OF YORK STREET)

Address: 2 Duke of York Street, SW1Y 6JP (☎ 020-7321 0782,
🖥 redlionmayfair.co.uk).
Opening hours: Mon-Sat, 11.30am to 11pm; closed Sun.
Transport: Piccadilly Circus tube.
Go for: A friendly, unpretentious, mirror-decked pub.

The Red Lion is the most common British pub name – there were over
600 at the last count – and this is another one in St James's, just off
Jermyn Street. It's a small, charming, traditional hostelry, built in 1821
on the site of an earlier tavern, remodelled in the 1870s and known for
its lovely interior featuring lots of mirrors and ornate glass.

This well-preserved Victorian pub has been owned by Fuller's since
2009 and serves the likes of London Pride, Timothy Taylor Landlord and
Hook Norton Old Hooky, plus guest ales, as well as solid homemade
food, notably pies. It runs to two small rooms and is a draw for workers
from the area's luxury retailers, so it can become rather busy.

Weather-permitting, many drinkers spill outside on to the pavement
along this side street. The Red Lion is one of the many London pubs
where Charles Dickens is said to have been a patron (along with
dozens of other pubs
– I don't know how
he found any time for
writing).

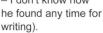

THE SALISBURY

Address: 90 St Martin's Lane, WC2N 4AP (☎ 020-7836 5863, 💻 taylor-walker.co.uk/pub/salisbury-covent-garden/c3111).

Opening hours: Mon-Wed, 11am to 11pm; Thu, 11am to 11.30pm; Fri-Sat, noon to midnight; Sun, noon to 10.30am.

Transport: Leicester Square tube.

Go for: One of London's most impressively glitzy pub interiors.

This Taylor Walker establishment (named after a 19th-century prime minister) is a notable example of Victorian pub design, with brass, etched glass, a horseshoe-shaped bar and mahogany and mirrors aplenty – one of London's best Victorian pub interiors. Take the time to gaze around and upwards to appreciate the full extent of the decorative detail.

It has a fair selection of beer, traditional pub grub and is proud to announce it's been 'sport-free since 1892'. This has served the Salisbury well, as despite being a large pub it's invariably full, sometimes packed, with a mixture of local workers, theatre-goers and tourists. But the staff are used to this and are quick and efficient. Afternoons are probably the quietest time and the best for viewing the impressive interior.

The pub has friendly, professional doormen in the evenings – partly to discourage the vagrants who are common in this part of town – who understand that intimidating genuine punters isn't part of a doorman's brief (which isn't the case at all venues).

THE SEVEN STARS

Address: 53 Carey Street, WC2A 2JB (☎ 020-7242 8521).
Opening hours: Mon-Fri, 11am to 11pm; Sat, noon to 11pm; Sun, noon to 10.30pm.
Transport: Chancery Lane or Holborn tube.
Go for: A charming atmosphere, real ale and a landlady who can really cook.

The Seven Stars is a tiny pub behind the Royal Courts of Justice. The building dates from the 17th century, one of the few in the area to survive the Great Fire of London in 1666. It doesn't require many punters for the pub to become crowded and there are plenty of good reasons to come here.

One of them is food: the splendidly-named landlady Roxy Beaujolais has a cookbook to her name – *Home from the Inn Contented* – so you can rest assured that you'll be well fed. There's an inviting real ale choice (Sussex's Dark Star brewery features regularly) and a short wine list by the glass. And it opens seven days a week, which is unusual in this part of town.

The interior has a long, narrow bar, with a snug at one end, while furnishings are simple but comfortable and the atmosphere congenial. Arrive early to bag one of the few tables. Given the location, the Seven Stars draws a lot of legal customers, another good sign, as barristers are usually discerning when it comes to food and drink.

1707

Address: Fortnum and Mason, 181 Piccadilly, W1A 1ER (☎ 020-7734 8040,
🖥 fortnumandmason.com).
Opening hours: Mon-Sat, noon to 9pm; Sun, noon to 6pm.
Transport: Piccadilly Circus tube.
Go for: A great wine selection in London's most famous food emporium.

This elegant, stylish wine bar was designed by the celebrated David Collins and is on the lower ground floor of the famous, exclusive grocer Fortnum and Mason. It's named after the year that the shop was founded, but is a modern, sleek operation, so leave the shopping trolley and cagoule at home!

It has a great wine list, including own-label choices made for 1707 by some lauded wine producers; the list includes an extensive selection available by the glass. There's a £10 corkage fee on the retail price of wines stocked by Fortnum and Mason's wine department, which is located close to the bar. There are also 'wine flights', whereby you can try several different wines for a fixed price, e.g. three different white Burgundies for £18.

Good food is served by friendly, efficient staff, but it doesn't come cheap. Next to 1707 is The Atrium, a sort of picnic area with tables, serving dishes from Fortnum's food counters (such as ham, pork pies and smoked salmon) and wines chosen to accompany them, which is a more reasonably-priced eating option.

SHAMPERS

Address: 4 Kingly Street, W1B 5PE (☏ 020-7437 1692, ▭ shampers.net).
Opening hours: Mon-Sat, 11am to 11pm; closed Sun.
Transport: Oxford Circus and Piccadilly Circus tube.
Go for: The knowledgeable wine list, reasonable prices and welcoming atmosphere.

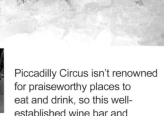

Piccadilly Circus isn't renowned for praiseworthy places to eat and drink, so this well-established wine bar and restaurant (it's been 'pouring since 1977', with the current owners at the helm since 1991) is a real find. Ignore the cheesy name – it's a minor quibble and, given the decade in which the bar was founded, forgivable – and just enjoy the wine.

Shampers has a serious wine selection (the owner, Simon, worked in the wine trade for eight years and it shows), the majority by small producers, many of whom use organic and/or biodynamic methods. A good number are available by the glass, with prices starting at a reasonable £4.50 per glass and around £17 a bottle. You can drink some pretty serious wines here at competitive prices, for example we recently spotted Contino 2005 (a high-end Rioja) for £42, while the retail price was £23-25.

The premises are clean, modern and simple, with wooden tables and chairs, and white tablecloths. Most of the food is British and main courses are generally in the £11.50-17.50 range. Tapas-style specials are served at the bar. Booking is recommended and is by telephone only.

THE SHOCHU LOUNGE

Address: 37 Charlotte Street, W1T 1RR (☎ 020-7580 6464,
🖥 shochulounge.com).
Opening hours: Mon-Fri, noon to midnight; Sat, 5.30pm to midnight; Sun,
5.30-10.30pm.
Transport: Goodge Street or Tottenham Court Road tube.
Go for: The Japanese spirit shochu, in a classy Far East-themed bar.

103

Shochu is a Japanese spirit, not
dissimilar to vodka, usually distilled
from barley, sweet potatoes or rice,
and flavoured with various fruits
and herbs. It's the speciality of this
high-quality bar, which sits below
the renowned Fitzrovia Japanese
restaurant Roka.

As well as the eponymous spirit,
you can choose from Japanese-
influenced cocktails and there's
also a wide choice of vodka, plus
an ample selection of non-alcoholic
cocktails and other drinks – which certainly isn't the case in all bars.
If you wish to eat, you can pick from the fine food available on the
restaurant menu.

The Shochu Lounge is chic, intimate and sumptuous, with
Japanese-influenced decor, including dark wood, red velvet and a
rustic-style bar. The dress code is smart-casual, the lighting dim and
the music low, so that it doesn't interfere with conversation. These
conspire to make it quite a romantic spot, providing you're willing to
splash the cash to impress your date.

THE STAR TAVERN

Address: 6 Belgrave Mews West, SW1X 8HT (☎ 020-7235 3019,
🖥 star-tavern-belgravia.co.uk).
Opening hours: Mon-Fri, 11am to 11pm; Sat, noon to 11pm; Sun, noon to
10.30pm.
Transport: Knightsbridge tube.
Go for: A cosy traditional pub with a criminal past.

104

Situated in an elegant Georgian building in a lovely, half-hidden mews just off Belgrave Square, this is another pub that claims to be where 1963's Great Train Robbery was planned (as does **The Anglesea Arms** – see page 210).

It's regarded as one of London's better Fuller's pubs and has featured in every CAMRA *Good Beer Guide*, as has the **Buckingham Arms** (see page 33). In the '50s and '60s it was a favourite haunt of the rich and famous, such as Diana Dors and Peter O'Toole, as well as the upper echelons of London's criminal fraternity, with whom the stars liked to hang out. Nowadays it has a more varied clientele than some of the other hostelries in this exclusive area.

The Star Tavern has a welcoming interior – warm and woody – an upstairs dining room and an attractive cobbled area in front of the pub, which is popular when the weather is mild. Bar and restaurant menus offer wholesome, fairly priced food, while there are the usual solid Fuller's beers on offer, plus a seasonal brew.

TERROIRS

Address: 5 William IV Street, WC2N 4DW (☎ 020-7036 0660,
🖥 terroirswinebar.com).
Opening hours: Mon-Sat, noon to 11pm; closed Sun.
Transport: Charing Cross tube/rail.
Go for: Tasty food and highly praised wine.

This attractive, buzzy wine bar and restaurant has been reaping the plaudits since it opened in 2008. It specialises in 'natural' wines, i.e. those produced organically and/or biodynamically ('cloudy reds and murky whites' as they put it, to describe wines made with minimal treatment, filtering and the use of sulphates). The list of around 200 wines is dominated by French wines, with some Italian and Spanish offerings, and a select few from further afield.

The food is another draw, well-presented French snacks, charcuterie and seafood being some of the tempting options. Terroirs is spread over two floors, each with its own menu – the ground floor is more of a wine bar, the basement more of a restaurant.

It's invariably full, therefore you usually need to book if you want a table. There are non-reservable seats at the bar on each floor, but you need to be lucky to bag one unless you arrive soon after opening. Terroirs' success has spawned two 'sister' venues: Soif at 27 Battersea Rise, SW11 1HG and Brawn at 47 Columbia Road, E2 7RG.

UPSTAIRS AT RULES

Address: 35 Maiden Lane, WC2E 7LB (☎ 020-7836 5314,
🖥 rules.co.uk/cocktailbar)
Opening hours: Mon-Sat, noon to 11.30pm; Sun, noon to 10.30pm.
Transport: Covent Garden or Leicester Square tube.
Go for: Classic cocktails in London's oldest restaurant.

Rules claims to be London's oldest restaurant – established in 1798 –
although its cocktail bar is a rather more recent arrival. It's reached via
a flight of stairs by the side of the restaurant and is an engaging mix of
a slightly camp cocktail bar with hints of a traditional gentlemen's club.

The dark wood, crimson fabric and open fire advertise the
fact that elegance and tradition are the watchwords here, so it's
no surprise that Rules specialises in classic cocktails rather than
new inventions. They are served by friendly staff from a shortish
list of beautifully prepared drinks (priced at around £13.50). The
mixologist is the experienced Brian Silva, one of whose mottos
is 'Don't try to be clever, just focus on making great drinks'. You
usually receive a sliver of cheese (good stilton invariably) and a
biscuit with each drink, another welcome touch.

As befits the environment and
ethos, there's a smart-casual
dress code, but this isn't a
pretentious or fashion-conscious
place, rather it's friendly and
relaxed.

VATS

Address: 51 Lamb's Conduit Street, WC1N 3NB (☎ 020-7242 8963,
🖥 vatswinebar.com).
Opening hours: Mon-Fri, noon to 11pm; closed weekends.
Transport: Russell Square tube.
Go for: Consistently good wine and food in a long-established wine bar.

This cosy wine bar and restaurant
in Bloomsbury sits on the attractive,
unusually-named Lamb's Conduit
Street. Vats retains design touches
from the era in which it was opened –
the early '70s – and has been owned
and run by the same husband-and-
wife team since 1985; consistency is
a byword here.

There's a large, traditional wine
list, running to over 100 bins – it's global but focuses on France and
is especially strong on claret (the reds of Bordeaux); half bottles are
priced from around £12.50, bottles from £19.50. The owners live in
East Sussex and source a lot of the food they serve locally. It's hearty
grub in the main, a mixture of English classics and modern European
dishes, and the menu changes in part every six weeks; main courses
are invariably in the £10-20 price range.

This is a cosy, unpretentious, professional establishment serving
enjoyable wine and food in a comfortable environment. The interior is
warm and woody, and it's popular with the area's professionals, who
form the backbone of the regulars (it's closed at weekends).

107

THE WONDER BAR

Address: Selfridges, 400 Oxford Street, W1A 1AB (☎ 020-7318 2476, 🖥 selfridges.com).
Opening hours: Mon-Sat, 9.30am to 9.30pm; Sun, 11.30am to 6pm.
Transport: Bond Street or Marble Arch tube.
Go for: A chance to sample small amounts of some exquisite wines.

Opened in 2007, this was one of the first venues in London to stock (the now increasingly popular) Enomatic machines that allow staff to dispense small measures of a selection of wines – around 50 in the case of the Wonder Bar – while preserving what's left in the bottle. Appropriately, the bar is on a mezzanine above Selfridge's wine department and has a modern, sleek look, with red and pale wood decor.

Since 2012, three wine sample sizes have been available – 25ml (a 'sip'), 125ml and 175ml; prior to 2012, 125ml was the minimum measure permitted by law. The so-called sip puts some extremely expensive wines within the reach of many more people at a (relatively and vaguely) affordable price.

The wines offered at the Wonder Bar are an interesting mixture of classics and a number of more unusual, off-the-wall choices, allowing you to compare and contrast different varieties of wine and expand your wine horizons. Cheeses, charcuterie and crustaceans are served to accompany them in this civilised venue. But be aware that even small sips soon add up and can lead to a big bill.

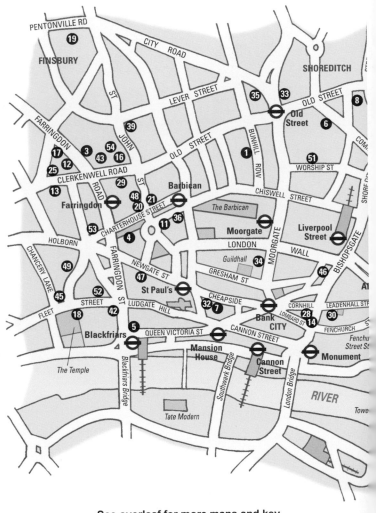

See overleaf for more maps and key.

CHAPTER 2

CITY & EAST LONDON

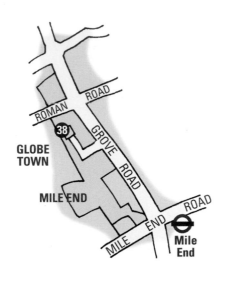

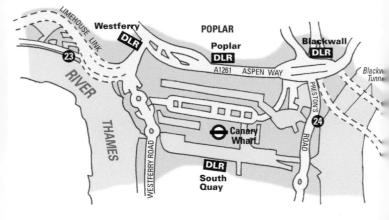

See previous page for main map.

Ref	Place	Page

THE ARTILLERY ARMS

Address: 102 Bunhill Row, EC1Y 8ND (☎ 020-7253 4683,
🖥 artillery-arms.co.uk).
Opening hours: Mon-Sat, noon to 11pm; Sun, noon to 10.30pm.
Transport: Old Street tube.
Go for: A tranquil, traditional pub with good beer and food.

Dating back to the 17th century,
this Fuller's establishment is well
located on a quiet, tree-lined street
opposite Bunhill Fields Burial
Ground. It's small and very much
a traditional pub, with a central
bar counter and two drinking and dining areas. The leather-seated
banquettes, dark wood, frosted glass and log fire in winter all combine
to generate a welcoming atmosphere.

As well as the usual solid range of well-kept Fuller's beer, the
Artillery serves seasonal ales and a range of wines, some by the
glass. The food is good, drawing discerning City and local punters for
pub grub classics and well-regarded Sunday roasts; lighter meals and
snacks are also available. As might be expected given its location on
the edge of the City, the food isn't cheap, but neither is it too wallet-
threatening.

Board games are available and there's a quiz on Sunday nights for
those who wish to exercise their grey cells along with their right arm.
The Artillery Arms also hosts a (recently-inaugurated) annual beer
festival – see website for details.

BEACH BLANKET BABYLON

Address: 19-23 Bethnal Green Road, E1 6LA (☎ 020-7749 3540,
🖳 beachblanket.co.uk).
Opening hours: Sun-Thu, 11am to midnight; Fri-Sat, 11 to 1am.
Transport: Liverpool Street tube/rail.
Go for: Good cocktails, amazing décor and a cool if chaotic vibe.

An offshoot of the original at 45 Ledbury Road, Notting Hill – which
was one of London's first Gothic style bars – this Shoreditch venue is
a bar-cum-gallery and is even more lavish and upscale. The décor is a
blend of boho chic and French country château, with gilded wallpaper,
over-the-top furniture and glitzy ornaments.

Spread over three floors of a former Victorian warehouse, BBB
'encapsulates the bohemian decadence of Cool Britannia', according
to the owners. The cocktail lounge can accommodate 300, the
restaurant seats 150 and there's also a 1,300ft² (120m2) gallery space
for exhibitions and special events. The total capacity is claimed to be
some 800, so it isn't exactly intimate
but is definitely somewhere to
impress a guest.

As for the all-important drinks,
there's a comprehensive choice of
cocktails and well-chosen wine and
champagne lists; cocktails start from
just under £9 but the sky's the limit
with champagne – some bottles
cost £400! The basement cocktail
lounge (there are two) is exotically
decked out with patterned flock
wallpaper and 18th-century and Art
Deco decoration, so you might like
to dress accordingly.

THE BETSEY TROTWOOD

Address: 56 Farringdon Road, EC1R 3BL (☎ 020-7253 4285, ⌨ thebetsey.com).
Opening hours: Mon-Wed, noon to 11pm; Thu, noon to 11.30pm; Fri-Sat, noon to 1am; closed Sun.
Transport: Farringdon tube/rail.
Go for: Good beer and entertainment in a pub that Dickens would approve of.

Named after a character in Charles Dickens's 1850 novel, *David Copperfield*, this Victorian pub is invariably known as the Betsey to its Clerkenwell regulars. It's a corner establishment, wedge-shaped like an iron, with a largish bar, a quieter upstairs room and a tiny basement; there's also a modest outside space, from where you can observe the goings-on along Farringdon Road and inhale the exhaust fumes.

Gigs are staged in the basement and the first-floor bar on some nights (usually Thu-Sat, with free admission or up to around £10), which partly determines the mood and the crowd; quite a lot of the bands seem to be indie, alternative country or folk, and there are also comedy performances, readings and disco nights. Otherwise,

it's a popular local, a mix of traditional and modern, which often becomes crowded with media and creative types.

The Betsey is a Shepherd Neame pub and serves the Kent brewery's well-regarded ales, as well as solid if unremarkable food, served by friendly staff. There's a good selection of whisky for those who enjoy a drop of the hard stuff.

THE BISHOP'S FINGER

Address: 9-10 West Smithfield, EC1A 9JR (☎ 020-7248 2341,
⌨ shepherdneame.co.uk/pubs/london/bishops-finger).
Opening hours: Mon-Fri, 11am to 11pm; closed weekends.
Transport: Farringdon tube/rail.
Go for: Beer and sausages, the diet of champions.

Another Shepherd Neame pub, this was the first London outlet for this Kent brewery (founded in Faversham in 1698) and is renowned for its beer and sausages, the latter a range of gourmet bangers from Smithfield Market just across the road.

117

As for the unusual moniker, the pub is named after one of Shepherd Neame's beers, described as 'Kentish Strong Ale' (5.4 per cent alcohol by volume/abv). 'Bishop's fingers' were unique to Kent, being fingerposts sited along the Pilgrims' Way to guide pilgrims to Thomas à Becket's shrine in Canterbury Cathedral. There's one on display in the pub.

Listed in *The Good Pub Guide*, the Finger has an attractive interior with a dark wood, single-roomed bar, an upstairs restaurant and some outdoor tables. To accompany your pint, there's a range of superior pub food (a bar menu and a restaurant menu), including sausage and mash (of course!), steak, fish and chips, etc., all well cooked and served by friendly staff. The Bishop's Finger becomes crowded at lunchtimes and in the evenings, and is regarded by some as one of the City's best pubs.

THE BLACK FRIAR

Address: 174 Queen Victoria Street, EC4V 4EG (☎ 020-7236 5474,
🖵 nicholsonspubs.co.uk/theblackfriarblackfriarslondon).
Opening hours: Mon-Thu, 10am to 11.30pm; Fri-Sat, 10am to midnight;
Sun, 10am to 11pm.
Transport: Blackfriars tube/rail.
Go for: London's most singular pub interior.

This wedge-shaped, Grade II listed pub is attractive outside, including
a glittering mosaic of its name, but inside it's nothing less than
spectacular. The elaborate and sumptuous decoration is a blend of Art
& Crafts and Art Nouveau styles, the latter a rarity in London. We're
lucky still to have this architectural gem, as it was only saved from
demolition by a campaign led by that great friend of historic buildings,
Sir John Betjeman.

The building dates from 1875 (with the interior refurbished in 1905
by architect H Fuller-Clark and artist Henry Poole) and is on the site
of a medieval Dominican Friary, which is reflected in the decoration:
friars feature everywhere in the pub's
cascade of intricate friezes, mosaics,
reliefs and sculptures.

It's a Nicholson's pub and has an
impressive range of ale, including guest
beers, wine from £11.95 a bottle and
good pub food. However, it's the striking,
singular interior that attracts gawping,
camera-wielding tourists. Many regulars
prefer to escape the hubbub by drinking
outside (weather permitting) where the
seating area is unusually generous for the
cramped City of London.

THE BOOK CLUB

Address: 100 Leonard Street, EC2A 4RH (☎ 020-7684 8618, 🖵 wearetbc.com).
Opening hours: Mon-Wed, 8am to midnight; Thu-Fri, 8am to 2am; Sat, 10am to 2am; Sun, 10am to midnight.
Transport: Old Street tube/rail or Shoreditch High Street rail.
Go for: Cocktails, a game of table tennis and to feed your brain.

119

Spread over two floors of a former Victorian warehouse, this bar and club describes itself as offering 'a cultural revolution to the East End's social scene' by providing a fusion of 'lively, creative events and late night drinking seven days a week'.

They're as good as their word, as the Book Club has club nights, talks, films, art events and more; there's even a ping pong table (which you pay a modest fee to use). But it's very much a drinking venue. The cocktail list is scribbled on the tiles surrounding the bar, and most are priced reasonably at around £7.50. There's also a choice of around 20 wines and champagnes, most also available by the glass, with prices from £4 per glass and £16 a bottle. Bottled beer is also available and a wide range of food, including light snacks, sharing food platters and breakfast, lunch and dinner menus.

There's usually an entrance fee – usually £5-10 – to join the crowd of mainly trendy 20-somethings who come here to drink, socialise and be entertained in this stimulating venue.

THE BOW WINE VAULTS

> **Address:** 10 Bow Churchyard, EC4M 9DQ (☎ 020-7248 1121,
> 🖳 bowwinevaults.com).
> **Opening hours:** Mon-Fri, 11am to 11pm; closed weekends.
> **Transport:** Mansion House or Bank tube.
> **Go for:** Good, reasonably-priced wine in an interesting part of the City.

Attractively situated in an atmospheric lane overlooked by the church
of St Mary-le-Bow ('true' Cockneys are supposed to be born within the
sound of its bells), the Bow Wine Vaults is in one of the most historic
and characterful parts of the City. It's a traditional wine bar, brasserie
and restaurant, which has been trading since 1987.

The Bow Wine Vaults has a nicely understated interior and a choice
of places to eat and drink. You can perch on a stool at the upstairs
bar, sit at one of its brasserie tables – the outdoor terrace tables are
especially sought-after and available all year – or eat downstairs in the
restaurant for a more luxurious experience.

There's a well-chosen range of around 50 wines, with around a
dozen also available by the glass. Prices are reasonable for the City,
with most bottles in the £20-30 range, while the house red is £18.10
a bottle and the white £18.50. The wine bar menu has good, simple,
filling food: Welsh rarebit, steak sandwiches, platters and so forth. In
short, it's a civilised, Gallic-leaning haven in the hectic financial district.

CALLOOH CALLAY

Address: 65 Rivington Street, EC2A 3AY (☎ 020-7739 4781, 🖥 calloohcallaybar.com).
Opening times: Sun-Wed, 6pm to midnight; Thu-Sat, 6pm to 1am.
Transport: Old Street tube/rail or Shoreditch High Street rail.
Go for: Cocktails in an imaginative, quirky environment.

Set on a cobbled side street and loosely Lewis-Carroll-themed – named after an expression in his nonsense poem *Jabberwocky* – this cocktail bar is a recent addition to Shoreditch's buzzy bar scene. It's been put together with imagination and definitely generates a sense of occasion.

Callooh Callay is split into three areas – The Bar, The Lounge and the Jubjub Members Bar – and you go through a 'wardrobe' (shouldn't that be a looking glass?) to reach the main bar area, which has a long bar counter and low purple seating. There are DJs at weekends. Cocktails are the drink of choice here and there's an interesting range to choose from – prices start from £8.50 – as well as imaginative, well-presented bar snacks.

Callooh Callay has quickly become popular and you sometimes have to queue to get in, therefore booking is recommended. It's worth the effort, as this venue is funky, quirky and swish (over-21s only and no hen or stag parties), if sometimes rather crowded and loud.

THE CAPTAIN KIDD

Address: 108 Wapping High Street, E1W 2NE (☎ 020-7480 5759).
Opening hours: Mon-Sat, noon to 11pm; Sun, noon to 10.30pm.
Transport: Wapping rail.
Go for: Exceptional riverside views.

This Sam Smith's pub by the river in Wapping is named after an infamous pirate who was hanged at nearby Execution Dock in 1701. Set in a recently-converted ('80s) warehouse, it doesn't look much from the street, but has the brewery's typical interior: smart and understated.

As well as the usual well-kept, keenly-priced beer in the two bars, the pub serves bar snacks, and there's also food available in the upstairs restaurant (it seems to divide opinion, from tasty and wholesome to typical pub grub or just okay). But for many, the main attraction of the Captain Kidd is its expansive river views from the terrace and riverside seats in the restaurant, which offer some of London's best windows on the Thames. Indeed, the river reaches right to the pub's walls, which can be slightly alarming for those of a nervous disposition (or those who cannot swim).

The Captain Kidd is also a fine spot from which to watch the comings and goings at the London River Police's moorings next door, providing one of London's most original Thames vistas to contemplate as you savour a drink.

THE CARPENTER'S ARMS

Address: 73 Cheshire Street, E2 6EG (☎ 020-7739 6342,
🖥 carpentersarmsfreehouse.com).
Opening hours: Mon-Wed, 4-11.30pm; Thu and Sun, noon to 11.30pm;
Fri-Sat, noon to 12.30am.
Transport: Bethnal Green tube.
Go for: Good beer, a warm welcome and an award-winning Sunday lunch.

123

Once owned by the infamous Kray family – Reggie and Ronnie bought it for their mum, Violet – the Carpenter's Arms is a stroll into Bethnal Green from the north end of Brick Lane. It was revamped and spruced up a few years ago and they've done a good job, turning it into an elegant, understated place to enjoy a drink, with dark wood, large windows and traditional fittings.

The pub was voted Best Newcomer 2008 by Fancyapint (🖥 fancyapint.com) due to its fine range of beer, which includes three hand pumps (Adnams' ales feature regularly) and a wide bottled selection. There's solid food too, including burgers, charcuterie, cheeseboards, homemade chips, pies and roasts, all fairly priced. The pub has also received a *Time Out* 'Best Sunday Lunch Award'. Arrive early on Sundays, as the word has spread and it quickly fills up.

The Carpenter's Arms is a popular venue, attracting a trendy crowd, and can become busy though rarely uncomfortably so. And as well as good beer and food, the atmosphere is a draw: cosy, relaxed and welcoming.

CELLAR GASCON

Address: 59 West Smithfield, EC1A 9DS (☎ 020-7600 7561,
🖳 www.clubgascon.com/cellar).
Opening hours: Mon-Fri, noon to midnight; closed weekends.
Transport: Farringdon tube/rail.
Go for: A great pairing of French food and wine.

A spin-off from next door's restaurant, Club Gascon, this is a must for lovers of French food and wine. Like its neighbour, it's particularly strong on the wines of southwest France (Gascony is the coastal region between Bordeaux and the Spanish border), but also stocks a good choice of wines from other regions, e.g. Alsace, Burgundy and the Loire Valley.

Cellar Gascon has a slightly club-like atmosphere, albeit a modern one, with leather banquettes and dim lighting (you can also sit at the bar), and this goes down well with the clientele, which includes a fair number of pinstriped City workers. They come to enjoy one of London's better specialist wine bars, offering a choice of around 200 wines at reasonable prices, with around 20 available by the glass – the choice changes regularly.

The food is excellent. Quality overrules quantity, and the emphasis is on small pates of delicious morsels. Dishes are meaty and a few are *foie-gras* based, so don't bring any squeamish eaters or vegetarians. In short, Cellar Gascon is a refined venue that demonstrates the wisdom of pairing local wines and regional cuisine.

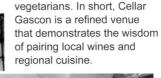

THE COACH & HORSES

Address: 26-28 Ray Street, EC1R 3DJ (☎ 020-7278 8990, 🖥 thecoachandhorses.com).
Opening hours: Mon-Fri, noon to 11pm; Sat, 6-11pm; Sun, 1-5pm. The pub isn't open every weekend, so check in advance.
Transport: Farringdon tube/rail.
Go for: A good all-round pub for beer, wine, food and atmosphere.

Sitting near Hatton Garden, this used to be a regular haunt of *Guardian* staff before the newspaper moved from Clerkenwell to King's Cross in 2008. There were fears that the loss of such famously (notoriously?) free-drinking customers would signal the decline of the Coach & Horses, but thankfully it's still going strong.

This is a good pub with enjoyable food (there's increasing emphasis on this aspect – the journalists presumably weren't interested in such distractions), and has the standard gastropub interior of wood-panelled walls, plain furniture, wooden floorboards, etched glass windows and arty prints. There are a number of outdoor tables, too.

Good beer is served and there's a well-chosen wine list, reasonably priced, with bottles from around £14 and a number of wines available by the glass. The food is modern British with main courses costing in

the £9.50-13.50 range. So, good drinks, enjoyable food, fair prices, professional service and a warm atmosphere – you can't ask for much more from a pub. How the *Guardian* hacks must miss it!

THE CRAFT BEER COMPANY

Address: 82 Leather Lane, EC1N 7TR (⌨ thecraftbeerco.com).
Opening hours: Mon-Sat, noon to 11pm; Sun, noon to 10.30pm.
Transport: Farringdon tube/rail.
Go for: One of Britain's broadest selections of craft beer.

What used to be the Clockhouse pub has, since summer 2011, been recast as this aptly-named brewpub which offers a vast selection of brilliant beers from around the world, many previously unavailable in the UK. (It also has outlets in Brixton, Islington and Brighton, Sussex.)

126

It isn't what you'd call a cosy, comfortable place – plain décor, white walls, and bright lights – but the focus is very much on the beer. There are 16 cask ales from Britain's finest independent microbreweries, and 21 keg beers, which is one of the UK's largest selections – unusually, the Craft Beer Company import the beers themselves. In addition, the bottled choice runs to over 400. There's a huge beer 'menu' to read through, and knowledgeable staff to give advice. Regular beer tastings take place if you want to expand your knowledge.

There's also a fair choice of wine and spirits, as well as good bar snacks of the pork pie and Scotch egg variety. Expect to pay high prices for some of the more exclusive beers; then again, this may be your only opportunity to try them.

THE CROSSE KEYS

Address: 9 Gracechurch Street, EC3V 0DR (☎ 020-7623 4824,
🖥 jdwetherspoon.co.uk/home/pubs/the-crosse-keys).
Opening hours: Mon-Thu, 9am to 11pm; Fri, 7am to midnight; Sat, 9am to
7pm; closed Sun.
Transport: Cannon Street tube/rail.
Go for: The City's widest choice of cask ale in an impressive environment.

JD Wetherspoon's pubs are too corporate for some tastes, but this
one is notable for its quite remarkable selection of cask ale, offering
what's probably the City's widest choice of beer, all at the pub chain's
usual keen prices.

The Crosse Keys is named after an old coaching inn that once
stood near the site, and has been a Wetherspoon's establishment
since 1999. In a previous life, the building was the London
headquarters of the HSBC bank and is an impressive space, with
many original features, including marble, pillars, rococo ceilings,
skylights and a tiled mosaic floor. A striking staircase leads to a
balcony with a variety of nooks and crannies.

As for the beer, there are between around 15 and 25, helpfully
listed on TV monitors above the bar. Fuller's and Greene King are
the only regulars, so this is a great venue for those seeking constant
variety, served by friendly staff. The Crosse gets busy during the
week, therefore Saturday is the best day to mull over the beer
selection.

127

THE DICKENS INN

Address: Marble Quay, St Katherine's Way, E1W 1UH (☎ 020-7488 2208,
🖥 dickensinn.co.uk).
Opening hours: Mon-Sat, 11am to 11pm; Sun, noon to 10.30pm.
Transport: Tower Hill tube/DLR.
Go for: A good pint in a lively environment with views of St Katherine Docks.

A large, touristy pub near Tower Bridge, the Dickens is different from
most of the other venues in this book, but it's a lively location with a
surprisingly good choice of beer.

The Dickens Inn (which, by the way, has no connection with the
author) was originally an 18th-century brewery building, later a spice
warehouse, and was transported to St Katherine Docks in 1976 from
its original location just to the east. Photos of its reconstruction on
the site are displayed inside. The pub is spread over three floors,
modelled in the style of a balconied 19th-
century inn, and different food is served on
each level: bar food on the ground floor,
pizza in the middle and more refined fare
on the top floor.

The terrace affords panoramic views
of the docks, where smart vessels bob
in the marina and warehouses have
been transformed into posh shops and
luxury apartments. While soaking up the
atmosphere you can enjoy a pint from
the well-chosen range, including Adnams,
Caledonian Deuchars IPA, Greene King
IPA, London Pride, Old Speckled Hen,
Sharp's Doom Bar and Wells Bombardier.

THE DOVETAIL

> **Address:** 9-10 Jerusalem Passage, EC1V 6JP (☎ 020-7490 7321.
> 🖳 dovepubs.com).
> **Opening hours:** Mon-Sat, noon to 11pm; Sun, 1-9pm.
> **Transport:** Farringdon tube/rail.
> **Go for:** Belgian beer, burgers and sausages in a quirky environment.

Situated just off Clerkenwell
Green, down an alleyway
that has associations with
the Order of St John (which
itself has long Clerkenwell
connections), this is a fine
Belgian bar. The décor is
an intriguingly quirky mix of
Gothic chairs, green tiled
tables, Tintin posters, and
a small marble and pewter
bar – the effect is that of a
slightly camp monastery.

129

The choice of beer is a big draw, with more than 100 brews to try,
ranging from the well-known to the obscure. Lovers of the grape are
catered for as well, with a fair choice of wine (from £15.95 a bottle),
some also available by the glass.

The food is good and eating is essential to help stave off the effects
of the high alcoholic content of some of the brews served; many are
in the range of 7-11 per cent
alcohol by volume (abv),
which is more than twice
as strong as British beers
– you have been warned!
Burgers and sausages are
a speciality, with the meat
sourced from farms in
Devon and Wiltshire,
and there's a beer and
cheese fondue, too.

THE EAGLE

Address: 159 Farringdon Road, EC1R 3AL (☎ 020-7837 1353).
Opening hours: Mon-Sat, noon to 11pm; Sun, noon to 5pm.
Transport: Farringdon tube/rail.
Go for: The original gastropub experience, still done well.

This falls into the must-visit-at-least-once category of London pubs – along with Soho's **Coach & Horses** (see page 42) and Blackfriars's **Black Friar** (see page 118) – and this is due to its trail-blazing role as arguably the UK's first gastropub.

It started serving posh pub grub in 1991 and still remains popular, while many imitators have fallen beside the wayside. This is understandable, as the Eagle does the gastropub 'model' well: it offers people a good pint or glass of wine with well-cooked food in a pared-back space of plain walls and wood (with large windows providing plenty of natural light), and all for a reasonable price.

Around six beers are available (usually including four real ales), there's a short wine list and even a few cocktails. The menu is chalked on blackboards and consists

mainly of well-executed Spanish & Mediterranean fare, which is cooked in full view of diners in an open kitchen. Friendly, efficient staff oversee a crowded, noisy pub with shared tables and a great vibe. There's no booking, so arrive early or late to ensure a place.

EL VINO'S

Address: 47 Fleet Street, EC4Y 1BJ (☎ 020-7353 6786, 🖳 elvino.co.uk).
Opening hours: Mon, 8.30am to 9pm; Tue-Fri, 8.30am to 10pm; closed weekends.
Transport: Chancery Lane or Temple tube.
Go for: Good wine, solid food and old school conviviality.

El Vino's was established in 1879 and is said to be the model for the fictional Pommeroys, the oft-frequented local wine bar of John Mortimer's barrister character, Horace Rumpole (*Rumpole of the Bailey*). It's now part of a small chain, which also includes outlets at London Wall, New Bridge Street, Mark Lane (trading as Ruskins) and Martin Lane – the latter, called the Olde Wine Shades, is the oldest wine house in the City.

131

Given El Vino's Fleet Street location, it used to be the haunt of the Fourth Estate's famously-thirsty journalists, but their industry has moved elsewhere and many of today's regulars are barristers, solicitors and other City types. These are often discerning folk who favour this traditional, old school wine bar and its dark wood interior, which also operates as a wine shop.

There's an extensive, well-chosen list of around 200 wines, simple but well-prepared food and friendly, well-informed staff, all to be enjoyed in an understated, relaxed environment. Booking is recommended for a venue where it's all too easy to while away the afternoon and suddenly realise it's last orders.

FILTHY MACNASTY'S WHISKEY CAFE

> **Address:** 68 Amwell Street EC1R 1UU (☎ 020-8617 3505,
> 🖳 filthymacnastys.co.uk).
> **Opening hours:** Mon-Sat, noon to 11pm; Sun, noon to 10.30pm.
> **Transport:** Angel tube.
> **Go for:** Whiskey, music… and more whiskey.

Sitting between Clerkenwell, Islington and King's Cross, this friendly, popular venue specialises in whiskey (or whisky, if you prefer) and Guinness. But it isn't a clichéd 'Oirish' theme bar, rather a grown-up venue for those seeking an interesting selection of drinks and a good time.

As you might reasonably hope, there's a great choice of whiskey/whisky – Irish, of course, but also Scotch, although the longest list details the bar's American offerings. There's also a fair selection for ale lovers, while there's pub grub as well as pizzas and a Sunday roast.

Filthy MacNasty's follows the Irish tradition of providing entertainment with the alcohol. It's noted for its live music – Pete Doherty apparently used to work behind the bar, and his band The Libertines played some of their first gigs here – and also stages music quizzes, literary readings and other events. It even supplies board games. All this takes place in a cosy, red interior with comfortable furniture. Note you'll need to arrive early if you want to bag a sofa.

FLUID

Address: 40 Charterhouse Street, EC1M 6JN (☎ 020-7253 3444,
🖳 fluidbar.com).
Opening hours: Mon-Wed, noon to midnight; Thu, noon to 2am; Fri, noon to
4am; Sat, 7pm to 4am; closed Sun.
Transport: Farringdon tube/rail.
Go for: Japanese drinks, sushi snacks and a nightclub vibe.

This popular, late-night, Japanese-themed venue is spread over
various levels and becomes less a bar and more a nightclub as the
weekend approaches. It's a fashionable place with some interesting
design touches, including a mural of Tokyo at night and retro table-top
arcade games.

Japanese drinks dominate the bar list, which includes sake, shochu
(a vodka-like spirit) and whisky – shots cost from £2.50. There's a
choice of beer, with bottles starting at £3.50, including Japanese brews
but also Guinness, cider and Belgian beer if you prefer. Cocktails are a
speciality, reasonably priced at around £7 and served 'with an eastern
twist'. Unsurprisingly, the food on offer is Japanese, too, and includes
sushi, tempura and various bento boxes. Don't leave it too late to order
as the kitchen shuts at 10pm (it's also closed Mondays).

133

Fluid features DJ slots most evenings and there's sometimes an
entry fee of £5-7 after 10pm on Fridays and Saturdays, depending on
who the DJ is. The dress code is casual, but a
bit of imagination won't go amiss. All in all, it's
place to stay up late and have fun.

THE FOX & ANCHOR

Address: 115 Charterhouse Street, EC1M 6AA (☏ 020-7250 1300,
🖥 foxandanchor.com).
Opening hours: Mon-Fri, 7am to 11pm; Sat, 8.30am to 11pm; Sun, 8.30am
to 10pm. Alcohol served from opening time onwards.
Transport: Farringdon tube/rail.
Go for: Attractive décor and a beer with breakfast, if you wish.

The Fox & Anchor is an attractive heritage pub in one of the most
historic parts of Clerkenwell. It has a striking exterior of mosaic tiles
and etched glass, and a classic late Victorian interior, with dark wood,
floor mosaics, mirrors, and a pewter bar and beer mugs. Tucked in the
back is The Fox's Den, a trio of cosy wooden booths. Upstairs, there's
accommodation, with six enchanting rooms.

The Fox has been serving the traders of Smithfield Market for
years, hence the early licensing hours. Smithfield starts trading at 3am
and finishes before noon, so its workers are hungry and thirsty by 8am
(it's 'lunchtime' to them).

The pub has a good choice of beer, including its own-label ale, plus
guest ales from brewers such as Adnams and Sharp's. There's also

a wide choice of bottled beers, as well
as whisky and wine. The Fox & Anchor
also serves excellent food, specialising
in simple, tasty British fare, although it's
become more 'gastro' over the years.
If you can manage it, the City Boy
Breakfast comes with a City Boy price
tag of £16.95 but does include steak,
liver, kidneys and a pint of stout!

THE GOLDEN HEART

Address: 110 Commercial Street, E1 6LZ (☎ 020-7247 2158).
Opening hours: Mon-Sat, 11am to midnight; Sun, noon to 10.30pm.
Transport: Liverpool Street tube/rail or Shoreditch High Street rail.
Go for: Tracey Emin art with your pint, perhaps a glimpse of Tracey, too.

This large, traditional, Truman pub is near Spitalfields and its clientele reflects the varied, changing nature of the area: a mix of old school locals, the odd City suit from up the road, traders from nearby Spitalfields Market and a number of arty trendies from the recent influx.

The art theme is carried further, as not only does Tracey Emin frequent the Golden Heart (she has a property in the area), but a number of her works have been

135

featured here, including one in neon outside marking the marriage of long-time landlady Sandra Esquilant to her (late) husband Dennis.

Apart from this, the pub's a traditional affair, with dark wood panelling and striped wallpaper, and a good range of drinks. Beers include Adnams and Leffe, and there's a well-priced wine list. It's a popular boozer and a good place for people-watching, but can become crowded, particularly on Friday nights and Sunday lunchtimes. Some people find the staff a touch brusque, while others think they're interestingly edgy and eccentric.

THE GRAPES

Address: 76 Narrow Street, E14 8BP (☎ 020-7987 4396, 🖳 thegrapes.co.uk).
Opening hours: Mon-Wed, noon to 3pm and 5.30-11pm; Thu-Sat, noon to 11pm; Sun, noon to 10.30pm.
Transport: Limehouse DLR.
Go for: Over 400 years of history and the chance of meeting Gandalf.

This attractive, riverside pub is one of the area's oldest, founded in 1583 and rebuilt in 1720. It's part of a Georgian terrace and backs on to the river, with a small wooden terrace close to the Thames. The Grapes is said to have been Charles Dickens's inspiration for the Six Jolly Fellowship Porters pub in his 1864 novel *Our Mutual Friend*.

It's a traditional pub, with bare floorboards, nautical decorations and wood panels. A narrow bar leads to a snug – The Dickens Snug (what else?) – and there's an upstairs dining room (with a good fish menu), which has glorious views towards the City and Canary Wharf. That said, many diners are happy with fish and chips or similar in the atmospheric bar.

They stock good ales, such as Adnams and Timothy Taylor, and some decent wines although the cheapest bottle is £22. Last, but not least, Sir Ian McKellen is one of the pub's leaseholders, so if you're lucky you might get to sip a pint next to Gandalf (or at least his earthly incarnation).

THE GUN

Address: 27 Coldharbour, E14 9NS (☎ 020-7515 5222,
🖥 thegundocklands.com).
Opening hours: Mon-Sat, 11am to midnight; Sun, 11am to 11pm.
Transport: Canary Wharf DLR.
Go for: Good beer, quality food and a singular view of the Dome.

Housed in a striking, Grade II listed, 18th-century building, the Gun was for many years a run-down boozer for local foundry and river workers, but it was given a makeover after a fire in 2001 and moved up in the world. It's now a popular, renowned gastropub, which is just a short walk from Canary Wharf and caters to the ranks of moneyed traders.

There's a good choice of beer, with the likes of London Pride and Adnams ales as regulars, an extensive wine list and good-quality food, including such delights as pheasant, oysters and salt-marsh lamb. Main courses range between £14 and £28 – trader rather than tourist prices – although less expensive food is available at the bar. In summer it has an al-fresco bar, called A Grelha, which serves Portuguese classics on a barbecue.

High-backed leather armchairs, smartly turned out waiters and impressive views of the O2 (the Millennium Dome, before the

rebranding) across the river are further draws for this popular venue, where booking is recommended.

THE GUNMAKERS

Address: 13 Eyre Street Hill, EC1R 5ET (☎ 020-7278 1022,
💻 thegunmakers.co.uk).
Opening hours: Mon-Fri, noon to 11pm; closed weekends.
Transport: Farringdon tube/rail.
Go for: A pint-sized pub serving a good pint and tasty food.

The Gunmakers is on a Clerkenwell side street and has an
understated black frontage with gold lettering. Its name comes from
the fact that this was a gunmaker's premises from the middle to the
end of the 19th century. It's a friendly, cosy, albeit tiny pub, although
the walls are lined with ornate mirrors that make it feel larger than it
is. There's no music or television to create a distraction, and it's an
excellent venue for a first date.

The food is French-influenced and good enough to earn the
Gunmakers a gastropub tag. The kitchen
is open noon to 3pm and 6-9.30pm,
with most mains priced in the £12-15
range. There's a well-chosen wine list
and, unusually for a gastropub, this is
also a destination for beer aficionados
– there are usually four ales on offer,
often including a Purity beer as well
as Adnams and Woodforde's, plus a
selection of guest brews.

The Gunmakers' formula works and
the pub soon fills up, attracting a smart
clientele. Booking is recommended to
be sure of getting a table.

HAWKSMOOR SPITALFIELDS

Address: 157 Commercial Street, E1 6BJ (☎ 020-7426 4856,
🖥 thehawksmoor.com/spitalfieldsbar).
Opening hours: Mon-Thu, 5.45-11pm; Fri, 5.45pm to midnight; Sat, noon to midnight; Sun, noon to 11pm.
Transport: Aldgate East tube or Liverpool Street tube/rail.
Go for: Classy cocktails, wine and beer in a super-stylish environment.

The original of a chain of four steakhouses and bars (the others are in Covent Garden, just off Regent Street and near the Guildhall), this is just down the road from architect Nicholas Hawksmoor's elegant Christ Church, Spitalfields – hence the name. The cellar bar has a striking décor, comprising copper wall panels and turquoise Victorian glazed bricks.

In trying to create London's best cocktail bars, Hawksmoor have apparently 'scoured our library of long out-of-print cocktail books to resurrect some great long-lost classics'. They've also invented a few of their own, with skilled bartenders working their magic from an extensive list, priced between £8.50 and £18.

There's also an excellent wine list (also online), with a number of wines sold by the glass; glasses cost from £5.50, bottles from £18. Beer drinkers can enjoy ales from Bermondsey's Kernel brewery and Greenwich's Meantime.

Hawksmoor Spitalfields' restaurant is a shrine to British meat, from porcine power breakfasts to serious steaks – and serious prices to match. But choose the bar menu and you can also tuck in to burgers and hot dogs (£8-9), and triple-cooked chips.

THE HOOP & GRAPES

Address: 47 Aldgate High Street, EC3N 1AL (☎ 020-7481 4583,
🖥 nicholsonspubs.co.uk/thehoopandgrapesaldgatelondon).
Opening hours: Mon-Fri, 10am to 11pm; closed weekends.
Transport: Aldgate tube.
Go for: A pub full of history and character, which also serves good ale.

140

This is one of London's oldest pubs, in one of the most historic parts of the capital: Aldgate dates back to Roman times and was the most easterly of the six London Wall gateways, which marked the old boundary between City and East End until its demolition in 1761.

The Hoop and Grapes was built in 1598 (originally called The Castle) and has the distinction of being one of the only remaining timber-framed buildings in London. It survived the Great Fire of 1666 by sheer good fortune; it's said the flames stopped just 50 yards (45m) from the front door. The building's structure has shifted over the centuries by around 18 inches (46cm), resulting in a pleasing 'wonkiness' which adds to its character, and while it was restored in the '80s, fortunately this was sensitively done.

Today, the Hoop is popular with City workers, and with tourists drawn by its history; it's on the route of walks which explore Jack the Ripper's gory crimes. It's also a proper beer-drinker's pub, with offerings such as Adnams ales, London Pride, Wadworth and Old Speckled Hen.

THE JAMAICA WINE HOUSE

Address: St Michael's Alley, EC3V 9DS (☎ 020-7929 6972,
🖳 jamaicawinehouse.co.uk).
Opening hours: Mon-Fri, 11am to 11pm; closed weekends.
Transport: Bank tube.
Go for: A historic old coffee house serving Kentish ale.

Set in a back alley off Cornhill, near the Royal Exchange, this is a
long-time draw for the pinstriped brigade, and has been refreshing
thirsty punters for more than 300 years. Although the current building
dates from the 19th century, the Jamaica is on the site of the City's
first coffee house, which opened in 1652. Samuel Pepys was a
regular back then.

The Jampot – as locals call it – has a nicely old-fashioned air,
wood-lined and full of welcoming nooks and crannies, and you can
step outside into the traffic-free alley when the sun shines. Despite the
name, it's more pub than wine bar, and is owned by the Kent brewery
Shepherd Neame, so there's a good range of well-kept Kentish ales,
as well as lager and wine. Downstairs, Todds Wine Bar is a recent
addition to the operation and here the focus is on the grape rather
than the grain. It serves good restaurant food,
with most mains under a tenner, or you can tuck
in to burgers and snacks in the Jampot's bar.

Mid-afternoon is the best time for a tranquil
pint, after the hectic lunch period and before the
evening rush.

141

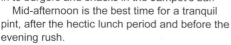

THE JERUSALEM TAVERN

Address: 55 Britton Street, EC1M 5UQ (☎ 020-7490 4281,
🖥 stpetersbrewery.co.uk/london-pub).
Opening hours: Mon-Fri, 11am to 11pm; closed weekends.
Transport: Farringdon tube/rail.
Go for: Good Suffolk beer in an atmospheric pub.

London outpost of St Peter's Brewery, a small specialist brewery
based in Suffolk, the Jerusalem Tavern is an old-fashioned inn which
occupies a building dating back to 1720, with a frontage added in
1810. The building didn't become a pub until 1996, but it looks as if
it should be one of the City's oldest watering holes. The name is a
reference to the Priory of St John of Jerusalem, which was founded
nearby in 1140.

The pub's interior is nicely higgledy-piggledy with a glass partition
that's a relic of the building's former life as a watchmaker's; it used to
separate the watchmaker's shop from his workshop and is now used
to mark off a seating area.

The Jerusalem Tavern is
a small pub and gets busy at
lunchtimes and early evenings.
It's popular with the area's
creative, media and legal types,
who come to enjoy the brewery's
excellent cask and bottled beers
as well as tasty pub grub. A
relaxing spot in which to enjoy
good beer, just as a traditional
pub should be.

St Peter's Brewery

THE LAMB TAVERN

Address: 10-12 Leadenhall Market, EC3V 1LR (☎ 020-7626 2454,
🖥 lambtavernleadenhall.co.uk).
Opening hours: Mon-Fri, 11am to 11pm; closed weekends.
Transport: Bank tube or Fenchurch Street rail.
Go for: An atmospheric Victorian pub in one of London's oldest markets.

A Young's pub, the Lamb Tavern is one of the City's better watering holes. It could scarcely have a better location, being at the heart of the elegant splendour of Leadenhall Market and near the iconic Lloyd's of London building, whose brokers and underwriters form a significant part of its clientele.

The pub originated in 1780, although the current, Grade II listed building dates from 1881. The covered market is a classical Victorian structure, but Leadenhall is one of London's oldest markets, dating back to 1309, and both market and pub are built on the site of the Roman Basilica from 50AD.

The Lamb has a rich red and gold-coloured frontage, a first floor dining room providing good views over the market, and a basement wine bar with attractive Edwardian tiles. As for drinks, there's a well-chosen wine list to appeal to City types, as well as Wells' and Young's ales and Sharp's Doom Bar. The best place to drink is outside the pub on the market cobblestones.

LOUNGELOVER

> **Address:** 1 Whitby Street, E1 6JU (☎ 020-7012 1234, 🖥 loungeloveruk.com).
> **Opening hours:** Sun-Thu, 6pm to midnight; Fri, 5.30pm to 1am; Sat, 6pm to 1am.
> **Transport:** Liverpool Street tube/rail.
> **Go for:** Unusual cocktails and unforgettable décor.

Housed in a former meat packing factory, this cocktail bar is run by the team behind next door's restaurant, Les Trois Garcons. Although it's been around since 2003, Loungelover is still regarded by those-in-the-know as a cool destination, which is no mean feat in the fickle world of trendy bar affiliation.

This may, in part, be down to its award-winning design which is high-camp kitsch, splendidly over-the-top (jarringly so to some eyes), consisting of a series of themed areas, including the Baroque, the Cage and the Gold Room. There's all sorts of stuff crammed in here – antiques, art, chandeliers, a disco ball, plants, even a stuffed hippo's head – all designed to give the place an air of stylish, inventive decadence.

Fashionable bar staff serve up tremendous, inventive cocktails – priced at £8.50-12 – and tapas-like snacks and nibbles, many with an Oriental influence (but watch out for added charges and tips). Loungelover gets busy at weekends when it's advisable to book a table.

144

MADISON

Address: One New Change, EC4M 9AF (☎ 020-8305 3088,
🖥 madisonlondon.net).
Opening hours: Mon-Sat, noon to midnight; Sun, noon to 8pm.
Transport: St Paul's tube.
Go for: Watching the sun set over St Paul's while enjoying a glass of wine.

Madison has a near-perfect location, on
the sixth floor of the One New Change
shopping and leisure development just
east of St Paul's, on one of Europe's
largest roof terraces. Reached by a glass
lift, it has a restaurant and cocktail/tapas
bar, both offering close-up views of the
iconic St Paul's Cathedral and beyond,
towards landmarks such as the London
Eye, Tate Modern and the Shard.

The bar is sleek and modern, designed to appeal to City workers,
with plenty of seating and large, slanted glass windows to maximise
the views. There's a wide choice of drinks, to suit a wide range of
budgets. Cocktails include classic mixes as well as faux-sexy blends
(e.g. Pornstar Martini), while there's a selection of spirits and beers.

Wine and champagne drinkers have a well-chosen list, including
some fine vintages with deep City pockets and tastes in mind.
Glasses start at £6, bottles from £19, which is reasonable given the
postcode. 'Tapas', priced from £6 upwards, include some tempting
seafood treats and an ice cream sundae!

NIGHTJAR

Address: 129 City Road, EC1V 1JB (☎ 020-7253 4101, ⌨ barnightjar.com).
Opening hours: Sun-Wed, 6pm to 1am; Thu, 6pm to 2am; Fri-Sat, 6pm to 3am.
Transport: Old Street tube/rail.
Go for: Vintage jazz, cutting-edge cocktails and a touch of old school glamour.

The anonymous entrance to this stylish Shoreditch basement bar sits incongruously between two cafeterias. Reminiscent of a '20s speakeasy, it specialises in cocktails, cabaret and jazz, and has a debonair atmosphere, describing itself as 'a hidden slice of old school glamour'. The interior is all dark wood, dim lighting and black leather booths – very much a place for grown-ups.

Cocktails are the thing here, both ancient and modern – some recipes date back to 1600 while others include unusual flavourings such as durian fruit and bee pollen syrup – and very good they are too, priced from £9. Beer, spirits and wine are also available; while bar snacks include cheese, charcuterie and tapas. Nightjar is popular and has a no-standing policy, therefore booking is advisable, certainly from Wed-Sat.

There's vintage live music from the cocktail era ('20s, '30s and '40s) from 9.30pm Tue-Sat. It's free on Tuesdays, but there's a door charge between 8.45 and 11 or 11.30pm on Wednesdays and Thursdays (£5), and Fridays and Saturdays (£7).

THE OLD DR BUTLER'S HEAD

Address: 2 Masons Avenue, EC2V 5BT (☎ 020-7606 3504,
🖥 olddoctorbutlershead.co.uk).
Opening hours: Mon-Fri, 11am to 11pm; closed weekends.
Transport: Moorgate tube/rail.
Go for: Fine beer and a rather unusual history.

147

Owned by Shepherd Neame, this oddly-named pub near Moorgate has an interesting past. Back in the 1500s, Dr William Butler wangled himself a position as James I's court physician, despite being a quack with no medical training. Among other creative 'cures', he developed his own medicinal ale and the name comes from the fact that pubs selling his brew displayed his portrait.

There's been a pub here since 1610, although much of what remains today is from much later. It doesn't give an impression of great age but is attractive and characterful – a rarity in this part of the City – with a Dickensian atmosphere, gas-lit and wood-panelled, and the opportunity to drink outside in the pedestrians-only Masons Avenue.

Many City workers come here to enjoy the range of well-kept Shepherd Neame ales, including the perennially popular Bishop's Finger and Spitfire; sadly, Dr Butler's ale is no longer served. The pub can be tricky to find, as it's hidden away down Mason's Alley, next to 30 Coleman Street, but is worth the effort.

THE OLD FOUNTAIN

Address: 3 Baldwin Street, EC1V 9NU (☎ 020-7253 2970, 🖳 oldfountain.co.uk).
Opening hours: Mon-Fri, 11am to 11pm; Sat, noon to 11pm; Sun, noon to 10pm.
Transport: Old Street tube/rail.
Go for: Great beer and live music in a convivial atmosphere.

Named after the medicinal springs for which this part of the City used to be famous, the Old Fountain is a freehouse – run by the Durrant family since 1964 – with a hospitable atmosphere. It's a serious beer-lovers' pub and was voted CAMRA (Campaign for Real Ale) 'East London and City Pub of the Year' 2011.

There are up to eight real ales at any one time (you can check out each day's ale listing on Twitter), with London Pride the house cask ale. Brodie's, Dark Star, Pitfield and York also put in regular appearances, and there's an interesting choice by the bottle. Good lager, wheat beer, fruit beer and real cider are available, too. You need hearty grub to soak up the ale, and favourites include roast beef, Cumberland sausage sarnies and homemade soups, as well as omelettes, jackets and salads (served between noon and 2.30pm).

The Old Fountain has a recently opened roof terrace for sunny days, and hosts live music on Saturday nights and some Sundays (see website for listings).

THE OLD RED COW

Address: 71-72 Long Lane, EC1A 9EJ (☎ 020-7726 2595, 🖥 theoldredcow.com).
Opening hours: Mon-Thu, noon to 11pm; Fri-Sat, noon to midnight; Sun, noon to 10.30pm.
Transport: Farringdon tube/rail.
Go for: A celebration of British and foreign beers.

Situated near London's premier meat market Smithfield, the appropriately-named Old Red Cow describes itself as a 'local beer house' and states its aim to be a 'delicatessen of beer', celebrating British and foreign microbreweries. This may sound pretentious but it's a warmly welcoming place to drink.

149

The interior is modern and understated, with some quirky touches, and the emphasis is firmly on the beer. There are four hand pumps dispensing real ale – such as Hophead and Wandle – while around a dozen taps along the

back of the bar have a changing selection of keg beer, including BrewDog, Camden, Redemption and Sambrook's. More choice is provided by a carefully chosen range of bottled beers.

Wine drinkers aren't neglected, with a reasonable selection, some available in two glass sizes as well as by the bottle; glasses cost from £3.90, bottles from £18. The food menu is a carnivore's treat (with some veggie options), ranging from bar snacks to sharing plates and priced from £3 to £30 – plus a Sunday roast for £14.50 – and all served by friendly, knowledgeable staff.

THE OWL & PUSSYCAT

Address: 34 Redchurch Street, E2 7DP (☎ 020-3487 0088,
🖥 owlandpussycatshoreditch.com).
Opening hours: Sun-Mon, noon to 11pm; Tue-Sat, noon to midnight.
Transport: Shoreditch High Street rail.
Go for: A gastropub with good beer and a garden.

It's sometimes difficult to remember that creative, self-consciously hip Shoreditch was, until recently, just a rundown corner of east London. But the gentrification continues and what was once a traditional East End pub has now had a gastro makeover. Fortunately, it hasn't forgotten that a pub should also serve good beer.

There's a downstairs bar, plus an upstairs restaurant specialising in modern British food. Main courses are generally priced around

£13-18, with cheaper options in the bar. The décor is typical understated gastropub design, with plenty of bare brick and wood.

As well as some good wines – several offered by the glass as well as the bottle – there are four rotating ales to hearten beer fans, including the likes of Brakspear and Marston's. There's also a pleasant back garden which is heated in winter. It's a popular location and soon fills up with a mixed crowd of local creative folk and City types. Staff are friendly and quite trendy – it's a trendy part of town – while prices are slightly above average but justified.

THE PALM TREE

Address: 127 Grove Road, E3 5BH (☎ 020-8980 2918).
Opening hours: Mon-Thu, noon to midnight; Fri-Sat, noon to 2am; Sun, noon to 1am. Last admission 10.45pm.
Transport: Mile End tube.
Go for: A genuine East End boozer in a green oasis.

The Palm Tree is a characterful East End freehouse in an unassuming building, tucked away in Mile End Park alongside the Regents Canal – a lovely if slightly isolated location. There are two bars with decidedly old school décor; indeed, the interior of the pub seems to come from a bygone age.

There's a lairy carpet, shelves of china plates, partially leaded windows and red velvet curtains. The noteworthy golden brown metallic wallpaper is responsible for the bright, warm atmosphere, as it casts light around the pub's interior.

This isn't really a place for wine drinkers but there are some good beers, including interesting guest brews. They're enjoyed by a nicely mixed clientele: students from the university across the canal, local hipsters, sporty types from the nearby climbing wall and residents

from the area's estates, all drawn by the atmosphere, late opening, weekend sing-alongs and live music, often jazz or old school crooning. Weather-permitting, you can drink your pint outside overlooking the (usually algae-covered) water.

THE PEASANT

Address: 240 St John Street, EC1 4PH (☎ 020-7336 7726, 🖵 thepeasant.co.uk).
Opening hours: Mon-Sat, noon to 11pm; Sun, 11.30am to 10.30pm.
Transport: Farringdon tube/rail.
Go for: Good beer, wine and food.

Sitting between Smithfield and Angel, the Peasant was one of London's pioneering gastropubs (the second to earn that label, according to some) and is still pulling in the punters. It occupies an imposing, well-restored Victorian public house, an inviting, civilised, light and airy place, with large arched windows, huge mirrors, a horseshoe bar and an old mosaic floor which is said to date from the 17th century.

152

The Peasant appeals to most drinkers, with an ever-changing choice of great ales, lagers and ciders, including many sold by the bottle, plus around 50 wines; you can even have cocktails if you must. There's a broad choice of bar food – from sharing plates such as ploughman's or Mediterranean mezze, to roast meats and

comfort puddings – while the upstairs restaurant serves an imaginative set menu (£20 for two courses, £24 for three).

In brief, this is a well-run, friendly place, reasonably priced and welcoming to children and dogs. Unsurprisingly, it's popular with locals and those from further afield and can get busy, therefore booking is recommended if you want a table.

THE PRIDE OF SPITALFIELDS

Address: 3 Heneage Street, E1 5LJ (☎ 020-7247 8933).
Opening hours: Mon-Sat, 11am to 11pm; Sun, noon to 10.30pm.
Transport: Aldgate East tube.
Go for: An old-school East End pub – and a Brick Lane curry.

The modestly-sized Pride of Spitalfields (it used to be called the
Romford Arms) is down a cobbled street off Brick Lane and provides
some respite from this East End thoroughfare's in-your-face, gaudy
charms.

It's very much an unreconstructed, old-school boozer, with red
upholstery, a wood-burning stove, a piano, and black and white
photographs portraying East End history. It's a bustling place with a
nicely mixed clientele of Cockneys, local trendies and fashionistas,
local workers and curry aficionados. Many pop in for a drink before
or after a meal in one of Brick Lane's famous curry houses (many of
which don't sell alcohol).

There are good, well-priced beers, including Brewers Gold, Doom
Bar, Fuller's ESB and London Pride, as well as simple, inexpensive
pub grub, much of it served
with chips – there are no gastro
pretensions here! It's a small
pub and can become crowded,
particularly at weekends, and on
Monday evenings when a group
of vinyl lovers gather at the Pride
to spin music all night.

153

THE PROSPECT OF WHITBY

Address: 57 Wapping Wall, E1W 3SH (☎ 020-7481 1095, 🖥 taylor-walker.
co.uk/pub/prospect-of-whitby-wapping/c8166).
Opening hours: Mon-Thu, noon to 11pm; Fri-Sat, noon to midnight; Sun,
noon to 10.30pm.
Transport: Wapping rail.
Go for: A chance to drink in history at a venerable Thames-side pub.

Built in around 1520, this claims to be London's oldest riverside
inn (as does the **Town of Ramsga**te, see page 157) and was once
a favourite with smugglers. Over the centuries, its regulars have
supposedly included just about everyone of note in London, including
Henry VIII, Samuel Pepys, Captain Cook, Charles Dickens, Princess
Margaret and Richard Burton.

Now Grade II listed, it's been altered a number of times but retains
an air of antiquity and its original flagstone floor, while period features
include a pewter bar, pillars fashioned from ships' masts and black
wooden beams. The terrace is a grand spot from which to admire the
Thames; the views are said to have inspired the painters JMW Turner
and James Abbott Whistler.

The pub has gone by various names. It was
once known as the Devil's Tavern, but adopted
its current name in the 19th century from a Tyne
collier that was berthed nearby. These days it's a
Taylor Walker outlet and offers a good range of
beer and lager, including Bombardier, Doom Bar,
London Gold and Staropramen. Traditional pub grub
is served, in keeping with the traditional atmosphere.

THE PUNCH TAVERN

Address: 99 Fleet Street, EC4Y 1DE (☎ 020-7353 6658, 🖳 punchtavern.com).
Opening hours: Mon-Wed, 7.30am to 11pm; Thu-Fri, 7.30am to midnight;
Sat-Sun, 11am to 7pm.
Transport: Blackfriars tube/rail or Temple tube.
Go for: A great all-round pub with a glorious Victorian interior.

155

Named after the now-defunct
satirical magazine that was dreamed
up here in 1841, this Grade II listed
pub is known for its magnificent
Victorian interior. The entrance lobby
is attractively decorated with glazed tiles, while the interior is a riot of
etched glass, Art Deco lighting, massive bevelled mirrors, a marble bar,
dark wood panelling and a series of Punch and Judy-themed paintings
from 1897, the year of Victoria's Diamond Jubilee.

There's been a tavern here since the 17th century – it used to
be called the Crown and Sugarloaf – and when Fleet Street was
the heart of the newspaper industry it was thronged with printers
and journalists. These days the pub attracts a mixed crowd of City
workers, lawyers and tourists.

The atmosphere is friendly and there's something for everyone:
long opening hours, good beer – Adnams Broadside, Marston's
English Pale Ale and Timothy Taylor Landlord – a comprehensive wine
list, coffee and excellent food, include a range of award-winning pies.
No doubt, the founders of *Punch* would approve.

THE THREE KINGS OF CLERKENWELL

Address: 7 Clerkenwell Close, EC1R 0DY (☎ 020-7253 0483).
Opening hours: Mon-Fri, noon to 11pm; Sat, 5.30 to 11pm; closed Sun.
Transport: Farringdon tube/rail.
Go for: Tasty beer, quirky atmosphere and good music.

The Three Kings of Clerkenwell is on a side street in an appealingly Dickensian part of London and is both a good locals' pub and a draw for visitors. As the amusing pub sign reveals, the regal threesome are Henry VIII, Elvis and King Kong – splendid bedfellows! The building dates from 1791, but the pub's interior is as eccentric as its name, incorporating autographed baseball photos, fairy lights and a fibreglass rhino's head.

The Kings is a freehouse and offers a range of beer and lager – Deuchars, Timothy Taylor Landlord and the like – as well as a notable selection of spirits and respectable pub fare to graze on. It's a popular watering hole, friendly and characterful, and when the weather is obliging, drinkers spill out into the small lane outside or sit on the steps of the church.

They like their music here. As well as DJ and band nights, there's a Monday night music quiz – this is taken seriously – and a vinyl jukebox in the quieter upstairs room, which includes some interesting rarities.

THE TOWN OF RAMSGATE

Address: 62 Wapping High Street, E1W 2PN (☎ 020-7481 8000,
🖥 townoframsgate.co.uk).
Opening hours: Daily, noon to midnight.
Transport: Wapping rail.
Go for: A drink in the footsteps of Captain Bligh.

Like the **Prospect Of Whitby** (see page 154), this is a Grade II listed inn which claims to be 'the oldest pub on the River Thames'. Its website asserts that there's been a tavern on this site since the Wars of the Roses, under an array of names, but it's been called the Town of Ramsgate since the early 19th century – a nod to the Ramsgate fishermen who used to sell their catch nearby.

157

This small corner pub is accommodates a long, narrow, wood-panelled bar, while outside there's a small area where you can enjoy panoramic views and some (bracing) river breezes. It's a sociable

spot, attracting a mixed crowd of locals, journalists and pin-stripes, and is generally less tourist-clogged than the Prospect. It has more for the beer drinker, too, including Doom Bar, London Pride and Young's ales, while guest brews include beers from Adnams, Batemans and Skinners.

One of the pub's most notable historic associations is as the tavern where HMS Bounty's crew enjoyed a last drink before setting off on their ill-fated voyage – there's a painting of Captain William Bligh in the bar.

28°-50° WINE WORKSHOP & KITCHEN

Address: 140 Fetter Lane, EC4A 1BT (☎ 020-7242 8877, 🖥 2850.co.uk/fetter).
Opening hours: Mon-Fri, 11am to 11pm; closed weekends.
Transport: Farringdon tube/rail.
Go for: A collection of special wines and food to complement them.

Named after the latitudes between which wine is produced (both north and south of the equator), this dimly-lit basement bar is a civilised haven for the wine lover. Over 30 wines are available by the bottle, carafe and glass, all of which 'are interesting, drinking well and offer good value'. The list changes often, so you'll probably be able to try different wines each time you visit.

In addition, 28°-50° operates as an agent for a number of wine collectors and sells wines on their behalf, so it has a fine 'collector's wine list' which gives you the chance to sample rare and/or iconic wines (which are also invariably expensive).

Wine is obviously the focus here, but the Kitchen serves excellent food from a short and thoughtful menu, much better than your average wine bar. Prices reflect the location near the City and legal London (there's also an outlet in Marylebone), as does the professional but friendly and unstuffy service. The 28°-50° is popular with discerning, well-heeled local workers, and booking is recommended.

VERTIGO 42

Address: Tower 42, 25 Old Broad Street, EC2N 1HQ (☎ 020-7877 7842,
🖵 vertigo42.co.uk).
Opening hours: Mon-Fri, noon to 4.30pm and 5-11pm; Sat, 5-11pm; closed Sun.
Transport: Liverpool Street tube/rail.
Go for: Views to die for and champagne to go with them.

A top-floor champagne bar
in what used to be called the
NatWest Tower, Vertigo 42 has
splendid, panoramic views over
London. However, you need to
put in some effort if you want
to enjoy those views. Entry is
only by advance booking and
you must negotiate airport-like
security gates and conform
to the smart-casual dress
code. Once there, it isn't a
cheap destination… but it's an
eminently memorable one.

159

The floor-to-ceiling windows
are lined with brightly-coloured
chairs facing outwards to provide a ringside seat to watch
the sun set over the City's iconic skyline. Even the
tables are glass, so nothing spoils the view. There's a
choice of 30 champagnes to sip, priced from £14 per
glass or £60 a bottle, and a dozen wines. There's also
a short cocktail list (around £14).

The bar food menu is classy but pricey – even a
dish of nuts costs more than a fiver. But if you're going
to worry about such things, better to stay on the ground
floor. This is a won-the-Lottery, will-you-marry-me,
treat-yourself destination, and worth every penny.

THE VIADUCT TAVERN

Address: 126 Newgate Street, EC1A 7AA (☎ 020-7600 1863,
🖳 viaducttavern.co.uk).
Opening hours: Mon-Fri, 8.30am to 11pm; closed weekends.
Transport: St Paul's tube.
Go for: The striking interior, a solid pint and some ghostly goings-on.

This Grade II listed pub was named after Holborn Viaduct – both pub and bridge were completed in 1869 – and boasts one of London's glitziest, gin-palace interiors. It's built on the site of a debtors' jail and the cellars are rumoured to have once seen service as cells of Newgate Prison, which was just across the road. As a result, the pub is believed to be haunted by a restless spirit (or two).

The Viaduct Tavern seems smaller inside, possibly because it's so highly ornamented. The sumptuous ceiling is made from Lincrusta, a Victorian concoction of pressed paper and linseed oil, while one wall features large paintings of three maidens, representing Agriculture, the Arts and Banking. There are striking mirrors, gilded and silvered, as well as a handsome cashier's office, from where the Victorian landlady dispensed gin tokens to customers.

This has been a Fuller's pub since 2006, so you can drink their reliable and popular London Pride and ESB as you soak up the atmosphere. There's also good food, with the emphasis on meat – Smithfield Market is a short walk away.

VINOTECA

Address: 7 St John Street, EC1M 4AA (☎ 020-7253 8786, 🖥 vinoteca.co.uk).
Opening hours: Mon-Sat, noon to 11pm; closed Sun.
Transport: Farringdon tube/rail.
Go for: Great wine selection, good food and Gallic charm.

A Smithfield wine lover's destination (with other outlets at 15 Seymour Place, Marylebone and 53-55 Beak Street, Soho) that describes itself as a 'bar and wine shop', and which also takes food seriously. Around 300 wines are on offer, not unreasonably priced for this fashionable corner of the City, and are described in detail on the lengthy wine list.

Licensing laws dictate that you must eat something, and bar snacks are reasonably priced from £2 upwards. There's also interesting bistro food from an open kitchen; the menu changes regularly and is listed on the website, with wine suggestions to accompany each dish. A Saturday speciality is the Farringdon's hot dog with a glass of champagne. Everything is served by enthusiastic staff who know their wines but who won't make you feel like an idiot if you're no Hugh Johnson or Jancis Robinson.

A cosy, relaxed wine bar, with an easy Gallic charm, it isn't difficult to see why Vinoteca is popular. You're advised to book at lunchtimes but it's first-come first-served in the evenings.

THE WHITE SWAN

Address: 108 Fetter Lane, EC4A 1ES (☏ 020-7242 9696,
🖥 thewhiteswanlondon.com).
Opening hours: Mon-Thu, 11am to midnight; Fri, 11 to 1am; Sat-Sun,
private parties only.
Transport: Chancery Lane tube.
Go for: A smart City venue with notably good food.

On the site of the former Mucky Duck pub, the White Swan (Pub &
Dining Room) is an attractive gastropub near Chancery Lane, popular
with the area's be-suited professionals. Downstairs is a traditional bar
and curved mezzanine, while upstairs is a bright, Art Deco-style dining
room. The emphasis is very much on food, and the main menu offers
hearty British fare, with a set price lunch of £27 for two courses (£31
for three). However, the bar menu has enough to keep most people
happy – try the Dexter beef burger or haddock and chips, both priced
under £16.

There are a number of draught ales on offer, including Adnams
Broadside and London Pride, along with several lagers and ciders.

Given the discerning punters, there's also a well-chosen wine list, with
around two dozen available by the glass. You can even drink cocktails
here, with a choice of around ten at £7.50 each.

The bar's décor is modern and understated, with wooden floors
and panelling, and plenty of seating, including a few outdoor pitches.
This is a smart, professional and justly popular venue, and can
become busy, notably on Friday evenings.

THE WINE LIBRARY

Address: 43 Trinity Square, EC3N 4DJ (☎ 020-7481 0415, 🖥 winelibrary.co.uk).
Opening hours: Mon, 10am to 6pm; Tue-Fri, 10am to 8pm; closed weekends.
Transport: Tower Hill tube.
Go for: A vast and varied selection of wine, to suit all pockets and tastes.

Reached by a slightly challenging spiral staircase, this plain, atmospheric cellar venue is a combination of wine bar, shop and restaurant. It's owned by a wine merchant and you can choose from a range of more than 400 wines and enjoy them at retail prices, plus a modest corkage charge – a welcome idea in the City, where the mark-up on wine can be outrageously high.

It isn't simply a wine list for moneyed aficionados, but includes bottles ranging from a modest £8.49 (retail) up to £750 for those celebrating a big deal or bonus. And staff are happy to help you negotiate your way through the vast choice available.

163

The Wine Library has stood the test of time and developed a vast band of regulars over the past 25 years, many of whom also come for the cheese and pâté lunch. There's also a buffet available from 11.30am to 3.30pm – booking is advised.

If you want to expand your knowledge of wine, the Wine Library holds regular public and private wine tastings – see website for details.

THE WORSHIP STREET WHISTLING SHOP

Address: 63 Worship Street, EC2A 2DU (☎ 020-7247 0015,
🖥 whistlingshop.com).
Opening hours: Mon-Tue, 5pm to midnight; Wed-Thu, 5pm to 1am; Fri-Sat,
5pm to 2am; closed Sun.
Transport: Old Street tube/rail.
Go for: Dickensian atmosphere and experimental drinks.

The sister bar to **Purl** in Marylebone (see page 94), the Worship
Street Whistling Shop (historically a spirit-shop, especially a secret
and illicit one) has gone for all-out Victoriana and its décor has a
distinctly Dickensian air with Chesterfield sofas, gas lamps, and staff
dressed in period clothing. It claims to combine 'the charm of Victorian
squalor with the elegance of grand gin palaces', which is surely a
good thing.

The Whistling Shop takes a similar attitude to its drinks which are
a cunning blend of old tyme and modern. Its mixologists experiment
with making flavour combinations using a range of elements and
equipment that wouldn't look out of place in a chemistry lab (blame
Heston Blumenthal!). This means you can sample unusual cocktails,
as well as barrel-aged spirit infusions based on gin, rum and more
unexpected ingredients. Fortunately, there's also a good range of
regular spirits – including blended, single malt and world whiskies – as
well as craft beer and well-chosen wines.

Food is available in the evenings and is mostly traditional fare such
as Scotch egg, pork pies and sharing platters of meat and cheese.

YE OLDE CHESHIRE CHEESE

Address: 146 Fleet Street, EC4A 2BU (☎ 020-7353 6170).
Opening hours: Mon-Fri, 11am to 11pm; Sat, noon to 11pm; Sun, noon to 4pm.
Transport: Chancery Lane or Temple tube.
Go for: Possibly the most historic pub in London.

One of the City's must-see pubs, the Cheese was already a century and a half old when it was rebuilt in 1667 after the previous year's Great Fire. Its vaulted cellars are even older, and are thought to have belonged to a 13th-century Carmelite monastery which once occupied the site.

Today, it's an attractive, creaky warren of bars, especially atmospheric in winter with a coal fire burning. It feels like a genuine history trip, and perhaps the long list of noted regulars and visitors has left its mark. This is surely the most illustrious for any pub, and includes Dr Johnson (who lived nearby), Sir Joshua Reynolds, Edward Gibbon, Charles Dickens (seemingly a regular at half of London's pubs), David Garrick, Thomas Carlyle, Alfred Lord Tennyson, WM Thackeray, Mark Twain, Theodore Roosevelt, Arthur Conan Doyle, GK Chesterton and WB Yeats.

The Cheese is a Sam Smith's pub, offering the brewery's usual range of well-priced ales and traditional pub fare. As well as plenty of tourists (it features in most guidebooks), the pub has a loyal local clientele.

165

YE OLDE MITRE TAVERN

Address: 1 Ely Court, EC1N 6SJ (☎ 020-7405 4751,
🖳 yeoldemitreholburn.co.uk).
Opening hours: Mon-Fri, 11am to 11pm; closed weekends.
Transport: Chancery Lane tube.
Go for: A 400-year-old pub with an inviting range of beer.

In a narrow lane off Hatton Garden, the Mitre once had a reputation as being difficult to find, secret even, but signs at both ends of the alley have changed that (to the regret of some). One of London's oldest pubs, it dates back to 1546, although the current building is from 1772 and has had subsequent rebuilds and refits. There's a surviving fragment of an ancient cherry tree near the entrance, which Elizabeth I is said to have danced around!

The pub consists of three rooms, including a panelled front bar, and there's an outdoor drinking area with barrel tables. The Mitre can get crowded, not only due to its historic attraction but its inviting selection of ales, which are a big draw for beer lovers. It's a Fuller's pub but features other beers and has won awards for its range. A few wines are also stocked – at around £15 a bottle – and there's a short menu of traditional pub fare.

Along with the **Olde Cheshire Cheese** (see page 165), the Mitre is usually listed in tourist guides, and has also 'starred' in films, including Guy Ritchie's crime caper *Snatch*.

THE ZETTER TOWNHOUSE

Address: 49-50 St John's Square, EC1V 4JJ (☎ 020-7324 4545,
🖳 thezettertownhouse.com).
Opening hours: Sun-Wed, 7am to midnight; Thu-Sat, 7am to 1am.
Transport: Farringdon tube/rail.
Go for: A feast for the eyes and cocktails to die for.

This is a cosy, friendly, stylish cocktail lounge on the ground floor of a Georgian townhouse next door to the boutique Zetter Hotel, hence the name. The décor is inviting and sumptuous, as well as inventive and sometimes quirky (as are the hotel's rooms), and the bar is positively crammed with curiosities, ephemera, portraits, photos, statues, urns, large comfy wingback chairs and even a stuffed cat in a frock. The end result resembles a cross between an antiques shop, an intimate gentlemen's club and the front parlour of an eccentric relative.

Despite the bizarre surroundings, cocktails are taken seriously here. They are excellent and creative, served by polite and knowledgeable staff, and not unreasonably priced at £8.50 for a house concoction. Tasty bar snacks and 'supper bowls' are available, as is a variety of wines and bottled beers.

Booking is recommended, but the Zetter limits the number of reservations (to keep space available for hotel guests?), so make yours in good time.

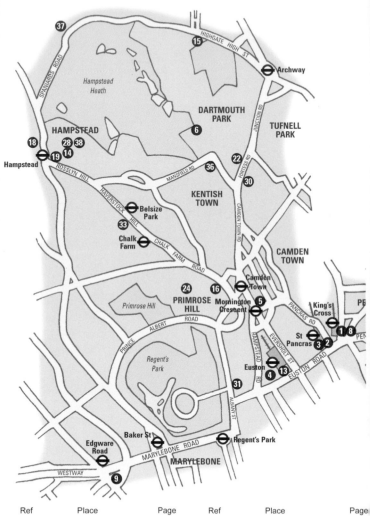

CHAPTER 3

NORTH LONDON

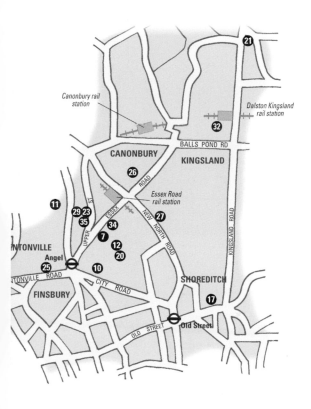

BAR PEPITO

> **Address:** Varnishers Yard, The Regent Quarter, N1 9FD (☎ 020-7841 7331, 🖳 camino.uk.com/pepito).
> **Opening hours:** Mon-Fri, 5pm to midnight; Sat, 6pm to midnight; closed Sun (but available for private hire).
> **Transport:** King's Cross tube/rail.
> **Go for:** Fine sherry and tasty tapas in a King's Cross 'bodega'.

Across the courtyard from its sister operation, **Camino Cruz del Rey** (see page 177), this rustic, Andalusian 'bodega' specialises in sherry in all its various guises. It's a tiny bar with a handful of tables, their tops made from sherry casks; and if there's any Spanish-style weather you can sit outside.

Around 18 sherries are stocked and you can sip them individually (from £4 for a 75ml glass) or take a sherry 'flight'. There are six flights to choose from, priced from £9.25-15, each comprising three 50ml shots, all served with a *tapita*, i.e. a bite of appropriate food. There's also a *Caminito de Pepito* (Pepito Road Trip) which is a journey through eight styles of sherry (50ml of each, £21.50). Best to hide the car keys after that lot!

If you prefer wine, Pepito has a dozen or so reds, whites and cavas, most available by the glass (two sizes), carafe or bottle; prices start at £4.25 per glass and £16 a bottle.

There's a short list of mainly cold tapas, plus Iberian hams and cheeses, as well as two puddings. The menu suggests a sherry to go with each.

THE BETJEMAN ARMS

Address: Unit 53, St Pancras International Station, Pancras Road, N1C 4QL
(☎ 020-7923 5440, 🖵 geronimo-inns.co.uk/thebetjemanarms).
Opening hours: Mon-Sat, 11am to 11pm; Sun, 11am to 10.30pm.
Transport: King's Cross tube/rail.
Go for: A grand view of London's most architecturally dazzling station.

Happily situated in the heart of St Pancras International Station, this pub is named after the poet who campaigned to save the station – a magnificent Victoria confection, now Grade I listed – from demolition in the '60s.

The pub has a huge terrace under the splendid arc of the station's glass and wrought iron ceiling. From here, you can watch Eurostar trains arrive and depart – it's a train spotter's dream – as well as admire the impressive architecture, while out front you can bask in the sun if the weather behaves. The outside space is impressive, so much so that it was chosen as one of *The Guardian* newspaper's 'Top Five Pub Gardens' in 2012.

As for drinks, there are four cask beers, including a Betjeman ale (re-badged Sharp's Cornish Coaster) and offerings from Adnams and Sambrook's. The wine list was chosen by

171

Master of Wine John Clevely and runs to around 35 bins, most available in one or two glass sizes and by the bottle; glasses cost from £4, bottles from £15.50. The Betjeman also serves good, gastropub food, from breakfast to desserts.

Sir John Betjeman

THE BOOKING OFFICE BAR

Address: St Pancras Renaissance Hotel, NW1 2AR (☎ 020-7841 3566,
🖳 bookingofficerestaurant.com).
Opening hours: Daily, 6.30pm to 3am.
Transport: King's Cross tube/rail.
Go for: Cocktails in a building from a bygone age.

This hotel bar and restaurant has the distinct advantage of being
housed in one of London's architectural highlights, St Pancras Station.
Even better, it's in the station's old ticket office and is attached to the
five-star St Pancras Renaissance London Hotel (formerly the Midland
Grand Hotel, first opened in 1873).

The bar echoes the building's cathedral-like Victorian magnificence
but with the added modern comforts you'd expect of a five-star hotel
bar. There's plenty of space and seating from which to enjoy the
original arched windows, ribbed vaulting and intricate, decorative
brickwork. Drinks are served from a 95ft (29m) long bar.

Cocktails are the speciality, reflecting the fact that the original
hotel was built 'at the height of the mixed drink explosion'. Some
172 recreate lost recipes from the era, while there are also bespoke and
seasonal offerings. There's also a selection of wines, and well-chosen
beers (not always the case in hotel bars) from breweries such as
Greenwich-based Meantime. The English food is solid rather than
remarkable, prices are quite high and
service can be slow – but that gives you
more time to enjoy the stunning setting.

THE BREE LOUISE

Address: 69 Cobourg Street, NW1 2HH (☎ 020-7681 4930,
🖥 thebreelouise.com).
Opening hours: Mon-Sat, 11.30am to late; Sun, noon to 10.30pm.
Transport: Euston tube/rail.
Go for: A great selection of fine ale, whisky and tequila.

West of Euston Station and
close to the popular vegetarian
Indian restaurants of Drummond
Street, this unassuming corner
pub stocks a fantastic selection
of cask ale. It self-confidently
describes itself as 'Euston's
best-kept secret' and was the
area's CAMRA 'Pub of the Year'
2009/2010 (it offers a modest
discount to CAMRA cardholders).

The pub consists of just
one room, with understated

173

decoration, and tables are often shared (although you can reserve
them). Some people find the Bree a bit uncomfortable, but others
regard it as refreshingly unreconstructed and non-trendy. There
are usually up to 17 beers on offer, 11 of which are gravity and six
on pump, and include offerings from BrewDog, Brodies, Dark Star,
Downton, Kernel, Redemption and Sambrook's, among others. There

are also 11 ciders and
perries from the cask
and box.

The ales and ciders
can change several
times daily 'due to
demand' and you can
check the current
selection via Twitter. If
you prefer your drinks
short, there are whisky
and tequila 'menus'.
The food is solid pub
fare and includes some
award-winning pies and
an interesting choice of
cheeses.

BREWDOG

Address: 113 Bayham Street, NW1 0BA (☎ 020-7284 4626,
🖥 brewdog.com/bars/camden).
Opening hours: Mon-Thu, noon to 11.30pm; Fri-Sat, noon to midnight; Sun,
noon to 10.30pm.
Transport: Camden Town tube.
Go for: Craft beer in a no-nonsense environment.

BrewDog is a craft brewery founded in Scotland in 2006, which claims
to be the antithesis of the corporate beer world. It makes 'beer for
punks' and produces a range of bottled and canned styles, some of
them also available in keg and cask. It currently has ten outlets in the
UK – this Camden bar opened in 2011 – with more to come; there's a
second London branch in Shoreditch.

It's conveniently situated close to Camden Town tube station and
has a bare, stripped-back interior with signs chalked on the walls. It
stocks BrewDog's innovative beers – here it's on tap, not cask – and
bottled offerings from other brewers. It isn't a cheap venue, but serves
good quality ales as well as tasty food.

174   This bar doesn't claim to be cutting edge and trendy, and the
BrewDog approach certainly isn't pretentious. Rather, they promise
'No Carling. No Tennents. No shots. No bullsh*t – just good honest
beer', which is eminently healthy in Camden where style sometimes
takes precedence over substance.

THE BULL & LAST

Address: 168 Highgate Road, NW5 1QS (☎ 020-7267 3641,
🖳 thebullandlast.co.uk).
Opening hours: Mon-Thu, noon to 11pm; Fri-Sat, noon to midnight; Sun,
noon to 10.30pm.
Transport: Kentish Town tube/rail.
Go for: Good beer, great food, a stone's throw from Hampstead Heath.

Situated close to the verdant
sweep of Hampstead Heath
and housed in a Grade II listed
Victorian building, this gastropub
builds on its natural advantages
by providing fine beer, wine and
food. The cooking is a particular
highlight, with separate lunch,
dinner and Sunday lunch menus
– the *Observer Food Monthly*
awarded the pub its 'Best
Sunday Lunch' gong in 2011. It
also offers a mean home-made ice cream.

175

The Bull and Last looks after its drinkers, too, and manages to
retain a traditional pub atmosphere. There's a good choice of ale,
including Black Sheep, Doom Bar and Mad Goose, while the wine list
is extensive and interesting, with many wines available by the glass
and carafe. A glass of wine costs from £4, a bottle from £16. The pub
also hosts 'wine events' such as talks and tastings matched with food
(see website).

This is a popular place and it's invariably full, therefore you may
have to wait to be served – or you could order one of the Bull's
hampers and picnic on the Heath.

THE CAMDEN HEAD

Address: 2 Camden Walk, N1 8DY (☎ 020-7359 0851, 🖳 camden-head.co.uk).
Opening hours: Sun-Wed, noon to 11pm; Thu, noon to midnight; Fri-Sat, noon to 1am.
Transport: Angel tube.
Go for: The fine Victorian interior and a warm welcome.

Tucked away in Islington's antiques quarter and dating from 1849, this impressive, ornate pub is Grade II listed, as befits such a well-preserved Victorian gin palace. It has high ceilings and a striking red bar top, and is noted for its glass work and mirrors. A number of other fine details remain, including tiles and attractive, original wooden features, which add warmth to the interior in winter. In summer the large beer garden is a big draw.

The pub has music hall connections, which are celebrated in some of the decoration, while the tradition of entertainment continues to this day with free comedy nights staged three times a week. A different form of entertainment is provided by the spirit world: the pub is said to be haunted by a ghost called George!

176 It's a Taylor Walker establishment and has a couple of good ales on tap – a Young's and a regional beer – as well as standard pub grub and sharing platters, enjoyed by a nicely mixed clientele. It also claims to have 'the friendliest bar staff this side of Dublin'.

CAMINO CRUZ DEL REY

Address: 3 Varnishers Yard, N1 9FD (☎ 020-7841 7331, 🖥 camino.
uk.com/kingscross).
Opening hours: Bar: Mon-Wed, noon to midnight; Thu-Sat, noon to 1am;
Sun, noon to 11pm.
Transport: King's Cross tube/rail.
Go for: All things Spanish – beer, wine, food and music.

177

A bar and restaurant in the
redeveloped King's Cross
area, this award-winning venue
is 'a place to enjoy the life,
vigour and tastes of Spain'.
Camino Cruz del Rey is part of
the Camino chain which also
has outlets in Canary Wharf and Monument, as well as **Bar Pepito**
(see page 170). The group is particular about the provenance of its
ingredients and claims to use only free-range, sustainable and organic
produce.

Camino is also serious about drinks, and has an extensive choice of
interesting wine from all over Spain, as well as cava and sherry. Many
are available by the glass and carafe; glasses cost from £4.25, bottles
from £16.

There are two draught beers: Estrella Damm ('the beer of
Barcelona') and Amstel, which is Spain's best-seller, as well as five
bottled beers (Mahou, Alhambra Reserva 1925, Ambar 1900 La
Zaragozana, Ambar Negra and Estrella Damm Inedit) and an Asturian
cider (El Gaitero). Cocktails are also available.

Samba, flamenco and other types of music – live and DJ sounds –
provide a suitably Spanish soundtrack.

THE CHAPEL

Address: 48 Chapel Street, NW1 5DP, ☎ 020-7402 9220,
🖥 thechapellondon.com.
Opening hours: Mon-Sat, noon to 11pm; Sun, noon to 10.30pm.
Transport: Edgware Road tube.
Go for: A glorious garden, plus award-winning food and drink.

One of London's earliest gastropubs (it opened in 1995), the Chapel has won awards from *The Good Pub Guide*, *The Restaurant Magazine* and *Time Out*. It has the typical gastropub interior – light and airy, with wooden floor and large windows – but also boasts a walled garden and terrace, a rare bonus for a city pub. They claim it's one of the largest in London, and it comfortably seats up to 60, with heated umbrellas for chilly evenings.

There's a selection of food menus – lunch, dinner, antipasti and canapés (see website for serving times) – while beer drinkers can choose from Adnams and IPA on draught, plus draught lagers which include Becks, Fosters, Hoegaarden and Kronenbourg. Bottled offerings comprise Fruli, Leffe, Sol and Tiger.

There's quite an extensive wine list, with around 15 available in two glass sizes, costing from £4, with bottles from £16, plus a good selection of spirits.

The Chapel is a popular place and deservedly busy. Arrive early if you want to sit outdoors.

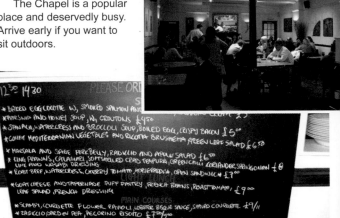

THE CHARLES LAMB

Address: 16 Elia Street, N1 8DE (☎ 020-7837 5040, 🖥 thecharleslambpub.com).
Opening hours: Mon-Tue, 4-11pm; Wed-Sat, noon to 11pm; Sun, noon to 10.30pm.
Transport: Angel tube.
Go for: A corner pub with a rustic atmosphere and a good reputation.

Dating from 1839, this small, friendly corner pub is near the Regent's Canal and Angel tube station. It was previously called the Prince Albert and was renamed in 2005 after the essayist Charles Lamb, who lived nearby in the late 18th century. It's now a gastropub and freehouse run by French-English owners, serving good food and wine as well as decent beer and cider.

179

The choice of beer is brief but well selected – Hophead and Alton's Pride plus interesting guest ales – and the pub specialises in locally produced brews. There's a well-chosen wine selection, which includes three Charles Lamb house wines from Domaine St Hilaire in the Languedoc, reasonably priced at £16.50 a bottle or £4 a glass.

The Charles Lamb remains a nice old pub with a surprisingly rustic feel, friendly, hospitable staff and board games to keep you entertained. Its website contains a host of favourable reviews, from the *Guardian*, *Observer* and *Time Out* among others, so it's understandably popular. See the website for kitchen opening times and arrive early to claim a table.

THE DRAPERS ARMS

Address: 44 Barnsbury Street, N1 1ER (☎ 020-7619 0348,
🖥 thedrapersarms.com).
Opening hours: Mon-Fri, 11am to midnight; Sat, 10am to midnight; Sun,
10am to 11pm.
Transport: Highbury & Islington tube/rail.
Go for: Fine food and drink in an elegant gastropub.

Drinkers and diners are both well catered
for at this superior Islington gastropub
and freehouse; while the owners state
their 'determination to serve rewarding
food and drink', they're also keen to
stress that theirs is a neighbourhood pub. The Drapers Arms certainly
looks the gastropub part. It's an elegant Georgian building with a
classic, stripped-down interior, lots of wood and a pale blue and green
decor, plus books, board games and a scissors mural, in homage to
the name. Outside, there's also an attractive, stylish beer garden.

The Drapers offers lunch and dinner menus which change daily
(they're posted on the website) and include gastro-treats such as ox
cheek terrine and confit duck leg. Prices are reasonable, with most
main courses in the £12-16 range and bar snacks around £3-8.

The pub has interesting ales, including Harvey's Sussex Best,
Truman's Runner, Dark Star Hophead, Thornbridge Jaipur and
Wandle, and there's also a good wine list of around 60 wines. A
number are available by the glass or half-litre carafe (two-thirds of a
bottle), with prices ranging from around £4 per glass and £11.20 a
carafe.

THE DUKE OF CAMBRIDGE

Address: 30 St Peter's Street, N1 8JT (☎ 020-7359 3066, 🖳 dukeorganic.co.uk).
Opening hours: Daily, 12.30 to 5pm, 6.30 to 11pm (closes 10.30pm Sun).
Transport: Angel tube.
Go for: An original organic pub.

This Islington back-street pub was one of the first to be certified as organic by the Soil Association and it remains one of only a handful in the UK. In fact, the Duke claims to be 'Britain's first and only certified organic pub', and this applies to the drinks as well as the food. It began operating in 1998 and has since been garlanded with awards. It's even published its own cook book.

Around 80 per cent of the fresh produce is sourced nearby in the Home Counties and the excellent (but slightly pricy) menu includes plenty of vegetarian options, served in a large, airy bar with shabby chic décor that also manages to be cosy and inviting.

The Duke's beer comes from the Freedom and Pitfield breweries, with Freedom lagers and a cider on draught as well as a wide range of bottled beer. There's also an interesting wine list, organic and biodynamic, from the Old and New Worlds, plus organic spirits and liqueurs.

The organic approach has obviously struck a chord in planet-friendly Islington and the Duke is hugely popular, drawing a trendy crowd.

THE EUSTON TAP

Address: West Lodge, 190 Euston Road, NW1 2EF (☎ 020-3137 8837, 🖵 eustontap.com).

Opening hours: Mon, noon to 11pm; Tue-Thu, Fri, noon to 11.30pm; Sat, noon to midnight; Sun, noon to 10pm.

Transport: Euston tube/rail.

Go for: One of Britain's best choices of craft beer in a unique location.

Opened in 2010, this is one of London's most adventurous beer venues. It's only small, a rectangular bar in an unusual setting: a Portland stone gatehouse dating from the 1830s in front of Euston station. A spiral staircase leads down to the small lounge and there's additional outside seating in a heated beer garden.

Wine and spirits are available but the focus is very much on beer, with eight rotating cask ales, 20 keg beers, 150 bottled beers, eight keg ciders on draught, and five varieties of still cider and perry (pear cider). It's an astonishingly fine selection, served by friendly staff. Regular cask ales include BrewDog, Dark Star, Purity, Riverhead and Thornbridge Old Swan, while you can also sample the likes of Bernard Pilsner, Erdinger Urweisse and Matuska Raptor IPA. Bar snacks include crisps and pork scratchings (no tapas here) or you can have one of Famous Ray's pizzas delivered to your table.

In short, this is a must-visit venue for beer lovers. To learn more, keep up with the ever changing selection of beers, events, launches and specials on Twitter and Facebook.

THE FLASK (HAMPSTEAD)

Address: 14 Flask Walk, NW3 1HE (☎ 020-7435 4580,
🖥 theflaskhampstead.co.uk).
Opening hours: Mon-Thu, 11am to 11pm; Fri-Sat, 11am to midnight; Sun,
noon to 10.30pm.
Transport: Hampstead tube.
Go for: A pint or glass of wine enjoyed in one of London's premier postcodes.

This impressive, welcoming Young's pub sits in a prime part of
Hampstead, one of London's most desirable areas and one which
has managed to retain its village-like charm. The Flask is one of its
best-known hostelries, situated on a quiet passageway, along with
bookshops and boutiques. It gets its name from the springs of potable
water that rose on Hampstead Heath and were bottled and sold in the
18th century to City taverns and coffee houses for threepence a flask.

The Flask dates from Victorian times, and the front saloon has
a number of original 1880s features, including painted panels by
(the appropriately named) Jan van Beers, making it rather more
characterful than the modern conservatory at the back; there's also a
plain public bar.

Young's beers are served, plus
guest ales and continental lagers,
and the Flask is strong on wine –
not always the case with Young's
pubs – which costs from £3.85
per glass and £15.50 a bottle. The
large dining room at the back is a
popular venue for traditional pub
grub and Sunday lunch.

THE FLASK (HIGHGATE)

Address: 77 Highgate West Hill, N6 6BU (☎ 020-8348 7346, ⌨ theflaskhighgate.com).
Opening hours: Mon-Sat, noon to 11pm; Sun, noon to 10.30pm.
Transport: Archway or Highgate tube
Go for: Ghosts, the garden and some famously good beer.

Another famous north London pub named after the containers of spring water once collected on Hampstead Heath, the Flask is a large coaching inn from the early 18th century, with a rustic feel and a cosy interior. It has wooden beams, an original shutter-window bar, bottle glass windows and a plethora of nooks and crannies. There are even a couple of ghosts: a Spanish barmaid who hanged herself and a uniformed Cavalier.

It's a Fuller's establishment and has an interesting range of beer: Fuller's ales, of course, plus Adnams, Butcombe and Hydes Original. There's also a well-chosen selection of bottled beers from Belgium and further afield, as well as an interesting range of single malt whisky.

This being well-to-do Highgate, the Flask isn't a cheap pub. But it has the added attraction of a large garden, which gets packed during decent weather, and you may spot famous faces from the media and entertainment worlds. Indeed, the pub has a long history of attracting the great and the good; the 18th-century painter and satirist William Hogarth is reputed to have been a regular.

GILGAMESH

Address: Stables Market, Chalk Farm Road, NW1 8AH (☎ 020-7428 4922, 🖥 gilgameshbar.com).
Opening hours: Bars: daily, 6pm to late; **restaurant:** daily, midday to midnight.
Transport: Camden Town tube.
Go for: Possibly the most OTT bar décor in London – and cocktails to match!

Named after a Babylonian demigod who was the son of a mortal king and a goddess (and why not?), this venue in Camden's Stables Market has a jaw-dropping interior, resembling the set of a '50s Hollywood biblical epic. It's actually a large, low-ceilinged cocktail bar and restaurant, slightly expensive but worth it for the head-turning experience.

The remarkably over-the-top décor includes masses of carved wood panels telling the story of Gilgamesh – a Mesopotamian saga from at least 2,500 BC – and a blue lapis lazuli stone bar, handcrafted by a 10,000-strong Indian team. It's all enhanced by an innovative lighting system with over 250 subtly changing colours.

The food is pan-Asian and good – if pricey – while bar fare

185

includes sushi, dim sum and spring rolls. There's a wine list and the odd beer available, such as Tiger (from Singapore). However, most people come for the Babylonian-themed cocktails which are the perfect refreshment in a venue that's as splendidly overcooked and glitzy as anywhere outside Las Vegas.

HAPPINESS FORGETS

Address: 8-9 Hoxton Square, N1 6NU (☎ 020-7613 0325,
📧 happinessforgets.com).
Opening hours: Mon-Sat, 5.30 to 11pm; closed Sun.
Transport: Old Street tube/rail or Shoreditch High Street rail.
Go for: Great service, good vibes and grown-up drinks.

Happiness Forgets is part of a recent trend, with a policy of table service only (no standing), a glass of water served with each drink and old school hospitality. In short, it's very much a place for discerning adults.

It's a tiny, dimly-lit basement bar, with hints of the speakeasy about it, lit by a warm, understated glow from '50s lamps and candles. Dark walls and wooden floorboards add to the subterranean atmosphere. It's relaxed and friendly, with a nicely mixed crowd, including local creatives and business suits. And it somehow avoids being yet another den of Shoreditch pretentiousness.

The drinks are great. There's a modest choice of good beer – by breweries like Meantime and Timothy Taylor – but cocktails are the speciality. Some are based on artisan British spirits, and prices are reasonable at between £7.50 and £9.

The website sums Happiness Forgets up nicely: 'High end cocktails, low rent basement,' it says, and 'Great cocktails. No wallies'. Bookings can be made by phone (after 4pm) for groups of two to eight people.

THE HOLLY BUSH

Address: 22 Holly Mount, NW3 6SG (☎ 020-7435 2892,
🖳 hollybushhampstead.co.uk).
Opening hours: Mon-Sat, noon to 11pm; Sun, noon to 10.30pm.
Transport: Hampstead tube or Hampstead Heath rail.
Go for: One of Hampstead's best pubs in a lovely location.

Housed in a building constructed for the painter George Romney in the 1790s, this noted Hampstead pub is hidden away in a warren of passages and narrow streets. It's on Holly Mount, which is reached via steep steps from Heath Street in the historic heart of lovely Hampstead. The pub's licence dates from 1802, although its origins apparently stretch back to 1643 – diarist James Boswell and polymath Samuel Johnson are reputed to have been patrons, while more recent regulars included the painter John Constable and scientist Michael Faraday.

187

The Holly Bush is spread over three bar areas and has a plain but inviting interior, with low ceilings, dark wood and original features, many of which are Victorian modifications. It was lit by gas lamps until quite recently.

The pub was a freehouse for many years but has recently been taken over by Fuller's and serves their ales, plus others such as Harveys Sussex Best, Becks, Blue Moon and Leffe. There's also a fine choice of bottled beer and enjoyable, quality food – as you would expect in Hampstead.

THE HORSESHOE

Address: 28 Heath Street, NW3 6TE (☎ 020-7431 6206,
🖳 camdentownbrewery.com).
Opening hours: Mon-Thu, 10am to 11pm; Fri-Sat, 10am to midnight; Sun,
noon to 10pm.
Transport: Hampstead tube.
Go for: Hampstead's take on an American brewpub.

Dating back to the 1880s, this striking corner premises was originally called the Three Horseshoes, but it underwent a complete refurbishment in 2006 and is now an outlet for Camden Town Brewery, which began its operation in the pub's cellar and is now based in Kentish Town (see below).

Inside, it's reminiscent of an American brewpub, as are some of its ales. Large windows making it light and airy, while the whitewashed brick and refectory tables are slick and stylish – it's the antithesis of the popular image of a fusty, specialist beer venue.

As well as Camden Town's fine ales, there's a guest brew from one of London's other producers, as well as a small but well-chosen bottled selection (British and international). There's also a reasonable wine list and good, gastro-quality food. The Horseshoe is usually busy, drawing a youngish clientele, therefore booking is recommended if you wish to eat. And there's a theatre upstairs if you fancy a spot of culture.

Camden Town Brewery has its own Brewery Bar at its Kentish Town premises (55-59 Wilkin Street Mews, NW5 3NN, ☎ 020-7485 1671, 🖳 camdentownbrewery.com, open Thurs-Sat noon to 11pm) where you can sup its beers at source.

THE ISLAND QUEEN

Address: 87 Noel Road, N1 8HD (☎ 020-7354 8741,
🖥 theislandqueenislington.co.uk).
Opening hours: Sun-Thu, noon to 11.30pm; Fri-Sat, noon to midnight.
Transport: Angel tube.
Go for: An attractive Victorian pub serving some of the world's best beers.

The Island Queen is on an Islington
back street near the Regent's Canal
and claims to be the only hostelry in
Britain to carry this exotic name. Built
in 1851 and remodelled in the 1880s
and '90s, it retains many attractive,
original features, including a wood
and glass frontage, mosaics, etched
glass screens, high ceilings, mirrors
painted with foliage and a curved
island bar. It blends the theatre
of the Victorian gin palace with a

calmer colonial air – comfy sofas, colourful rugs and warm dark wood
furniture make it cosy and inviting.

The website also asserts that the pub has 'nine of the world's best
beers on tap' and there's certainly an interesting selection, including
such names as Doom Bar, Timothy Taylor Landlord, Fruli, Leffe,
Paulaner, Pilsner Urquell, Schneider Weisse, Sierra Nevada and
Staropramen. Around 20 wines are offered, most available by the glass.

There's an extensive menu of superior pub food, which includes a
reasonable fixed price menu (£10 for two courses, £13 for three), and
outdoor tables on the 'south-facing street terrace' – all of which make
for a proper pub with a good atmosphere.

THE JOLLY BUTCHERS

Address: 204 Stoke Newington High Street, N16 7HU (☎ 020-7241 2185, 🖥 jollybutchers.co.uk).

Opening hours: Mon-Thu, 4pm to midnight; Fri, 4pm to 1am; Sat, noon to 1am; Sun, noon to 11pm.

Transport: Stoke Newington rail.

Go for: A fine selection of quality beer and a menu to go with it.

What was once an unpleasantly grungy pub was transformed in 2010 into a beer aficionados' delight. The interior is plain and open plan, so as not to detract from its main attraction: beer.

The Butchers describes itself as 'north London's premier real ale, cider and craft beer house', which isn't a hollow claim as it received a CAMRA nomination after just one year in business. It stocks around seven cask and ten keg beers, a selection of 25-30 bottled beers, and five ciders. Crouch Vale, Dark Star, Redemption and Thornbridge feature regularly, plus a range of guests which are often from small London outfits – Brodie's, BrewDog, Camden Town, Kernel and Meantime are favourites. Check what's on offer on the website under 'This Week's Brewers'.

An ever-changing menu of food follows the recent trend for suggesting beers to go with different dishes, demonstrating that like wine, beer can be a serious accompaniment to food. The Jolly Butchers isn't cheap and you'll probably have to share space with some of the area's trendies, but beer lovers will find this a happy home.

JUNCTION TAVERN

Address: 101 Fortess Road, NW5 1AG (☎ 020-7485 9400, ⌨ junctiontavern.co.uk).
Opening hours: Mon-Thu, 5-11pm; Fri, noon to 11pm; Sat, 11.30am to 11pm; Sun, noon to 10.30pm.
Transport: Tufnell Park tube or Kentish Town tube/rail.
Go for: A CAMRA-approved gastropub with a garden terrace.

A large, corner establishment, the Junction Tavern is a welcoming local gastropub with an envious reputation. It's a typical Victorian affair, with a warm, dark wood interior, as well as large tables in the front bar, an airy conservatory and a large, heated garden terrace.

It serves sophisticated seasonal food, with menus that change daily – main courses are in the £12.50-20 range or around the London average for superior gastro fare. Weekend options include Saturday brunch (11.30am to 4pm) and all-day Sunday lunch (until 9pm). Drinkers are also well catered for. The in-house real ale is Sambrook's Wandle, while there's an ever-changing list of guest beers, many from local producers, such as Ascot, Brodies, East London, Exmoor, Meantime, Redemption, Timothy Taylor, Tring and Wye Walley. A pint costs £3.80.

The Junction has been voted CAMRA 'North London Pub of the Year' in the past, and stages regular beer festivals (see website for details).There's also a comprehensive wine list, with many available in two glass sizes (from £3.20) and bottles from £15.50.

THE KING'S HEAD

Address: 115 Upper Street, N1 1QN (☎ 020-7226 4443,
🖳 kingsheadtheatrepub.co.uk).
Opening hours: Mon-Wed, noon to 1am; Thu-Sat, noon to 2am; Sun, noon
to 12.30am.
Transport: Angel tube or Highbury & Islington tube/rail.
Go for: The late licence, music, theatre and good beer.

There's been a King's Head
pub on this site since the
16th century, as noted in
Samuel Pepys's diaries;
the name supposedly refers to Henry VIII who would stop here for
refreshment en route to see one of his mistresses (he must have
stopped at many taverns – and had many mistresses – as it's one of
the commonest pub names in the country!).

The current building dates from 1860 and is a splendidly original
affair, with high ceilings, a slightly bohemian air and roaring fires in
winter. There's free music most nights from 9.30pm – generally swing,
rock and roll, blues or jazz (full listings on the website).

The King's Head also hosts London's oldest pub theatre which,
when founded in 1970, was the first to be established in England since
Shakespeare's time. Its boards have been trodden by such stellar
performers as Steven Berkoff, Rupert Graves, Alan Rickman and
Prunella Scales, and 37 of its shows have transferred to the West End.
See the theatre website (🖳 kingsheadtheatre.com) for more information.

If you just want a drink, there are reasonably priced beers,
including solid offerings from Adnams, Bass, Tetley, Young's and
Wadworth, as well as wines and spirits.

THE LANSDOWNE

Address: 90 Gloucester Avenue, NW1 8HX ☎ 020-7483 0409,
🖥 thelansdownepub.co.uk).
Opening hours: Mon-Fri, noon to 11pm; Sat, 10am to 11pm; Sun, 10am to 10.30pm.
Transport: Chalk Farm tube.
Go for: Upmarket gastropub with some good beer.

Founded in 1992, the Lansdowne is one of the stalwarts of the gastropub scene, serving standards such as roast cod and samphire to the gilded Primrose Hill set. It's quite likely you'll see a familiar face from music, film or television as you jostle for space at one of the wooden tables or try to grab a spot in front of its welcoming winter fire.

The downstairs bar serves a more basic menu, including good-quality pizzas and pastas, while the upstairs restaurant presents a concise but classic list of gastro grub – main courses are generally priced between £10 and £20. There are also a few outdoor tables, much sought after when the sun appears. As for drinks, the Lansdowne stocks good ale, such as Adnams, Truman's Runner and Wells Bombardier, and there's an extensive wine list, with many wines available in three glass sizes as well as by the bottle.

Although the Lansdowne's tables are a bit too close together and the staff have a reputation for brusqueness, the pub must be doing something right, as it's almost always full. But it probably isn't one for fans of traditional boozers.

THE LEXINGTON

Address: 96-98 Pentonville Road, N1 9JB (☎ 020-7837 5371,
🖥 thelexington.co.uk).
Opening hours: Mon-Thu, noon to 2am; Fri-Sat, noon to 4am; Sun, noon to
midnight.
Transport: Angel tube.
Go for: A feast of bourbon and indie music.

This dubs itself 'Islington's finest
new music venue and lounge bar'
and is housed in a large, majestic
building with a ground floor bar and
an upstairs music venue. The latter
specialises in indie music – live bands
and DJ sounds (entry fee applies).

The bar is in the American lounge style, with décor described as
'bordello baroque': red curtains, plush upholstery, mood lamps, flock
wallpaper and cows' skulls. It draws a lot of drinkers from upstairs,
especially before and after the bands have done their stuff.

There's a good choice of US beers, including offerings from
Brooklyn Brewery, Flying Dog and Goose Island, as well as UK beers
such as Sambrook's and often another London brewer. You can also
choose from a wide selection of US whiskey, including more than 40
bourbons, while the wine list has a choice of 20 or so, around half
available in two glass sizes as well as by the bottle (glasses from
£4.10, bottles from £14.50). Food is of the burgers and bangers
variety.

If you really know your music, the Lexington hosts the Rough Trade
Records pop quiz on Monday nights.

THE MARQUESS TAVERN

Address: 32 Canonbury Street, N1 2TB (☎ 020-7354 2975,
🖥 themarquesstavern.co.uk).
Opening hours: Mon-Thu, 5-11pm; Fri, 4pm to midnight; Sat, noon to midnight; Sun, noon to 10.30pm.
Transport: Angel tube or Highbury & Islington tube/rail.
Go for: Award-winning food in a classy location.

Located in a leafy, residential area, this Young's establishment is housed in an impressive, detached, 19th-century building which has the slight air of a wedding cake about it. The interior décor is classic gastropub: neutral, light and airy, with high ceilings, wooden floors and leather Chesterfield sofas to sprawl on.

The food has won a number of awards over the years from the likes of the *Islington Gazette* and *Observer Food Monthly*, and from 2012 was being prepared by the much-lauded team from *A Little of What You Fancy* in Dalston. There's emphasis on locally grown British ingredients, with meals being served in the lovely dining area at the back. This is also a relaxed destination for drinkers, with a wide choice of beer, wine and spirits, including around 40 bottled beers and 30 malt whiskies.

Like any north London gastropub, a trip to the Marquess Tavern doesn't come cheap, but it does its thing well and has a lively atmosphere and helpful staff. Booking is recommended if you want a table. There's a pub quiz on Tuesdays and a Supper Club on the last Thursday of the month.

THE NORTH POLE

Address: 188-190 New North Road, N1 7BJ (☎ 020-7354 5400, ⌨ thenorthpolepub.co.uk).
Opening hours: Mon-Thu, 11am to 11pm; Fri-Sat, 11am to midnight; Sun, 11am to 10.30pm.
Transport: Essex Road rail.
Go for: An excellent selection of craft beer – and you can take some home also.

Recently reopened after refurbishment (it was formerly the North Star but has reverted to the name it had when it first opened in the 1860s), the North Pole dubs itself 'Islington's home of craft beer, real ale and home-cooked food'. It lives up to the billing and is a great destination for fans of London's current craft beer revival.

It's an unpretentious place, with an understated interior featuring wooden floorboards and furniture, and a decked area outside. The hints of gastropub are reflected in its good-quality American food – jerk chicken, salt beef hash, pulled pork and chilli dogs – but its fine beer is the main draw.

The North Pole stocks 22 draught beers and ciders, plus another 30 by the bottle. The ten hand pumps feature ale and cider from independents (many London-based), with a constantly rotating choice. On keg are beers from Anchor, Brooklyn Brewery, Flying Dog, Harbour Brewing, London Fields and Meantime, among others. There's also a take-away service, which is a brilliant idea as these brews can be hard to track down in the shops.

THE OLD WHITE BEAR

Address: 1 Well Road, NW3 1LJ (☎ 020-7794 7719, ⌨ theoldwhitebear.co.uk).
Opening hours: Mon, 5-11pm; Tue-Wed, noon to 11pm; Thu-Sat, noon to 11.30pm; Sun, noon to 10.30pm.
Transport: Hampstead tube.
Go for: Excellent gastropub serving modern European cuisine.

This used to be a traditional boozer called Ye Olde White Bear, and has been updated into a gastropub serving excellent modern European food – although the makeover in 2010 didn't go down well with some Hampstead traditionalists. It's an old tavern, dating back to 1704, although the current building is Victorian rather than Georgian.

197

The interior is cosy and inviting, with a central bar, colourful tiled tables, 19th-century English pine furniture and an open fire. It's popular with walkers on nearby Hampstead Heath and with shoppers attracted to the area's prestigious retailers, who are willing and able to pay the above-average – although not excessive – prices.

The food is good and includes sausages from the local butcher alongside antipasti and French cheeses (there are separate lunch and dinner menus), while there's an extensive wine list, and a fair number of wines which are available by the glass (two sizes). Beer drinkers have less choice, with only a couple of brews available, but at least they're solid offerings such as London Pride and Greene King Abbott Ale.

THE PIG AND BUTCHER

Address: 80 Liverpool Road, N1 0QD (☎ 020-7226 8304,
🖵 thepigandbutcher.co.uk).
Opening hours: Mon-Wed, 5-11pm; Thu-Sun, noon to 11pm; Fri-Sat, noon to 1am.
Transport: Angel tube.
Go for: Fine meat from the in-house butcher and a choice of craft beer.

Housed in an attractive mid-19th century building, the Pig and Butcher is a smart, well-run pub and restaurant which takes pride in the way it sources its food. It lives up to its name by butchering its rare-breed meat carcasses on site, which allows the chef to offer unusual cuts at keen prices. Fish comes from the south coast and is line caught on day boats, while vegetables are fresh from Kent.

The pub's interior décor is sleek, in muted shades of grey with large windows providing lots of light. The menu changes daily (and is posted on the website) but is always inventive and hearty – 'think of food as Granny used to make!' Main courses are priced roughly between £10 and £20 and include such delights as venison faggots, pearl barley risotto and guinea fowl.

Craft beer is a speciality, with a well-selected list of 25-30 bottles from the UK, Belgium, Germany and the US, including BrewDog, Camden, Goose Island, Hackney, Meantime and Sharp's. There's also a good wine list with around 50 bins, a number of which are available by the glass and carafe.

THE PINEAPPLE

Address: 51 Leverton Street, NW5 2NX (☎ 020-7284 4631).
Opening hours: Mon-Sat, noon to 11pm; Sun; noon to 10.30pm.
Transport: Kentish Town tube/rail.
Go for: Good beer, tasty Thai food and a warm welcome.

This good-looking pub is located in a Grade II listed building dating from 1868, slightly off the beaten track in an area of Kentish Town terraces. It was snatched from the jaws of property developers following a Save the Pineapple campaign which won the support of broadcaster Jon Snow, actor Rufus Sewell and politician Ken Livingstone, among others, so has influential friends.

199

Its centrepiece is a fancy, carved Victorian bar counter, with a conservatory at the back and a lovely garden beyond. Its foodie USP is a Thai kitchen, so you can have a green curry with your pint. Beer drinkers are well served, with a varying selection of ale, including something local from brewers such as Redemption and Sambrook's, as well as Adnams, Becks and Staropramen. They also host beer festivals here.

The pub is called the Pineapple because the exotic fruit is an old symbol of hospitality. It suits this friendly venue, that's clearly valued by its local community – every neighbourhood should have one like it!

THE QUEEN'S HEAD AND ARTICHOKE

Address: 30-2 Albany Street, NW1 4EA (☎ 020-7916 6206, 🖥 theartichoke.net).
Opening hours: Mon-Sat, 11am to 11pm; Sun, noon to 10.30pm.
Transport: Warren Street or Regent's Park tube.
Go for: A wide selection of tapas and ales at a pub with royal connections.

200

Originally dating from the 16th century, the Queen's Head and Artichoke was once a royal hunting lodge in what later became Regent's Park. It's said the tavern was once run by Elizabeth I's head gardener – which may explain the name. It was relocated to its current site in 1811, although the present building dates from around 1900 and is an attractively restored late Victorian pile with wood panelling and leaded windows.

It's one of London's more recently created gastropubs, offering a daily menu of modern English food and an extensive and popular tapas menu, with many of its small dishes priced under a fiver. Beer drinkers can enjoy a wide range of beers, including Adnams, Bitburger, Doom Bar, Marston's Pedigree, San Miguel, Sharp's Cornish Coaster, Timothy Taylor Landlord and others.

Cocktails are available at £7-9.50 and you can choose from around 50 wines, a number of which are available in by the glass (from £2.80) as well as the bottle (from £14.80). In short, it's a pub which caters to most tastes.

THE RAILWAY TAVERN

Address: 2 St Jude Street, N16 8JT (☎ 020-0011 1195).
Opening hours: Mon-Sat, noon to 11pm; Sun, noon to 10.30pm.
Transport: Dalston Kingsland rail.
Go for: The Thai kitchen, range of ales and friendly atmosphere.

Reopened after a well-conceived restoration in 2011, this was once Old Henry's Freehouse but has reverted to the name it was given back in 1896. It's an attractive, curved, corner pub with a convivial atmosphere and is a welcome addition to this area, on the border between Dalston and Islington.

Staff are friendly and the interior is inviting, with plenty of original features alongside modern touches. The décor is pastels and greys, with film posters, railway memorabilia (of course!) and a fireplace. On some nights there's live music.

The Railway describes itself as an 'ale house' and the emphasis is mainly on beer, with Adnams, BrewDog, Meantime, Purity and Redemption lining up at the bar, along with some good German beers such as Leicher Weizen wheat beer. The interesting bottled selection includes samples from some of the capital's microbreweries.

Like at the **Pineapple** (see page 199), the main menu is Thai. This may not be everyone's idea of the perfect accompaniment to beer, but it goes down well with the locals.

THE SIR RICHARD STEELE

Address: 97 Haverstock Hill, NW3 4RL (☎ 020-7483 1261,
🖳 www.faucetinn.com/sirrichardsteele).
Opening hours: Mon-Sat, 11am to midnight; Sun, noon to midnight.
Transport: Belsize Park or Chalk Farm tube.
Go for: An atmospheric, traditional pub with lively décor.

Named after the Irish writer and politician who founded *The Spectator* magazine and sought to promote well-informed social interaction, this is a large, rambling, traditional pub with an appealingly louche atmosphere.

Situated on the hill that runs from Chalk Farm to Belsize Park and Hampstead, it's an attractive Victorian building with a comfortable, dimly-lit interior, well supplied with sofas, tables and chairs. The décor is a deliberately mismatched melange of portraits and old photographs, vintage advertisements, old mirrors, book-lined shelves, stuffed animal heads and other paraphernalia. There are open fireplaces for chilly nights and a terrace with parasols for fine-weather days.

Four real ales are served – including Dark Star Hophead and Timothy Taylor Landlord – to a lively, mixed, good-humoured clientele;

there's also a range of entertainment, including live music, comedy and quiz nights (see website for details). It's a formula which works well with the liberal, creative, well-heeled folk of north London and one which would have found favour with Sir Richard.

69 COLEBROOKE ROW

Address: 69 Colebrooke Row, N1 8AA (☎ 07540-528593, 💻 69colebrookerow.com).
Opening hours: Sun-Wed, 5pm to midnight; Thu, 5pm to 1am; Fri-Sat, 5pm to 2am.
Transport: Angel tube.
Go for: Some of the best cocktails in the capital.

203

Though named after its address, this is also known by its tongue-in-cheek nickname of the Bar with No Name and has impressive cocktail credentials. It's a sister venue of the **Zetter Townhouse** (see page 167), and the man who mixes the cocktails here (and at the Zetter) is the dapper, award-winning Tony Conigliaro.

Opened in mid-2009, 69 Colebrooke Row is a small, intimate venue tucked away behind an anonymous exterior. Both cosy and elegant, the décor takes second billing to the drinks which are the real stars of the show.

The cocktail list is concise but well-conceived and the drinks are clever combinations which leave you wanting more. Moreover, they're all priced at £9, and are served by smartly turned-out staff, who know what they're talking about and are big on old school charm. Another nice touch is the hand-written bills. You can also drink wine or beer, of course, but why would you in this cocktail drinkers' mecca?

If you want to learn more about what goes into the perfect cocktail, there are regular masterclasses, some hosted by Tony, priced from £40 (see website for details).

SLIM JIM'S LIQUOR STORE

Address: 112 Upper Street, N1 1QN (☎ 020-7354 4364,
🖥 slimjimsliquorstore.com).
Opening hours: Mon-Wed, 4pm to 2am; Thu, 4pm to 3am; Fri-Sat, noon to 3am; Sun, 6pm to 2am.
Transport: Angel tube or Highbury & Islington tube/rail.
Go for: Spirits, heavy rock and a dive bar vibe.

If you're an aspiring rocker or enjoy the darker side of the American dream, this could be the place for you. It dubs itself 'the UK's first LA-style dive bar' and is a venue where you half expect to see Lemmy and Slash discussing guitars and groupies over a bottle of Jack Daniels.

Jim's has bare brick walls, a long bar, '50s-style bar stools and plywood diner booths. Lighting is by candles and neon, which gives a hazy glow. On some nights there's entertainment with guest DJs; otherwise you're serenaded by a heavy rock soundtrack, which is 'predominantly guitar-based rock and roll, from AC/DC to Led Zeppelin and everything in between'.

204 As for the drinks, you can select from 'a connoisseur's choice of fine spirits'. The list is especially strong on hard liquor – whisky, bourbon, tequila and rum – but there's also wine on the menu as well as a range of cocktails, including the eponymous Slim Jim.

Casual rather than smart is the dress code among the young, lively crowd who come here to let their hair down (sometimes literally) into the wee small hours.

THE SOUTHAMPTON ARMS

Address: 139 Highgate Road, NW5 1LE (🖥 thesouthamptonarms.co.uk).
Opening hours: Daily, noon to midnight.
Transport: Kentish Town tube.
Go for: A tremendous selection of ale and cider from independent producers.

205

A sign outside proclaims this to be an 'Ale & Cider House' in what used to (see pic!) be a tatty old pub. Since 2009, however, it's become one of London's must-visit beer bars, specialising in ale and cider from small independent producers. A couple of Camden Town beers are regulars, while the rest of the list is constantly changing.

The Southampton Arms has a long bar, wooden floorboards, old furniture – including church pews – and white tiles on the walls, with a small patio garden at the back. The 18 handpulls serve around ten real ales and eight real ciders and perries, while the food is simple and wholesome: pork pies, sausage rolls, Scotch eggs and, many people's favourite, hot meat in baps, perfect for soaking up the alcohol.

There's often a pianist on Wednesdays and Sundays, and the venue is forthright in stating that it doesn't have a phone, take bookings, reserve seats or accept payments by card. It draws a mixed crowd of beer aficionados and local trendies, and becomes crowded. Go in the afternoon if you like things quieter.

THE SPANIARDS INN

Address: Spaniards Road, NW3 7JJ (☎ 020-8731 8406,
🖥 thespaniardshampstead.co.uk).
Opening hours: Mon-Sat, noon to 11pm; Sun, noon to 10.30pm.
Transport: Hampstead tube and then a 15-minute walk or catch the 603 bus.
Go for: A famous tollhouse inn with history, atmosphere and good beer.

A 16th-century coaching inn close to Hampstead Heath, the Spaniards Inn is a local landmark with a great many historic and literary claims to fame – though some should be taken with a pinch of salt. Charles Dickens immortalised the pub in *The Pickwick Papers*, while Bram Stoker used it as inspiration for Dracula, and it's said the poet John Keats wrote *Ode to a Nightingale* in the garden. Some say that Dick Turpin was born here in 1705; certainly, its location on the lonely heath made it popular with highwaymen.

The building dates back to 1585, and while there have been plenty of modifications and additions since, it remains a quaint and atmospheric pub, with a glorious garden. It's popular with walkers – there's an automatic dog wash for mucky pups – as well as locals and tourists.

The Spaniards has some good beers, such as Adnams Broadside, St Austell Tribute, Doom Bar, Timothy Taylor Landlord and Leffe, and serves seasonal British food. It isn't a cheap venue, but is worth visiting for its unique position and glorious past.

THE WELLS

Address: 30 Well Walk, NW3 1BX (☎ 020-7794 3785, 🖳 thewellshampstead.co.uk).
Opening hours: Daily, noon to 11pm.
Transport: Hampstead tube.
Go for: Fine food and wine in a lovely Georgian building near the Heath.

A short walk from Hampstead Heath, the Wells Tavern was associated with the area's well (or spa) from the early 18th century. In 2003 it was taken over and transformed into the Wells, now a popular gastropub. Some original features of the Georgian inn remain, and are combined with modern decorative touches to make for an eye-catching venue.

The main dining area is upstairs and the ground floor bar serves food, while there are also some outdoor tables. The wine list is well-considered, with wines categorised by character rather than grape; a few are available by the glass (small, medium or large). Beer drinkers have less choice, although solid favourites such as London Pride and Black Sheep are often served.

The Wells is a smart place in a smart area with a well-heeled clientele, although while its prices are far from bargain bin they aren't too wallet-threatening either. The team behind the pub certainly believe in their enterprise: 'The pub and restaurant you've always been looking for,' is how they modestly describe it. Pay a visit and see if they're right.

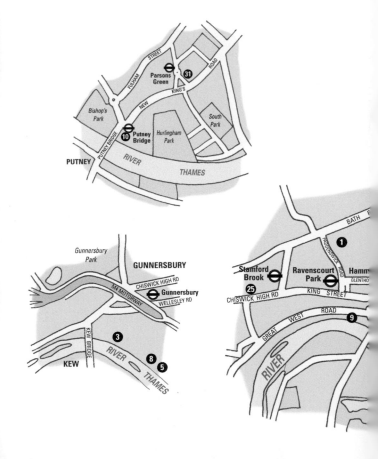

CHAPTER 4

WEST LONDON

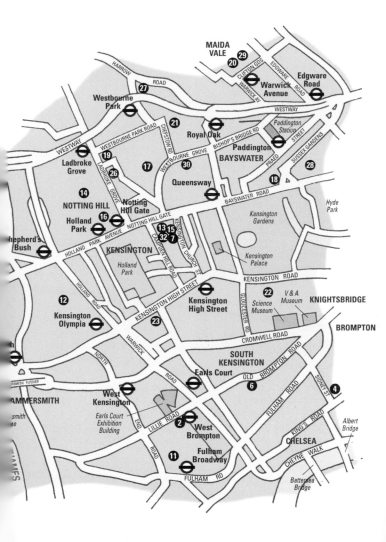

THE ANGLESEA ARMS

Address: 35 Wingate Road, W6 0UR (☎ 020-8749 1291,
🖥 anglesea-arms.com).
Opening hours: Mon-Sat, 11am to 11pm; Sun, noon to 10.30pm.
Transport: Goldhawk Road or Ravenscourt Park tube.
Go for: One of the original and best gastropubs.

One of several pubs which claim to be where the Great Train Robbery was planned (another is **The Star Tavern** – see page 104), this Shepherd's Bush pub became one of London's first gastropubs and remains one of the best. It's situated on a residential street off the Goldhawk Road and has wood-panelled walls, a Chesterfield sofa, wooden chairs and well-used tables; in short, the classic gastropub interior.

The bar is understated yet inviting – helped by a welcoming open fire when it's cold – and there's a dining room behind it, or you can eat on the front terrace when the sun shines. The atmosphere is lively and welcoming, and the pub is usually busy.

Beer lovers can enjoy Devon's Otter ales plus guest beers and lagers, while there's a fair selection for wine drinkers, including around 20 wines available by the glass. The British-style food isn't cheap, but is of good quality and rightly popular, and it's especially well-regarded for its home-made ice creams and sorbets. Booking is recommended.

THE ATLAS

Address: 16 Seagrove Road, SW6 1RX (☎ 020-7385 9129,
🖥 theatlaspub.co.uk).
Opening hours: Mon-Sat, noon to 11pm; Sun, noon to 10.30pm.
Transport: West Brompton tube.
Go for: An excellent all-round pub/gastropub.

Appearances can be deceptive: this plain-looking pub in a Fulham backstreet is actually a notable gastropub. Its menu is a trip around the Mediterranean, with Italian, Moroccan and Turkish influences, and its mains are priced around the London average (£11.50-17.50) for gastropub fare.

The Atlas is also serious about its drinks (rather than just paying lip service to them, as some dining pubs do). There are four real ales on offer at any one time, which may include Caledonian Deuchars IPA, Hog's Back GFB, London Pride, Otter Ale, Sharp's Doom Bar, St Austell Tribute or Timothy Taylor Landlord. There's also a good wine list – detailed tasting notes are provided – including a fair number available in two glass sizes costing from £4.10, with bottles from £15.90. Indeed, the Atlas is sufficiently interested in the grape to host wine workshops by The London Wine Academy.

211

The décor is downbeat and unpretentious – glazed tiles, wood panelled walls and stone fireplaces – and there's a small garden. In short, a civilised place to enjoy great food, beer and wine.

THE BELL & CROWN

Address: 11-13 Thames Road, W4 3PL (☎ 020-8994 4164,
🖥 bell-and-crown.co.uk).
Opening hours: Mon-Sat, 11am to 11pm; Sun, 11am to 10.30pm.
Transport: Kew Bridge rail or Gunnersbury tube/rail.
Go for: A tranquil spot from which to enjoy riverside views.

Located on a lovely part of the River Thames towpath near Kew
Bridge, this friendly, traditional pub became the Bell & Crown in 1787
although a tavern probably existed here in earlier times. West London
brewer Fuller's acquired it in 1814, rebuilt it in 1907 and enlarged it
in the '80s. The pub's cellars were reputedly once used by smugglers
to store contraband, and according to local folklore, a resident ghost
used to turn on the beer pumps in the middle of the night.

All is calm now at the Bell, which is a good all-year venue: it has a
patio, picnic benches along the towpath and a conservatory, so you
can enjoy the views when it's cold. Sitting on this peaceful stretch of
the Thames, it's easy to forget how close you are to central London.
The pub has competition from several other riverside boozers but
remains popular and busy with locals and those from further afield.

Beers include the
usual range of Fuller's
ales, and most of the
wines can be ordered
by the glass. Food is
good-quality pub grub,
including steaks, platters
and pies.

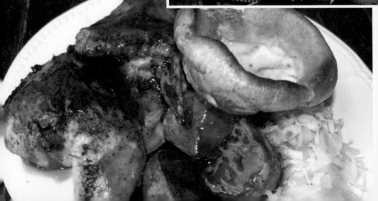

THE BUILDER'S ARMS

Address: 13 Britten Street, SW3 3TY (☎ 020-7349 9040, 🖥 geronimo-inns.co.uk/thebuildersarms).

Opening hours: Mon-Wed, 11am to 11pm; Thu-Sat, 11am to midnight; Sun, noon to 10.30pm.

Transport: South Kensington tube.

Go for: Civilised eating and drinking with the Chelsea set.

213

There's nothing rough and ready about this popular Chelsea gastropub which belies its workaday name with a stylish interior and excellent food. It occupies a three-storey Georgian building on a side street near St Luke's Church and its glorious garden. There's a main bar and a dining area, and the atmosphere is relaxed and inviting, with artwork, bookcases and comfy banquettes. You can also sit outside.

They take food seriously here, serving imaginative bar snacks and a brief but tempting lunch and dinner menu (most mains are priced between £12 and £20), but it's also a good all-round pub. There's a great wine list assembled by Master of Wine John Clevely, and mark-ups aren't unreasonable (considering you're a stone's throw from the King's Road), with glasses costing from £4 and bottles from around £15. The list includes some unusual selections, e.g. a Slovenian white, and a wine club on Wednesdays offers punters the chance to try a selection of wines. Beer drinkers have a choice of three ales on pump plus a choice of lager.

Not surprisingly, the Builder's is popular and soon fills up, especially at weekends.

THE BULL'S HEAD

> **Address:** 15 Strand on the Green, W4 3PQ (☎ 020-8994 1204,
> 🖥 chefandbrewer.com/pub/bulls-head-chiswick-london/c6789).
> **Opening hours:** Mon-Sat, 11am to 11pm; Sun, noon to 10pm.
> **Transport:** Gunnersbury tube/rail or Kew Bridge rail.
> **Go for:** River views, history and tranquillity.

Blessed with an enviable position overlooking the Thames a short
distance from Kew Bridge, this rare Grade I listed pub is old, rambling
and oozing with history.

In the centre of the river opposite the pub is Oliver's Island, an eyot
(river island) named after Oliver Cromwell. It's said that the Bull was
his headquarters on a number of occasions during the English Civil
War and that he sometimes hid out on the island. Since the pub's
licence only goes back to 1722, this may be more fiction than fact, but
the Bull does have a tangible sense of age, which is reinforced by its
low ceilings, exposed wooden beams and creaking floorboards.

Some people regard Chef and Brewer pubs as bland and this
isn't a venue for the drinks purist or the dedicated foodie. But there's
reasonable pub grub, some cask
ales and six lagers, while the house
wines are keenly priced at just
£9.99 a bottle. Besides which you
don't visit this pub for fine dining or
great ale; it's all about the history,
the location and the views.

CAPOTE Y TOROS

Address: 157 Old Brompton Road, SW5 0LJ (☎ 020-7373 0567,
🖳 cambiodetercio.co.uk).
Opening hours: Tue-Sat, 6-11pm; closed Sun-Mon.
Transport: Gloucester Road or South Kensington tube.
Go for: Sherry, wine and tapas – a true taste of Spain.

215

A celebration of Spain, this small, narrow, convivial wine bar is brash
and bright, in shades of orange and pink, with a wall displaying
bullfighting photographs and hams suspended from the ceiling. The
website suggests you'll feel like you've entered 'a neighbourhood bar
in downtown Cadiz' rather than one in the Old Brompton Road.

Capote y Toros claims to have the largest sherry list in the UK –
some 110 varieties – as well as 350 wines; it's no wonder the wine
list is a heavy tome. It will appeal to fans of the classic Spanish
wine regions – notably Rioja and Ribera del Duero – but also to
those wishing to sample something from lesser-known regions.
The speciality, however, is sherry and there's a vast choice to try by
the glass, from sandpaper dry to tooth-strippingly sweet. It's even
incorporated into many of the dishes on
offer, including the ice cream!

The tapas are authentic and
meaty – there are a few veggie
options – and teamed with the bar's
other specialities: Iberico ham and
charcuterie from southern Spain. It's
all done well, and with sherry and
tapas on a wave of popularity, Capote
y Toros is deservedly busy.

THE CHURCHILL ARMS

Address: 119 Kensington Church Street, W8 7LN (☎ 020-7727 4242,
🖥 churchillarmskensington.co.uk).
Opening hours: Mon-Wed, 11am to 11pm; Thu-Sat, 11am to midnight; Sun,
noon to 10.30pm.
Transport: High Street Kensington or Notting Hill Gate tube.
Go for: Flowers, food and Fuller's ale in a pub that pays homage to a great
leader.

This civilised Fuller's pub sits at the Notting Hill end of Kensington
Church Street and dates from 1750. Its name comes from its
connection to Winston Churchill's family – his grandparents were
regulars in the 19th century, and the pub was renamed in the great
man's honour after the Second World War.

It's rambling and cluttered, eccentrically decorated with portraits
of prime ministers and American presidents; there are chamber pots
hanging from the ceiling, Churchill memorabilia scattered around and
even souvenirs of the County Clare hurling team (the landlord is Irish).
The Churchill is also a visual treat outside, festooned with hanging
baskets and a regular winner in its class in the London in Bloom
competition.

It claims to have been the first pub in London to offer Thai food,
and the authentic curries and noodles, served in the butterfly-themed
conservatory, provide excellent value for money in an exclusive part of
town. To go with them there's the usual range of reliable Fuller's ales,
a changing special and some interesting bottled beers.

THE CITY BARGE

Address: 27 Strand on the Green, W4 3PH (☎ 020-8994 2148,
🖥 gkpubs.co.uk/pubs-in-london/city-barge-pub).
Opening hours: Daily, noon to 11pm (10.30pm Sun).
Transport: Gunnersbury tube/rail or Kew Bridge rail.
Go for: The archetypal historic riverside pub.

There's been a pub on this picturesque Thames-side site since at
least 1484. The current incarnation has been known as the City Barge
since the early 19th century in recognition of the Lord Mayor's state
barge that was moored nearby in winter. The building took a direct hit
in the Second World War and has been substantially rebuilt, but one
of the original two bars survived, and the place still feels lost in time.

Attractively wonky, the City Barge is right on the towpath, a few
steps from the river and opposite an eyot (a small island). You could
be in the country, so tranquil is this spot. The outside tables are a
great vantage point from which to watch the river activity, and although
the towpath is liable to flood at high tide,
you'll be dry and cosy inside – the heavy
front door is watertight!

217

There's a selection of good cask
ale, including Greene King IPA and Old
Speckled Hen, while the house wine is just
under £3 per glass. And the food menu is
tasty and imaginative. But it's the views
and atmosphere that will keep you coming
back for more.

THE DOVE

Address: 19 Upper Mall, W6 9TA (☎ 020-8748 9474,
🖥 dovehammersmith.co.uk).
Opening hours: Mon-Sat, 11am to 11pm; Sun, noon to 11pm.
Transport: Hammersmith or Ravenscourt Park tube.
Go for: Great views, history and the world's smallest bar.

Another of London's must-visit pubs, the Dove is one of the capital's oldest, most characterful waterside taverns. There's been a pub here since the 17th century, so it's soaked in history: Charles II and Nell Gwynne shared trysts at the Dove, while the poet James Thomson wrote *Rule Britannia* in one of its rooms.

The pub has also hosted some notable patrons, including Ernest Hemingway, Dylan Thomas, Alec Guinness and Graham Greene. And it has appeared in the Guinness Book of World Records for having the world's smallest bar room – you need sharp eyes to spot the entrance just to the right of the bar.

If the interior is cosy and Dickensian in atmosphere, the riverside terrace and leafy conservatory are prime spots from which to watch the activity on the river, in particular the annual Boat Race between crews from Oxford and Cambridge universities.

The Dove is a Fuller's pub and serves their ales, plus a seasonal selection and some decent bottled beers. There's good (if pricy) pub grub; Sunday lunch is particularly popular at this, the best of Hammersmith's old riverside pubs.

218

THE EIGHT BELLS

Address: 89 Fulham High Street, SW6 3JS (☎ 020-7736 6307).
Opening hours: Mon-Sat, 11am to 11pm; Sun, noon to 10.30pm.
Transport: Putney Bridge tube.
Go for: A 'proper' local with a sense of history.

Sitting across the bridge from Putney, this small Georgian pub dates from 1629 and may well be Fulham's oldest. It was originally called the Bell, but in 1729 the nearby All Saints Church had its six bells recast and two more added – and the pub was renamed to reflect this momentous occasion.

It was once on the main road to Putney Bridge, but when the old river crossing was replaced in 1886, the new bridge was built just to the west. So the Eight Bells is a bit off the beaten track, tucked behind a Premier Inn, but is well worth seeking out. It's an atmospheric, wood-panelled venue with a U-shaped bar, and is just the sort of civilised pub many people would love to have as their local. It has a loyal following of customers, and can become busy, especially when Fulham FC is playing at home.

The friendly crowd can enjoy a pint of London Pride or Sharp's Doom Bar, or one of a number of draft lagers, and the most popular seats are on the pavement outside.

THE HARWOOD ARMS

Address: Walham Grove, SW6 1QP (☎ 020-7386 1847, 🖥 harwoodarms.com).
Opening hours: Mon, 5-11pm; Sun and Tue-Thu, noon to 11pm; Fri-Sat, noon to midnight.
Transport: Fulham Broadway tube.
Go for: A great pub serving Michelin-star food.

A friendly pub on a back street north of Fulham Broadway, the Harwood Arms is also a food-lover's mecca. It's received many accolades for its cooking and was the first London pub to be awarded a Michelin star. Unlike some gastropubs, however, the 'pub' bit hasn't been forgotten. The owners emphasise that the Harwood is still a traditional pub and can get noisy.

There's a rural feel to the Harwood Arms – it's described on the website as 'where the country comes to the town' – and that also reflects the bill of fare which includes a lot of wild game and foraged food. Most mains cost up to £20, so it isn't cheap, but neither is it outrageous considering that all-important star! Booking is recommended if you want to eat at a table, although there are good bar snacks available, including such tempting morsels as venison Scotch egg and rabbit rissoles.

As for drinks, there's a good range of draught real ale, including Black Sheep Bitter and Ruddles County, and more than 30 wines available by the glass – a glass of the house red or white costs just £4.

THE HAVELOCK TAVERN

Address: 57 Masbro Road, W14 0LS (☎ 020-7603 5374,
🖥 havelocktavern.com).
Opening hours: Mon-Sat, 11am to 11pm; Sun, noon to 10.30pm.
Transport: Shepherd's Bush tube or Kensington (Olympia) tube/rail.
Go for: An original gastropub that's still a real pub.

Opened in 1996, this is one of London's earliest gastropubs, and one which hasn't forgotten its roots; it's a pub that serves food, rather than a restaurant serving beer.

The distinctive blue-tiled frontage reveals a 'classic' gastro interior: light and airy with bare wooden floorboards and plain walls. There are outdoor tables for sunny days. The food isn't cheap but has won awards and recommendations from *Michelin* and the *Good Pub Guide*, therefore is worth pushing the boat out for.

Fortunately, the Havelock Tavern takes its beer seriously and has a rotating selection of cask ales – usually four – supplied by Adnams, Purity, Sambrook's and Twickenham Fine Ales, among others. Wine is taken seriously, too, and one of the pub's suppliers is the well-regarded Caves de Pyrene, known for its organic and biodynamic wines. A number of wines are available by the glass or carafe, as well as by the bottle. Prices start from £4.25 a glass.

It's slightly out of the way, but the Havelock Tavern rewards the effort of getting there.

THE HILLGATE PUB

Address: 24 Hillgate Street, W8 7SR (☎ 020-7727 8566, ⌨ thehillgate.com).
Opening hours: Mon-Sat, 11am to 11pm; Sun, noon to 10.30pm.
Transport: Notting Hill Gate tube.
Go for: Good beer and fair prices in trendy Notting Hill.

A handsome, welcoming corner pub in an attractive corner of Notting Hill, the Hillgate is popular with the area's moneyed residents and also attracts visitors from further afield. It used to be your archetypal local (and not a very pleasant one, either) but has been refurbished and taken in the gastro direction by its new owners.

The interior is understated, light and airy, with dark wood and a cream and purple decor, wooden floors and patterned rugs; there are also several outdoor tables. It retains a U-shaped, dark wood bar and has pretty dimpled glass in the windows.

The superior food is reasonably priced (see the website for meal times) and there are tasty bar snacks available all day. There is also good ale on offer, such as Sambrook's Wandle and Sharp's Doom Bar. The wine list runs to around 30 bins, with a number by the glass as well as the bottle, priced from £3.50 and £14 respectively – cheaper than might be expected in this part of London. If you're feeling brainy, there's a quiz at 8pm on Mondays.

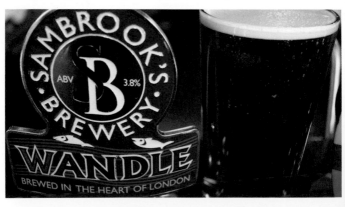

JULIE'S BAR

Address: 135 Portland Road, W11 4LW (☏ 020-7229 8331, 🖵 juliesrestaurant.com).

Opening hours: From around 10 or 10.30am to midnight (see website for exact times).

Transport: Holland Park tube.

Go for: People-watching in a renowned champagne bar.

A landmark bar in Holland Park, Julie's is a wine bar (and restaurant) which has been keeping its customers happy since 1969. It's comfortable, friendly and has the bonus of a terrace, so plenty of people are happy to pay the elevated prices (the food in particular isn't cheap), including a number of celebrity faces you might recognise.

223

Wine and champagne are the drinks of choice, with a well-conceived list including Julie's own-label offerings; around a dozen wines are available in two glass sizes starting from £5 a glass, while champagne is £10. Bottled cider and beer are also available, as are cocktails (around £10).

The atmosphere at Julie's is convivial and slightly boho, but in an sophisticated, refined fashion – it describes itself as 'Portland Road's enduring bohemian haunt' and is on a pedestrianised stretch surrounded by exclusive boutiques. Some of its customers come across as rather snooty – but then this is Holland Park. Fill your wallet, open your mind and see how the other half live.

THE KENSINGTON WINE ROOMS

Address: 127-9 Kensington Church Street, W8 7LP (☎ 020-7727 8142,
🖥 greatwinesbytheglass.com).
Opening hours: Daily, midday to midnight.
Transport: Notting Hill Gate tube.
Go for: Serious wines available by the glass and tasty 'snacks'.

A stylish, inviting wine bar, the Kensington Wine Rooms was named 2010's Newcomer of the Year by *Decanter* magazine, (it has a sister outlet, the Fulham Wine Rooms, at 871-3 Fulham Road). The KWR has a warm atmosphere, helped by its décor – a colour scheme of deep reds and dark wood, with dried hams suspended temptingly over the bar.

224

The dining space serves Mediterranean and French-influenced food, with recommended wines for each dish, while there are bar plates featuring British cheeses and Spanish charcuterie if you just want something to complement the wine. The bar area seats around 40 but there's plenty of standing room.

More than 150 wines are listed and 40 are available by the glass, including some truly special wines – this is made possible by the

use of Enomatic wine dispensers (🖥 enomatic. co.uk) which keep the rest of the bottle fresh. There are regular wine classes, too. The bar also sells beers brewed in Greenwich and gin and vodka distilled in Hammersmith. In all, it's a slick, high-quality operation.

THE LADBROKE ARMS

Address: 54 Ladbroke Road, W11 3NW (☎ 020-7727 6648,
💻 capitalpubcompany.com/our-pubs/the-ladbroke-arms).
Opening hours: Mon-Fri, 11.30am to 11pm; Sat, noon to 11pm; Sun, noon to 10.30pm.
Transport: Holland Park tube.
Go for: A pretty pub with good food in an upscale destination.

225

A freehouse on a tranquil Holland Park residential street, the Ladbroke Arms is slightly off the beaten track, between Notting Hill Gate and Ladbroke Grove, but it's a destination pub for many drinkers attracted by its eye-catching exterior, welcoming vibe, good beer, tasty food and extensive wine list (is that all?).

In summer, the pub is festooned in an award-winning display of hanging baskets, while inside the look is pure gastropub: light and airy, with wooden floors, rugs, arty prints and plain wooden furniture. The small terrace is popular when the weather permits.

People come here for the well-presented, upmarket food (most mains come in at £12-18), organic natural wines, and seasonal and guest ales such as Sambrook's, Sharp's and Twickenham Spring Ale.

The Ladbroke is an upscale gastropub in a part of London inhabited by successful, 40-somethings who form the core of its clientele, therefore it isn't your average local boozer. It's invariably busy, however, so it must be doing something right.

THE LONSDALE

Address: 48 Lonsdale Road, W11 2DE (☎ 020-7727 4080, 🖳 thelonsdale.co.uk).
Opening hours: Tue-Thu, 6pm to midnight; Fri-Sat, 6pm to 1am; closed Sun-Mon.
Transport: Ladbroke Grove or Notting Hill Gate tube.
Go for: Great cocktails in a hyper-trendy environment.

A noted feature of Notting Hill's bar scene for the last decade or so, this large, stylish, award-winning venue is spread over three floors on a quiet residential street. Its impressive décor has futuristic touches, like the bronze half spheres embedded in the walls, but the atmosphere is anything but stark; rather, it's inviting, relaxed and lounge-like.

The Lonsdale is noted for its drinks, especially the extensive list of cocktails (they call it the Cocktail Bible). There are more than 80 to choose from, ranging from classic blends to innovative new mixes. The bar also stocks over 200 spirits – it's particularly strong on whisky – around 40 wines and champagnes (a few can be ordered by the glass) and serves tapas-like snacks. The restaurant was recently revamped and the quality of the food now matches that of the drinks.

It attracts a mixed clientele – generally quite trendy, as are the staff – and can become crowded and noisy, especially on DJ nights. And it isn't cheap… but what do you expect in fashionable Notting Hill?

THE MITRE

Address: 24 Craven Terrace, W2 3QH (☏ 020-7262 5240,
🖥 mitrelancastergate.com).
Opening hours: Mon-Thu, noon to 11pm; Fri-Sat, noon to 00.30am; Sun, noon to 10.30pm.
Transport: Lancaster Gate tube or Paddington tube/rail.
Go for: A Victorian pub with a popular basement serving cocktails and craft beer.

The Mitre is a friendly Young's pub on a Bayswater corner, which proudly displays its various CAMRA awards. It's housed in a Grade II listed building dating from the 1850s that retains many original features, including etched glass, open fireplaces and mosaic floors.

The pub is divided into three areas: the pub, the upstairs grill restaurant and a basement bar. The Mitre (pub) proper has dark wood, armchairs and Chesterfield sofas, creating a traditional pub atmosphere. In addition to Young's ales and Wells Bombardier, there's Erdinger, Heineken, Kirin Ichiban, Peroni and more. Wine drinkers have a reasonable choice, too. The pub grub is solid and fairly priced for this part of town, but if you want something more substantial you can head upstairs to the Lord Craven Grill (Tue-Sat, 7-10pm), with its traditional grill menu featuring dry aged steaks.

The basement is home to Old Mary's, named after a kitchen maid who was murdered in the scullery and (allegedly) still haunts the building. Cocktails, craft beers and hot dogs are on the fare here.

All this, and the Mitre is just a stone's throw from Hyde Park.

MONTGOMERY PLACE

> **Address:** 31 Kensington Park Road, W11 2EU (☎ 020-7792 3921.
> 🖳 montgomeryplace.co.uk).
> **Opening hours;** Mon-Thu, 5pm to midnight; Fri, 5pm to 1am; Sat, 2pm to
> 1am; Sun, 5-11.30pm.
> **Transport:** Ladbroke Grove tube.
> **Go for:** A stylish and grown-up cocktail bar.

228

If you want a cosy, sophisticated, dimly-lit cocktail lounge serving grown-up drinks, this is the place for you. Inspired by 'the roaring era of Hemingway' and 'the rebirth of cool', Montgomery Place has a refined atmosphere, redolent of the '40s and '50s, and lets its cocktails do the talking.

The bar is long and narrow, with comfortable banquette seating, but can accommodate no more than around 40 people, so it's an intimate and exclusive venue. It's also relatively expensive, but worth it for the wide choice of cocktails, listed by spirit and including both traditional and innovative mixes. There are around 60 in total, most costing in the £9-12 range, and beautifully prepared. There are also some interesting wines, from around £5 per glass or £20 a bottle, while champagne costs from £9.50 a glass (£50 a bottle). You can mitigate the effects of the alcohol with an enticing range of American-style bar snacks.

If you're planning to take someone on an important date, Montgomery Place would certainly create the right impression. You can book online for groups of four or more.

THE PRINCE ALFRED

Address: 5A Formosa Street, W9 1EE (☎ 020-7286 3287,
🖳 theprincealfred.com).
Opening hours: Mon-Sat, noon to 11pm; Sun, noon to 10.30pm.
Transport: Warwick Avenue tube.
Go for: A stunning Victorian pub interior and good choice of food and drinks.

One of *The Times* newspaper's 'Top Ten Heritage Pubs' in London,
this is a fine example of a Victorian hostelry, close to Little Venice's
charming canals. Built in 1863, the pub's exterior is rich in plate glass
and wood, while the interior is utterly splendid, the decorative bar area
divided into 'snugs' by original wood and glass panels. If you prefer,
you can sit outside on the tiled terrace.

As well as being great to look at, the Prince Alfred (& Formosa
Dining Room) is a good place to drink, with well-kept cask beers such
as Wells Bombardier and Young's Bitter and Double Chocolate Stout,
plus a range of lager and cider, some bottled. Wine drinkers have a
choice of around 50 bottles, almost half which are available by the
glass (from £3.80 per glass, £15.50 a bottle). You can even drink
inexpensive cocktails (£4-6.50).

Food-wise, you can either graze on bar snacks and platters, or
pop next door to the Formosa Dining Room, where there's a great
seasonal menu and a good-value set meal (two courses for £11.50,
three for £15.50). An absolute steal in this part of town!

THE PRINCE BONAPARTE

Address: 80 Chepstow Road, W2 5BE (☎ 020-7313 9491,
🖳 theprincebonapartew2.co.uk).
Opening hours: Mon-Fri, noon to midnight; Sat, 9am to midnight; Sun, 9am
to 11pm.
Transport: Notting Hill Gate tube.
Go for: One of Notting Hill's most well-regarded pubs.

The Prince Bonaparte is one of those gastropubs that also manages
to be a proper pub and doesn't make drinkers feel unwanted. It's
a large, striking corner establishment, with high ceilings, bare
brick, neutral colours, open fires and picture windows. Despite its
spaciousness and lack of clutter, it still manages to feel cosy at night,
partly due to the light cast by its lamps.

The bar seats around 70, the dining room 38, offering decent
food (at Notting Hill prices, of course). It's popular with discerning
locals although many diners travel from further afield, so you're
recommended to book well in advance if you want a table to eat.

Beer drinkers have a fair time of it here, with a varying selection,
including the likes of Adnams and Sharp's ales, plus various lagers
and ciders. And there's an interesting wine list which is particularly
strong on whites, with around 40 wines in total and around 15
available by the glass.

Well worth a visit, whether or not you're hungry.

THE QUEENS ARMS

Address: 30 Queen's Gate Mews, SW7 5QL (☎ 020-7823 9293, 🖳 thequeensarmskensington.co.uk).
Opening hours: Mon-Sat, noon to 11pm; Sun, noon to 10.30pm.
Transport: Gloucester Road tube.
Go for: Good beer and potato vodka near the Albert Hall.

Regarded by many as one of Kensington's best pubs, the Queen's Arms is half hidden away on the corner of a narrow mews. It was built to cater to the servants of the wealthy in 19th-century Kensington – a number of workers' hostelries were opened in mews – and it's thought to be part of the pub's charm that it's difficult to find (actually it isn't that secluded, just a short walk south from Kensington Gardens).

The Queen's Arms is an understated pub with a plain wood interior, light and airy, and with board games available. In good weather, drinkers spill outside into the mews. The Royal Albert Hall is nearby and the pub can become busy before and after performances.

There are around 20 beers and ciders on tap, including London Pride, Bass and Sharp's Doom Bar, as well as a range of Belgian and speciality bottled beers. They also stock English potato vodka, which sounds reassuringly dangerous, and a reasonable selection of wines. The food is good; roasts and Bloody Marys are a Sunday speciality for those recovering from the excesses of the night before.

THE SCARSDALE TAVERN

Address: 23A Edwardes Square, W8 6HE (☎ 020-7937 1811,
💻 scarsdaletavern.co.uk).
Opening hours: Mon-Sat, noon to 11pm; Sun, noon to 10.30pm.
Transport: High Street Kensington tube.
Go for: A pie and a pint in Bodie and Doyle's local boozer.

Well located on an attractive square on an attractive square in 'deepest Kensington', this Fuller's pub is one of the area's best. It isn't so much a gastropub as a pub with good food; it's upscale but doesn't make a meal of it (pun intended).

The pretty front terrace garden is a real draw and popular in good weather, the perfect spot to work your way through a jug of Pimm's on a sunny afternoon. If the weather is more typically English, then the pub's interior is dark and cosy with an open fire. Bar snacks are available, or there's a restaurant in the back – booking is recommended if you want to eat dinner here. There's a well-considered list of (mostly expensive) wines, and a good choice of well-kept ale such as London Pride and Butcombe Bitter, plus some interesting European beers.

The Scarsdale is a friendly place with an inviting atmosphere but best of all, perhaps, it featured as Bodie and Doyle's local in the legendary, splendidly cheesy '70s cop series, *The Professionals*.

THE STONEMASONS ARMS

Address: 54 Cambridge Grove W6 0LA (☎ 020-8748 1397,
🖳 stonemasons-arms.co.uk).
Opening hours: Mon-Sat, 11am to 11pm; Sun, noon to 11pm.
Transport: Hammersmith tube.
Go for: Tasty gastropub fare with good beer and entertainment.

233

Another Fuller's pub, this friendly hostelry is a little off the beaten track in Hammersmith (although only a short walk from the tube station) and one of the area's best pubs – it manages to be both a friendly local and a noted gastropub. Inside, it's sleek, clean, airy and modern, with wooden furniture, bare brick, a roaring log fire and large windows that flood the bar with light.

Professional, friendly staff serve good ale, wine and food. The menu features generous portions of 'English favourites and continental creations' (check the website for meal times). There's a choice of beer, including Fuller's ales and seasonal selections, plus Leffe, Peroni and Staropramen. The wine list features around 40 bins, a number of which are available by the glass and carafe.

There's a terrace for when the sun shines, a pub quiz on Wednesdays and regular appearances by the Hammersmith Ukulele Group (HUG), so the Stonemason's Arms has something for everyone and does most things well.

It's close to Earls Court, Olympia and the Hammersmith Apollo, therefore it's busier than usual when there are concerts or exhibitions on.

THE TABARD

Address: Bath Road, W4 1LW (☎ 020-8994 3492, ⌨ taylor-walker.co.uk/
pub/tabard-chiswick/m2617).
Opening hours: Sun-Wed, noon to 11pm; Thu-Sat, noon to midnight.
Transport: Turnham Green tube.
Go for: Arts and Crafts architecture and a tiny fringe theatre.

The Tabard in Chiswick is a rare and unique Arts and Crafts pub. It was designed by architect Norman Shaw and built in 1880 as part of the development of the Bedford Park estate, which was one of London's first garden suburbs. Its dark interior features Arts and Crafts tiles by William de Morgan and Walter Crane. The pub is named after the type of tunic worn by a herald and may recall the ancient Tabard

234

Inn on Borough High Street, which was demolished in 1875 (and which featured in Chaucer's *The Canterbury Tales*).

A Taylor Walker pub, the Tabard has five hand pumps, which dispense a range of ales, such as Caledonian Deuchers IPA, Purity, Timothy Taylor Landlord and Tetley and others. There's also a good wine list and tasty pub grub.

On the first floor of the pub is the Tabard Theatre, a 79-seat fringe theatre which is run independently of the pub. It hosts its own productions and is also used by comedians as a pre-tour warm-up venue. Al Murray, Harry Hill and Russell Brand have all performed here (and survived).

TRAILER HAPPINESS

Address: 177 Portobello Road, W11 2DY (☎ 020-7313 4644,
🖳 trailerhappiness.com).
Opening hours: Tue-Sat, 5pm to midnight; closed Sun-Mon.
Transport: Ladbroke Grove or Notting Hill Gate tube.
Go for: Tiki cocktails in a tacky environment (in the nicest possible way).

This Notting Hill basement bar describes itself as a 'lounge bar, den
and kitchen' and a 'retro-sexy haven of cosmopolitan kitsch and
faded trailer park glamour'. It doesn't take itself at all seriously – the
décor is a mix of palm trees, bright colours and '60s art – which is
a healthy change in this part of town. The nicely tacky interior aims
for lo-fi glamour and there are DJs most nights, so it isn't a classic
cocktail bar.

The drinks are of good quality, with classic and contemporary
cocktails spread across three menus: House Favourites (£6.50), Tiki
Classics (£7-15) and Homage Drinks (£6.50-8). Martinis are £4 or £6.
You can also choose from ten wines, four champagnes and two beers.

The nibbles and finger food are good,
and some thought has gone into them.

235

This is a relaxed, affordable venue
with a happy, friendly crowd, in an area
of London that's usually expensive
and tries too hard to be boho-chic and
super-cool. Hardly surprising, then, that
it's popular.

THE UNION TAVERN

Address: 45 Woodfield Road, W9 2BA (☎ 020-7286 1886,
🖥 union-tavern.co.uk).
Opening hours: Mon-Thu, 11am to 11pm; Fri-Sat, 11am to midnight; Sun,
noon to 10.30pm.
Transport; Westbourne Park tube.
Go for: Canal-side location, great ale and delicious food.

Formerly called the Grand Union and recently reopened, the 'unique selling point' of this Victorian pub in Maida Vale is its location overlooking the canal. It makes the most of this, with a couple of dozen tables on the waterside terrace. Such is the allure of sipping a drink next to any stretch of water (regardless of the views), that it gets very busy.

236

The Union Tavern's interior is attractive, too: light and modern, with wooden tables and chairs, and large brown leather sofas. Beer is taken seriously here and there's an unusually large number of guest ales for a Fuller's pub, which include brews from various parts of London and further afield: Bermondsey, Camden, Chiswick, Hackney and Windsor, plus Belgium, Germany and the US. The staff are apparently regular visitors to the London breweries, so are well informed about the drinks they serve.

The food is another draw, featuring home-smoked meat and fish and freshly made bread – the two combine to make spectacular sandwiches – as well as tasty pies and sharing platters. They also serve a popular Sunday roast.

THE VICTORIA

Address: 10A Strathearn Place, W2 2NH (☎ 020-7724 1191,
🖥 victoriapaddington.co.uk).
Opening hours: Mon-Sat, 11am to 11pm; Sun, noon to 10.30pm.
Transport: Lancaster Gate tube or Paddington tube/rail.
Go for: A traditional boozer with some famous friends.

Yet another Fuller's establishment and their Pub of the Year in 2007
and 2009, the Victoria is something of a beacon in a part of London
sadly lacking in decent pubs. Built in 1838, legend has it that Queen
Victoria stopped here on her way to Paddington Station (which was
built at around the same time as the pub) and the hostelry was named
after her.

The interior is quite grand and decorative, friendly with a good
atmosphere. There are five hand pumps serving Chiswick Bitter,
London Pride, Discovery and ESB, plus a seasonal ale. Around 20
wines are available, half of which can be bought by the glass (from
£3.50). Traditional pub grub is served, as you'd expect in a traditional
local boozer.

The Victoria has built up a list of famous patrons over the years,
including Winston Churchill, Ronnie Wood, Liam Gallagher, Damian
Hirst and Keira Knightley. The
Dracula Society used to meet
here and (almost inevitably)
Charles Dickens was a
regular and apparently wrote
part of *Our Mutual Friend*
while propped up at the bar.
Appropriately, the pub's décor
is suitably Dickensian.

237

THE WARRINGTON

Address: 93 Warrington Crescent, W9 1EH (☎ 020-7592 7960,
🖳 www.faucetinn.com/warrington).
Opening hours: Mon-Thu, noon to 11pm; Fri-Sat, noon to midnight; Sun,
noon to 10.30pm.
Transport: Maida Vale tube.
Go for: A lovely, eye-catching Victorian pub.

Built in 1857, this striking Grade II listed pub was a hotel in the late
19th century and is rumoured to have once been a brothel. Situated
at the end of one of Maida Vale's elegant curving crescents, The
Warrington was part of TV chef Gordon Ramsay's restaurant and pub
stable until 2011, when he sold it to Faucet Inns.

The entrance porch is attention-grabbing, with columns covered
with colourful glazed tiles and two large rare lamps standing on
either side. Inside, the large bar is dominated by a marble-topped bar
counter, with a carved, dark wood base, above which is a riot of fancy
detailing, with cherubs gazing down on drinkers. The bar also has Art
Nouveau touches, including glasswork, mahogany, marble columns
and plasterwork.

It's a striking, memorable place to drink and it will be interesting to
see how it develops under the new owners. Initial indications suggest
a few teething troubles, including slow service, but it's early days,
and this notable example of pub architecture in an attractive part of
London deserves to become a destination venue once again.

WESTBOURNE HOUSE

Address: 65 Westbourne Grove, W2 4UJ (☎ 020-7229 2233, 🖳 westbournehouse.net).

Opening hours: Mon-Thu, 11am to 11pm; Fri, 11am to midnight; Sat, 9am to midnight; Sun, 9am to 10.30pm.

Transport: Bayswater or Royal Oak tube.

Go for: Fairly-priced cocktails in a stylish environment.

Westbourne House is a cocktail venue with both substance and style. The décor is reminiscent of a Baroque nightclub, with a hint of Parisian salon. It's candlelit with a fire in winter, lots of mirrors and a zinc-topped bar counter. In summer, there are outdoor tables.

239

It's something of a temple to the history of the cocktail, most of which are priced between £8 and £10; indeed, its literature proclaims that 'what cocktails will not cure, there is no cure for'. There are also 20 wines and ten champagnes; eight wines and one bubbly are available by the glass, with wine costing from £5 per glass and £24 a bottle, champagne from £9 and £48 respectively. There's a brunch menu and a longer list for evening dining, including everything from a plate of olives to rib-eye steak.

This is a polished, sophisticated venue which attracts a smart clientele and would be a suitable place for a date. Prices are reasonable by London cocktail bar standards, but that means that it tends to get crowded at weekends.

THE WHITE HORSE

Address: 1-3 Parsons Green, SW6 4UL (☎ 020-7736 2115,
💻 whitehorsesw6.com).
Opening hours: Sun-Wed, 9.30am to 11.30pm; Thu-Sat, 9.30am to midnight.
Transport: Parsons Green tube.
Go for: A London 'village' pub that understands ale.

Formerly a coaching inn (since at least 1688, perhaps even earlier),
this high-ceilinged Victorian pub has also been nicknamed the
Sloaney Pony, as it's supposedly filled almost exclusively with the
young British upper classes (the so-called Sloane Rangers). This is
rather unfair as it attracts a mixed clientele, although it does include a
regular supply of public schoolboy rugger types.

They're drawn by the excellent choice of ale: Adnams, Harveys
and Oakham, plus five interesting guests and a great selection by
the bottle (over 135), especially strong on offerings from Belgium and
the US. The pub's owners are sufficiently serious about beer to host
beer festivals, as well as education and training events. There's also a
good choice of wine, some by the glass, and good food, all served by
friendly, well-informed staff.

The pub's interior is light and airy, thanks to the large windows,
and features dark wood, giant tables,
leather wingback chairs, and wooden
floors. There are also outdoor tables
facing the green, much sought
after when the weather is good. In
short, it's a delightful pub in a lovely
location.

THE WINDSOR CASTLE

Address: 114 Campden Hill Road, W8 7AR (☎ 020-7243 8797,
🖥 thewindsorcastlekensington.co.uk).
Opening hours: Mon-Sat, noon to 11pm; Sun, noon to 10.30pm.
Transport: Notting Hill Gate tube.
Go for: Good beer, potato vodka and a fine interior.

Built in 1835, this attractive Georgian pub feels like a country tavern, perhaps because Kensington was an agricultural backwater until the late 19th century. The Windsor Castle is supposedly named after the view it enjoyed before it was surrounded by subsequent development, although given its distance from Windsor, this is somewhat fanciful.

It's a lovely traditional tavern and has one of the most original, unaltered 19th-century pub interiors in London, spread over three bars: the Campden Bar, Private Bar and Sherry Bar. It's Dickensian in atmosphere, characterful and nicely cramped and gloomy, with wooden panelling, pews and booths, and plenty of nooks and crannies. There's also a walled garden, including a heated area for al fresco dining, and outside bar.

There's a range of draught and bottled beer, including Sambrook's Wandle, Timothy Taylor Landlord and five draught ciders, as well as various wines and food, notably a good range of sausages and popular Sunday roasts. The Windsor Castle even offers English potato vodka and describes itself as Kensington's friendliest pub.

241

CHAPTER 5

SOUTHWEST LONDON

THE ALMA

Address: 499 Old York Road, SW18 1TF (☎ 020-8870 2537,
🖥 almawandsworth.com).
Opening hours: Mon-Sat, 11am to midnight; Sun, noon to 11pm.
Transport: Wandsworth Town rail.
Go for: Good beer, food and sport in a Victorian pub with a modern twist.

Built in 1866, this archetypal Victorian pub was named after the Battle of Alma in 1854, the first conflict in the Crimean War, and shares the name with nearby Alma Road. It's a large, imposing pub which was extended in 2010 to provide 23 boutique-style hotel rooms. It's only a few hundred yards from the site of the old Young's brewery – which may explain why the Alma and many other pubs in the area are Young's establishments.

The interior is a now a large, open space, with three round mosaics on the walls sporting the pub's name, plus painted mirrors and a low island bar. Food is important here; there's a large dining area serving appetising fare as well as reasonable bar food, which includes meat platters, sausages and burgers.

A vast, pull-down TV screen draws sports fans in to watch rugby and soccer matches (if you don't like rugger buggers, avoid the place on important egg-chasing days), but otherwise it has a nicely mixed clientele. Beer drinkers are well served with ales from Sambrook's, Twickenham, Wells and Young's, plus a selection of over 30 wines.

THE BOATHOUSE

Address: Brewhouse Lane, SW15 2JX (☎ 020-8789 0476,
🖳 boathouseputney.co.uk).
Opening hours: Daily, noon to 11pm.
Transport: Putney Bridge tube or Putney rail.
Go for: Exceptional views from any angle and fishy treats to eat.

Another Young's outlet, the Boathouse's calling card is its fine
riverside location in Putney Wharf, between Putney Bridge and the
railway bridge. It makes the most of this with a wide front terrace from
where punters can observe the ebb and flow of the Thames.

It's a modern bar in a Victorian building, with a touch of the ski
chalet about its exterior. There are three floors – a downstairs bar, an
upstairs space with comfortable chairs and sofas, and a third-floor
terrace – and the glass front makes for great river views, even if you're
sitting inside. Food is served on all three floors – well-made, modern
fare with an emphasis on fish and seafood – and the ales come, of
course, from Wells and Young's.

The Boathouse is too smooth – corporate even – for some tastes,
but it's pleasantly relaxed and does its thing well. Some people find
the regulars a bit 'Putney poser', and it can get crowded on sunny
days, but don't let that put you off visiting one of the best-situated
pubs in southwest London.

245

THE BOTANIST BREWERY & KITCHEN

Address: 3-5 Kew Green, TW9 3AA (☎ 020-8948 4838, 💻 thebotanistkew.com).
Opening hours: Mon-Thu, noon to 11pm; Fri-Sat, noon to midnight; Sun, noon to 10.30pm.
Transport: Kew Gardens tube/rail.
Go for: Craft beer from a microbrewery in an elegant corner of London.

Just south of Kew Bridge, this airy, light bar and restaurant resembles one of the glasshouses at nearby Kew Gardens. It used to be a row of shops and the interior is divided into a number of different areas, which together add up to a sleek, modern venue.

246

The in-house microbrewery is a major draw, producing the bar's own craft beer. The Botanist also stocks an extensive range of British, American and continental bottled beers and lagers, has a good wine list and even serves cocktails. The website has details (under Brewery) of what's currently being produced by the microbrewery, which might include a pale ale, bitter, German Kolsch-style beer, organic wheat beer, traditional London Porter and organic fruit beer. There's a takeaway beer service from around £1.50 a pint.

Food consists of bar snacks, sharing boards and more substantial dishes, with mains costing from £11 to £17.50. Wednesday night is quiz night, and there's live music on some Saturdays. Sunday lunch is popular with families, so expect a lot of toddlers with your beer.

THE BRICKLAYER'S ARMS

Address: 32 Waterman Street, SW15 1DD (☎ 020-8789 0222,
🖥 bricklayers-arms.co.uk).
Opening hours: Mon-Sat, noon to 11pm; Sun, noon to 10.30pm.
Transport: Putney Bridge tube or Putney rail.
Go for: A classic English pub with brilliant British beer.

The Bricklayer's is one of the oldest pubs in Putney, dating from 1826, and has a rural feel about it – a small but perfectly formed Victorian pub. In 2012 it was voted into third place in a list of Top 10 English pubs by *National Geographic* magazine.

It's a beer specialist's venue, a freehouse that dubs itself 'London's Permanent Beer Festival' and has been garlanded with a number of awards by CAMRA. It also stages 'real' beer festivals each year. The 12 handpumps serve such popular brews as Acorn, Dark Star, Rudgate and Sambrook's, plus regular guest beers, while two dispense real cider and perry. There's a wide range of lagers, and wine lovers can chose from a list that includes 15 English wines. The décor is understated, with wood, brick and an open fire, and there are outdoor tables in the small garden.

247

Avoid the Bricklayer's on annual Boat Race day (around Easter – see 🖥 the boatrace.org), when this and all the surrounding hostelries are jammed to the rafters. It'll still be there on the other 364 days of the year.

THE CAT'S BACK

Address: 86-88 Point Pleasant, SW18 1PP (☎ 020-8874 7277,
🖥 thecatsback.com).
Opening hours: Mon-Sat, 11am to 11.30pm; Sun, noon to 10.30pm (but
check in view of impending refurbishment).
Transport: Putney Bridge tube or Wandsworth Town rail.
Go for: Good Sussex ales in a friendly, traditional atmosphere.

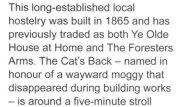

This long-established local
hostelry was built in 1865 and has
previously traded as both Ye Olde
House at Home and The Foresters
Arms. The Cat's Back – named in
honour of a wayward moggy that
disappeared during building works
– is around a five-minute stroll
from the river and sits amid stark high-rise blocks of flats. However,
it has nothing in common with the bland, chain-like establishments
commonly found in such spots, but is a valued local with a bohemian
tinge and a choice of real ale.

In 2012 it was purchased by the lauded brewer Harveys, of
Lewes, Sussex (founded in 1790), becoming only its second London
outlet (47th in total), the other being **The Royal Oak** in Borough (see
page 298). Drinkers can choose from at least four Harveys offerings,
including Sussex Bitter, Knots of May, Armada Ale and Olympia.

The pub is a work in progress and there may be further changes
(so check before visiting) but if the born-again Cat's Back becomes as
popular as The Royal Oak, it will be a fine addition to Wandsworth's
roster of hostelries.

THE DEVONSHIRE

Address: 39 Balham High Road, SW12 9AN (☎ 020-8673 1363,
🖥 dukeofdevonshirebalham.com).
Opening hours: Daily, noon to midnight.
Transport: Balham tube/rail.
Go for: An appealing, well-run pub in an upmarket area.

The Devonshire is a vast, attractive Young's pub which used to be
called the Duke of Devonshire. It was always an atmospheric, friendly
place but since having its name clipped it's been smartened up – and
has some seriously funky furniture, both inside and out.

The striking open-plan interior manages to be smart and
welcoming at the same time. There's no shortage of seating, with
stools, chairs and sofas scattered around. There's a sectioned-off
dining room with a lovely mural, and plenty of outdoor space in the
pleasant beer garden, which has a BBQ island (with its own menu).
The parasols have heaters, so you can pretend that it's summer all
year round!

The house beers are from Wells and Young's, while the wine
list is more extensive than is usual in Young's venues, running to
around 40 bins; it's a reflection of clients' tastes in this upwardly-
mobile part of London. The Devonshire is a friendly, professionally-
run venue, although not the cheapest and perhaps a touch
yuppiefied for some.

249

THE DRAFT HOUSE (NORTHCOTE)

Address: 94 Northcote Road, SW11 6QW (☎ 020-7924 1814,
🖥 drafthouse.co.uk).
Opening hours: Mon-Fri, noon to 11pm (Thu-Fri, midnight); Sat, 10am to
midnight; Sun, 10am to 10.30pm.
Transport: Clapham South tube or Clapham Junction rail.
Go for: A fine specialist beer bar with interesting food.

Opened in 2009, this is one of a small group of pubs which are 100
per cent focused on sourcing, cellaring and serving the best beers.
It has a changing selection of beers on draft from various parts of
the world, which usually includes something from London breweries
Meantime and Sambrook's, and it serves them in three glass sizes:
a pint, a half or a third (around 190ml). In fact the Draft House
dubs itself the 'Home of the Third' and it's a clever idea as smaller
measures allow drinkers to sample a range of (strong) ales without
becoming insensible.

The Draft House also has a great choice of bottled beers, including
some notable and/or rare offerings from American microbreweries,
and beers from Belgium, Czechoslovakia and Germany. The food
is also good, although it's more American diner than UK boozer,
with an emphasis on burgers, fried chicken and mac 'n' cheese. But
everything is served by friendly staff in a clean, modern interior with a
relaxed atmosphere.

It you enjoy the formula, there are
another four Draft House outlets in
Battersea, East Dulwich, Goodge Street
(W1) and Tower Bridge – although this
one is generally the favourite.

THE DUKE'S HEAD

Address: 8 Lower Richmond Road, SW15 1JN (☎ 020-8788 2552,
🖳 dukesheadputney.com).
Opening hours: Mon-Thu, noon to midnight; Fri-Sat, noon to 1am; Sun,
noon to 10.30pm.
Transport: Putney Bridge tube.
Go for: Great views, entertainment and a convivial atmosphere.

A grand Victorian tavern overlooking the Thames, this Young's establishment dates from 1832. It was rebuilt in 1864, altered again in 1894 and is now Grade II listed, therefore should stay as it is for the foreseeable future. It has an enviable position, right next to the spot where the annual Oxford vs. Cambridge Boat Race begins and is one of the favourite venues from which to watch the contest.

It's classy inside, with a nicely ornate original bar and huge bay windows providing great views, especially in the front rooms where the river is visible on three sides. The lower ground floor is home to the Rowing Club, which hosts live music, comedy and film screenings, but in good weather the only place to be is the towpath.

In addition to solid Wells and Young's beer, there's a reasonable wine list, some available in two glass sizes as well as by the bottle; glasses cost from £4.10, bottles from £15.90. The Duke's Head has a good bar menu or you can eat in the Coxswain Dining Room. Either way, steaks, roasts and pies compete with gastropub fare.

THE EARL SPENCER

Address: 260-2 Merton Road, SW18 5JL (☎ 020-8870 9244,
🖥 theearlspencer.co.uk).
Opening hours: Mon-Thu, 4-11pm; Fri-Sat, 11am to midnight; Sun, noon to 10.30pm.
Transport: Southfields tube.
Go for: Fairly-priced food and cask ale in a celebrated gastropub.

The Earl Spencer was given a gastro makeover in 2003, but has managed to remain a 'proper' pub and a destination for drinkers as well as diners – not always an easy compromise. It's housed in an attractive, high-ceilinged Edwardian building with a long, low bar connecting two large spaces; there are also outdoor tables for those rare days when the sun shines.

252

Three cask ales are stocked, including the likes of Fuller's London Pride, Hook Norton's Old Hooky and Sharp's Doom Bar. There's also a list of around 30 wines, a few of which are available in two glass sizes as well as by the bottle; glasses cost from £3.40, bottles from £13, which is keenly priced, especially in up-and-coming Southfields.

The food is also reasonably priced and has won some good reviews. The menu changed daily (check the website, also for serving times) and includes such treats as home-smoked Atlantic prawns, devilled kidneys on toast and beef, bacon and pearl onion stew.

Needless to say, the Earl is usually filled with locals who are very supportive of this lively and welcoming pub.

THE FOX AND GRAPES

Address: 9 Camp Road, SW19 4UN (☎ 020-8619 1300,
🖳 foxandgrapeswimbledon.co.uk).
Opening hours: Mon-Sat, 11am to 11pm; Sun, 11am to 10.30pm.
Transport: Wimbledon tube/rail.
Go for: A superior gastropub in a stunning location.

The Fox and Grapes enjoys a fine position on the edge of Wimbledon
Common where you feel as if you're in the country rather than a
London suburb. Once a rather bland pub, the Fox was taken over
in 2011 by Claude Bosi of Hibiscus and is now a superior gastropub
(with a seasonal British menu), which is managed by Claude's brother
Cedric. It also has three upstairs guest rooms for when you've over-
indulged and cannot stagger home.

It's more a venue for foodies than a pub, although drinkers are
well catered for with some excellent ale such as Black Sheep Bitter
and Sharp's Doom Bar, as well as Symonds cider and Amstel. The
short, evolving wine list concentrates on 'small growers dedicated
to producing terroir-driven, sustainable wines' and is chosen by the
noted St James's wine merchant, Berry Brothers and Rudd.

This is an unashamedly exclusive gastropub overseen by a two
Michelin-starred chef, and isn't cheap (although the Early Bird menu is
worth checking out
– three courses
for under £20).
But if you want to
raise a glass to
great British food
in a lovely part of
London, the Fox is
the place to do it.

THE LEATHER BOTTLE

Address: 538 Garratt Lane, SW17 0NY (☎ 020-8946 2309,
🖳 leatherbottlepub.co.uk).
Opening hours: Mon-Thu, noon to 11pm; Fri-Sat, noon to midnight; Sun,
noon to 10.30pm.
Transport: Earlsfield rail.
Go for: The wonderful beer garden and barbecue.

A pub has been on this spot for over 300 years, and the current huge,
sprawling Young's operation is well known for its beer garden. The
website boasts that it's 'the largest pub garden in London' – and very
civilised it is too. The pub is also a draw when the weather's poor as it
has comfortable sofas, snug corners and open fireplaces.

It's slightly off the beaten track, so
attracts a lot of local people, notably
on Sundays when lunch is popular
(booking is essential). Food is also
an attraction at other times, with a
selection of lighter bites and sharing
platters, and a choice of classic
main courses and daily specials,
generally in the £10.95-13.95
range, with pheasant a popular
choice. There's a barbecue menu in
summer if you prefer to sit outside.

As well as Wells and Young's
beer, there's a longish wine list, including some superior bottles. A
pub quiz is held on Wednesdays and there's always a big crowd for
sporting events like the Six Nations rugby tournament (Twickers isn't
far away), for which you can book a table.

LOST SOCIETY

Address: 697 Wandsworth Road, SW8 3JF (☎ 020-7652 6526,
🖥 lostsociety.co.uk).
Opening hours: Thu, 5pm to midnight; Fri-Sat, 5pm to 1am; Sun, 2-7pm.
Transport: Clapham Common tube or Wandsworth Road rail.
Go for: Innovative cocktails, stylish decor, entertainment and a party vibe.

There's a nicely decadent feel to this Art Deco-themed bar and party
venue, which is located just north of Clapham Common. The bar is
divided into different zones, for eating, drinking and dancing, each with
a different style and mood and décor to match. There's even a small
courtyard garden where you can sip cocktails.

The overall effect is a blend of gentleman's club and boudoir, with a
friendly and quirky atmosphere. You can book space for parties Mon-
Thu, while weekends see a range of entertainment, including cabaret,
burlesque and DJs. The drinks are a major draw. The cocktail list runs
to around 60 drinks, including some innovative mixes, and there are
some interesting bottled beers, primarily from the UK and US.

At weekends, the entry policy is over-21s only and there's a £5
charge after 9pm on Saturdays. Or for something completely different, 255
you can hold a tea party or join in a cocktail-mixing class.

The owners run another venue in the area, Lost Angel (🖥 lostangel.
co.uk), which is a well-regarded blend of traditional pub, modern bar
and restaurant.

THE MANOR ARMS

Address: 13 Mitcham Lane, SW16 6LQ (☎ 020-3195 6888,
🖳 themanorarms.com).
Opening hours: Mon-Thu, 11am to 11pm; Fri-Sat, 11am to 1am; Sun, noon
to midnight.
Transport: Streatham rail.
Go for: Child-friendly pub with good food and a pleasant garden.

This large Edwardian pub is just off Streatham's main thoroughfare
and was successfully refurbished a few years ago. The dark wood
interior marries original Art Deco touches with modern features; it
features a bar made from pewter and oak and original '30s oak-
panelled walls.

It's known for its excellent food. Main courses on the a la carte
menu are in the £9-17 range, but you can enjoy a great value prix fixe
menu for just £10 (two courses) or £14.50 (three courses), either as a
weekday lunch or dinner on Mon-Thu. Other options include Sunday
lunch and barbecues in the walled garden.

Wine drinkers are well served, with bottles from £15; the list
includes some imaginative choices, such as the lauded Chateau
Musar from Lebanon. There's also a solid real ale selection including
such brews as Adnams, Doom Bar, Meantime London Pale Ale, Purity
Mad Goose and Sambrook's Wandle.

The Manor Arms is particularly child-friendly and has won plaudits
from Mumsnet for its welcome. It runs a kids' club every morning and
serves healthy children's meals.

POWDER KEG DIPLOMACY

Address: 147 St John's Hill, SW11 1TQ (☎ 020-7450 6457, ✉ powderkegdiplomacy.co.uk).
Opening hours: Mon-Fri, 4pm to midnight; Sat-Sun, 10am to midnight.
Transport: Clapham Junction rail.
Go for: Fine drinks in colonial splendour with a touch of Victorian drama.

The décor of this neighbourhood bar and restaurant takes its cue from 'a combination of colonial Britain, Victoriana and hints of the industrial'. It's a warm, dimly-lit, welcoming place, perfect for a genial evening. There's a restaurant serving good, creative, British food, or you can fill up on 'tiffin and titbits' (bar snacks to you and me), but the excellent choice of drinks is the main draw.

The wine follows the colonial theme, with most bins from Australia, New Zealand and England, although there's the odd surprise, such as an Indian Zinfandel and a Cabernet France from Canada. A selection of wines are sold in two glass sizes and by the carafe, as well as by the bottle (glasses cost from £3, bottles from £16.90).

The extensive beer and cider list includes Meantime seasonal ales, Thatcher's Gold Cider and Williams Brothers' Joker IPA on tap, backed up by a wide bottled choice. There are also some interesting cocktails and punches, many made from old recipes (try a Beetroot Fizz or Sherry Cobbler), priced around £8.

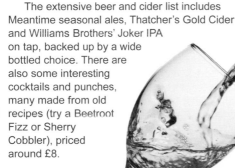

THE PRIORY ARMS

Address: 83 Lansdowne Way, SW8 2PB (☏ 020-7622 1884,
🖥 theprioryarms.co.uk).
Opening hours: Mon-Sat, noon to 11pm; Sun, noon to 10.30pm.
Transport: Stockwell tube or Wandsworth Road rail.
Go for: A real London local with good food and great beer.

Just down the road from Stockwell's architecturally impressive bus garage, this beer lover's destination is a freehouse and a genuine community pub. It's quite small, with a busy downstairs bar, a quieter lounge upstairs and an outside terrace. The interior is smart, with wooden floors, high stools and leather sofas to lounge on, while large windows allow in natural light.

The beer mats and clips on display announce this as a serious ale venue and there are usually around five available (London independents are regular features), which may include Camden Town Redemption, Hop Back Summer Lightning, Sambrook's, Sharp's and Twickenham Fine Ales. There are also guest draught beers from Belgium and Germany, and an exhaustive choice of bottled beers.

The Priory Arms has a short, keenly-priced wine list, some available by the glass (from £3.80) as well as by the bottle (from £13). There's good food, strong on burgers and international tapas (booking is recommended for Sunday lunch), as well as board games, so it's a local which ticks all the boxes and a few more besides.

PUTNEY STATION

Address: 94-8 Upper Richmond Road, SW15 2SP (☎ 020-8780 0242,
🖥 brinkleys.com/putneystation.asp).
Opening hours: Mon-Thu, 5pm to midnight; Fri, 5pm to 1am: Sat, 11am to
1am; Sun, 11am to 11pm.
Transport: East Putney tube.
Go for: Bargain wine and food in pricy Putney.

259

Putney Station is part of
the Brinkley's chain of six
restaurants/wine bars, which
trade under various names across London; others are in Kensington,
Marylebone and Wandsworth. The Putney outlet is (appropriately)
opposite East Putney tube station and offers keenly priced food and
wine in a generally expensive area.

It's a roomy bar and restaurant with large windows, potted plants,
pavement tables and a patio garden. The menu is modern British and
European with a Mediterranean influence, and keenly priced. Pizzas
cost £5-7.50, while mains start from £8; the Early Burger special is
just £6 and available until till 8pm (see website).

The interesting, well-priced wine list is a major draw. Brinkley's
claim to sell its wines at retail rather than restaurant prices and this
is probably the only bar in Putney where house wine is sold for £10 a
bottle. In addition, there are around 45 bins from various parts of the
world, priced up to £45, with fizz from £20-68; that said, the choice
by the glass is limited. Cocktails are also served and there's a happy
hour from 5-7pm.

THE ROEBUCK

Address: 130 Richmond Hill, TW10 6RN (☎ 020-8948 2329, 💻 taylor-walker.co.uk/pub/roebuck-richmond/s5628).
Opening hours: Mon-Thu, noon to 11pm; Fri-Sat, noon to midnight; Sun, noon to 10.30pm.
Transport: Richmond tube/rail.
Go for: One of London's most iconic views.

A steady climb from the centre of handsome Georgian Richmond, this pub sits at the top of Richmond Hill and is favoured with unmatched views. From here you can look down Terrace Field towards rural Petersham and soak up a wonderful panorama of the Thames – on a clear day you might even catch a glimpse of Windsor Castle. The vistas have inspired writers and painters, from William Wordsworth to JMW Turner, and can turn even the most average pint into the nectar of the gods.

A former hotel, the Roebuck is now a Taylor Walker establishment with plain décor, friendly staff and an above-average selection of beer, including Fuller's and interesting guests from Ascot, Bath and Downton, as well as some sold pub grub.

But the Roebuck's location is its key attraction, and it really doesn't matter what you drink if you can secure a perch on one of the outside benches overlooking that fabulous view. You may also spot some famous faces from Richmond Hill's community of rock royalty; Mick Jagger and Pete Townshend have both been spotted here.

THE ROOKERY

Address: 69 Clapham Common, SW4 9DA (☎ 020-8673 9162,
🖥 therookeryclapham.co.uk).
Opening hours: Mon-Thu, 5.30 to 11pm; Fri, 3pm to midnight; Sat, 12.30pm
to midnight; Sun, 12.30-10.30pm.
Transport: Clapham Common or Clapham South tube.
Go for: Craft beer, fine wine and seasonal food on the common.

A meandering quote from the
owners sums up this venue rather
well: 'Craft beers from around the
world; interesting wines by smaller
producers; classic cocktails;
and simple, seasonal food. All
overlooking Clapham Common.'

The Rookery has a New York
vibe, with trendy staff and stripped
back décor including bare brick,
white tiles and skylights. If the
weather permits, there's an outdoor
area, west-facing and with a
canopy, which is across the road

261

(albeit a busy one) from Clapham Common and is a popular spot for
Sunday lunch.

It's a good destination for wine drinkers as the well-chosen list runs
to more than 40 bins, some available by the glass, carafe or bottle,
priced from £4.20, £10.90 and £16.50 respectively. There's also a
selection of cocktails, and a decent choice of beer which can include
Anchor Steam, Meantime and Sambrook's, plus a good bottled
selection. A wide choice of spirits will appeal to those who enjoy the
hard stuff.

If you want to
eat, there's a short
seasonal menu of
mainly British fare
– main courses are
mostly in the £10-15
range – and there's
a bar menu of lighter
bites.

THE SHIP

Address: 41 Jew's Row, SW18 1TB (☎ 020-8870 9667, 🖥 theship.co.uk).
Opening hours: Sun-Wed, 11am to 11pm; Thu-Sat, 11am to midnight.
Transport: Wandsworth Town rail.
Go for: A riverside pub where they know how to party.

Conveniently located near the station and next to Wandsworth Bridge, the Ship is a well-known and well-loved riverside pub. There's been an inn on the site since 1786, although the current building dates from the early 19th century and was first leased by Young's brewery in 1832. It has one of the quirkiest pub signs you'll ever see.

It's a large pub, with a comfortable interior – lots of mirrors, plenty of nooks and crannies – as well as a conservatory and a large deck overlooking the Thames. On sunny days, these are usually packed while the bars stay relatively quiet. One side of the conservatory is a dining area serving respectable, gastro fare, for which booking is recommended, and the pub also hosts barbecues when 'the temperature creeps above 14 degrees'.

As well as Young's beer, there are up to four guest cask ales at a time, including offerings from Sambrook's. There's also a reasonable wine list, designed to appeal to the pub's clientele of young professionals, who come here to enjoy the buzzy atmosphere. Regular live music events include jazz, blues and Irish acoustic sessions.

THE SPREAD EAGLE

Address: 71 Wandsworth High Street, SW18 2PT (☎ 020-8877 9809).
Opening hours: Sun-Thu, 11am to 11pm; Fri-Sat, 11am to midnight.
Transport: Wandsworth Town rail.
Go for: The splendid Victorian interior.

263

A coaching inn next to the site of the original Young's brewery, there's been a pub here since at least 1780. It was acquired by Young's in the 1830s and completely rebuilt in 1898 to incorporate a grand interior, typical of a late Victorian, 19th-century town hostelry, and has been Grade II listed accordingly.

It's also impressive from the outside, retaining its original iron canopy above the entrance, while inside is a large main bar with a number of original features, including wood panelling, fine etched glass, pillars and a huge bar, while there's a dining room and lounge at the back. It's an imposing space, especially noted for its glasswork, which some people think compares with that of the noted **Princess Louise** in High Holborn, one of London's finest gin palaces (see page 92).

As for drinks, there are the usual solid Wells and Young's ales, plus some bottled offerings, to be enjoyed while seated on leather benches and admiring the impressive details of this authentic Victorian pub.

SUGAR CANE

Address: 247-249 Lavender Hill, SW11 1JW (☎ 020-7223 8866, ⌨ thesugarcane.co.uk).
Opening hours: Sun and Tue-Thu, 5-11pm; Fri-Sat, 4pm to 1.30am; closed Mon.
Transport: Clapham Common tube.
Go for: Typically tropical cocktails.

Sugar Cane is unashamedly a party venue and does it well. It promises 'a taste of the Tropics in south London', and was designed by the same people behind Mahiki (a nightclub favoured by Prince Harry), so there's a definite cool quotient there.

The décor is typically Tiki tacky, with exotic flowers, palm trees, wicker furniture, rum barrel tables and bamboo knick-knacks. The atmosphere is friendly and relaxed – it's somewhere to let your hair down and chill out.

The drinks are a major attraction. There are 11 wines, six available by the glass from £3.90 (bottles from £14.90) and six champagnes (from £36 a bottle), while beer drinkers can choose from seven bottles (including a coconut beer). But cocktails are king, presented across four menus which include classics, Tiki (tropical classics such as Mai-Tai and Zombie), Sugar Cane's own blends and cocktails for sharing, which include the dangerous-sounding Tiki Death Punch. Prices range between £6 and £10 or up to £35 (for up to eight drinkers sharing). If you like rum and prefer it served straight, the rum menu includes 30 shots.

264

THE SULTAN

Address: 78 Norman Road, SW19 1BT (☎ 020-8542 4532, 🖥 hopback.co.uk/our-pubs/the-sultan.html).
Opening hours: Sun-Thu, noon to 11pm; Fri-Sat, noon to midnight.
Transport: Colliers Wood or South Wimbledon tube.
Go for: Fine Hop Back ale in a community pub.

Named after a 19th-century racehorse, this award-winning venue is a 'roadhouse' style public house, typical of the suburban '30s, which is now an inviting community pub on a residential road. It's the only London outlet of Salisbury's celebrated Hop Back microbrewery which has nine pubs across the UK.

Behind the plain exterior is a cosy interior, with two bars, wooden tables and open fires; the saloon bar is named after *The Archers* cast member Ted Higgins (who was devoted to good beer). Decent pub grub is served and the patio hosts barbecues in summer.

The beer draws many ale aficionados. Hop Back's cask ales (Entire Stout, GFB and Summer Lightning) are always on, plus a guest or seasonal ale, usually from the associated operation the Downton brewery. The pub also stocks Hop Back's fine bottled real ales, as well as some from Downton. There's a beer festival in the autumn.

The Sultan has previously been voted southwest London CAMRA pub of the year, and is well worth making the journey for.

265

THE SUN INN

Address: 7 Church Road, SW13 9HE (☎ 020-8876 5256,
🖥 thesuninnbarnes.co.uk).
Opening hours: Sun-Wed, 11am to 11pm; Thu-Sat, 11am to midnight.
Transport: Barnes Bridge rail.
Go for: A beer on the village green.

The Sun Inn benefits from a splendid position in the centre of the
exclusive southwest London 'village' of Barnes. It's a large, rambling
establishment in a striking, whitewashed building, and although it
doesn't have a riverside location, it has the next best thing, being just
over the road from the pond on Barnes Green.

The interior has an island bar and several different places to sit,
with comfy sofas and homely mismatched furniture. The daily menu
has a gastro edge but is fairly priced, and there are Saturday brunch
and Sunday roast options, too, as well as sandwiches. Wine costs
from around £13 a bottle, and there's English potato vodka if you want
to sample a different type of spirit. But most punters come for the beer,
and there are over 20 ales and ciders on tap and some good bottled
beers, including Adnams, London Pride, Sharp's Doom Bar and
Timothy Taylor Landlord.

The pub's terrace is a popular place in decent weather, or you can
take your beer over to the pond and drink it with the ducks.

THE TRINITY ARMS

Address: 45 Trinity Gardens, SW9 8DR (☏ 020-7274 4544, 🖥 trinityarms.co.uk).
Opening hours: Mon-Thu, 11am to 11pm; Fri, 11am to midnight; Sat, noon to midnight; Sun, noon to 11pm.
Transport: Brixton tube or rail.
Go for: Tasty beer and a warm welcome.

A (longish) stone's throw from Brixton High Street, surrounded by elegant Georgian terraces, this attractive Young's pub sits on a quiet, leafy square, and is a haven of tranquillity in often busy Brixton. Built in 1850, it's named after the Trinity Asylum in nearby Acre Lane, which was founded in the 1820s to help 'pious aged women'.

267

The pub's comfortable interior has an island bar and traditional décor and has a much friendlier mien than many of the area's bars, which strive to be as cutting-edge as possible. Approachable staff serve well-kept Wells and Young's ales – it's a CAMRA award-winning pub – as well as generous portions of good, fairly-priced food (available all day). There's also a good selection of single malt whisky.

The Trinity Arms attracts a mixed crowd of locals and is generally regarded as the area's best spot for decent beer. It can become crowded with gig-goers when there are bands on at the nearby Brixton Academy.

THE VICTORIA

Address: 10 West Temple Sheen, SW14 7RT (☎ 020-8876 4238, 🖥 thevictoria.net).
Opening hours: Mon-Sat, 8.30am to 11pm; Sun, 11am to 10pm.
Transport: North Sheen or Mortlake rail.
Go for: A 'country' pub with a TV chef in the kitchen.

Voted 'Best Gastro Pub in London' at the Great Pub Awards 2011, the Victoria describes itself as a 'public house, dining room, hotel'. What it feels like is a lively country pub, being located in a quiet road close to Richmond Park in a building dating from the mid-19th century, when East Sheen was mainly comprised of rural estates.

The Victoria's chef and co-owner is Paul Merrett, a familiar face if you watch foodie TV programmes, and

the emphasis is firmly on fine food, which you can eat in the bar or the conservatory dining room. The menu isn't cheap but neither is it exorbitant. The two-course set meal served Mon-Thu is excellent value at £12.50, while most bar mains are under a tenner.

As you'd expect, there's a good wine list of around 70 bins, including some interesting and unusual choices. Around 25 are available by the glass, with glasses costing from £4, bottles from £17.

Beer drinkers aren't ignored either, with London Pride, a Timothy Taylor beer and a guest ale, and there's a reasonable choice of spirits.

THE WHITE CROSS

Address: Riverside (off Water Lane), TW9 1TH (☎ 020-8940 6844, 💻 thewhitecrossrichmond.com).
Opening hours: Mon-Sat, 10am to 11pm; Sun, 10am to 10.30pm.
Transport: Richmond tube/rail.
Go for: A wonderful riverside location.

The White Cross is a large, historic Young's pub on the river near to Richmond Bridge. The building dates from the mid-18th century (when it was called the Waterman's Arms) and has some unusual features, such as a fireplace tucked under a window; however, the main draw is the outdoor terrace, which becomes crowded on sunny days. Views are also good from the River Room.

Wells and Young's ale are on tap here, along with seasonal and guest ales from other breweries. There's a reasonable wine list, with a fair choice by the glass, plus upmarket pub grub with the emphasis on the provenance of the ingredients.

The White Cross draws a nicely mixed clientele of locals, tourists and rugby types on Twickenham match days, with big games screened for those who can't secure a ticket. It's glorious on sunny

days, but just as atmospheric in winter, especially at high tide when the river can reach almost to the door. Tide times are given in a link from the website and you may need to bring your wellies!

YE WHITE HART

Address: The Terrace, SW13 0NR (☎ 020-8876 5177, 🖳 whitehartbarnes.co.uk).
Opening hours: Mon-Thu, 11am to 11pm; Fri, 11am to midnight; Sat, 10am to midnight; Sun, 10am to 11pm.
Transport: Barnes Bridge rail.
Go for: A prime spot to watch the climax of the Boat Race.

Ye White Hart is the oldest pub in the area, dating from the 1660s, and was extensively rebuilt at the end of the 19th century. Today it's a three-storey Victorian pile, one of the capital's largest riverside boozers, with splendid river views.

An inviting inn, with lots of dark wood, comfortable sofas and open fires, it's been owned by Young's since 1857 and stocks their usual ales. The food menu is solid and satisfying, and cheaper than you'd expect for such a great setting. The upstairs sports bar and live music on some Friday nights are also big draws.

The Hart makes the most of its enviable location and has plenty of outside tables and benches on the river towpath, predictably popular during warm weather, less so during high tides. It really comes into its

own on Boat Race weekend, as the pub is located near the finish line at Chiswick Bridge. Predictably, it's absolutely jammed on that day (see 🖳 theboatrace.org), but also busy the rest of the year, notably when big rugby matches are screened.

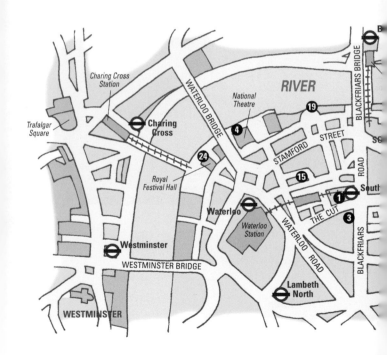

CHAPTER 6

SOUTHEAST LONDON

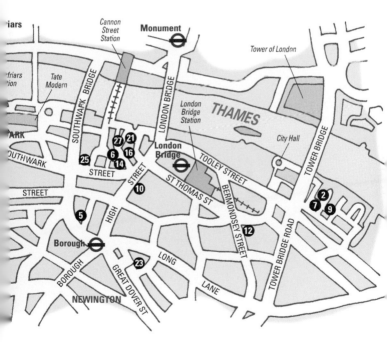

See overleaf for more maps.

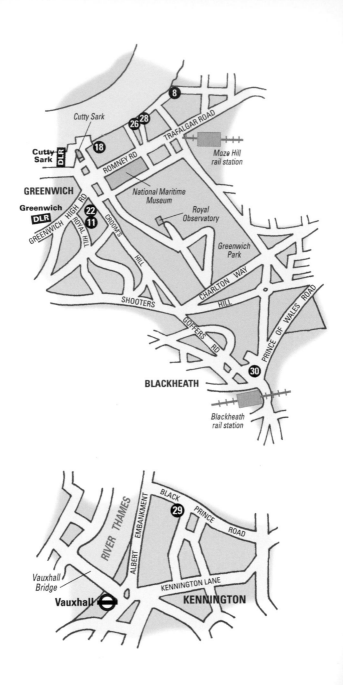

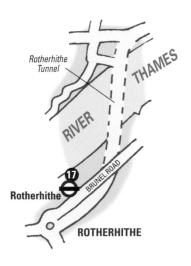

See previous pages for more maps and key.

THE ANCHOR & HOPE

Address: 36 The Cut, SE1 8LP (☎ 020-7928 9898).
Opening hours: Mon, 5 to 11pm; Tue-Sat, 11am to 11pm; Sun, 12.30-5pm.
Transport: Southwark rail or Waterloo tube/rail.
Go for: A famous, no-frills gastropub.

Just down the road from the Young Vic theatre, the Anchor & Hope is one of London's best-known gastropubs. It's a no-frills venue, with minimal decor, bare wood tables and art to brighten the walls, while the menu is chalked on a board and presented in plain and simple terms. The food is robust British fare, served in 'hearty portions using the finest fresh ingredients' (as the kitchen explains).

It's popular and generally busy, attracting everyone from food tourists to theatre goers. The 'no reservations' policy (which is only relaxed for Sunday lunch) means you may have to wait for a table, although you can relax in the pub and sample something from the short but comprehensive wine list, which includes a reasonable choice by the glass and bottles. There are bargain cocktails priced at around £5, and beer choices include St Austell Tribute, Young's, Wells Bombardier and Red Stripe.

If you're planning an intimate tête-à-tête, be aware that you may end up seated on one of the Anchor's communal tables which are sociable, or noisy, depending on your perspective.

THE ANCHOR TAP

Address: 28 Horsleydown Lane, SE1 2LN (☎ 020-7403 4637).
Opening hours: Mon-Sat, noon to 11pm; Sun, noon to 10.30pm.
Transport: Tower Hill tube.
Go for: Keenly-priced beer in the area's best traditional pub.

The Anchor Tap is tucked away in a warren of streets just south of Tower Bridge and offers a real refuge in an increasingly touristy part of SE1. It's named after the old Anchor Brewery, one of many that sprang up in Southwark from the 16th century onwards. 'Tap' was the name for the pub nearest its brewery, where the brewery's workers could sample the fruits of their labours.

The Anchor brewery closed in the '80s and the pub is now owned by Yorkshire brewer Sam Smith's, and stocks its usual range of keenly priced beer. It's very much a traditional pub for local residents and workers, and is a down-to-earth antidote to the trendy bars which have mushroomed in and around the renovated warehouses along Shad Thames and in nearby Bermondsey.

This area used to be a haunt of dockers and sailors, and the Anchor is a plain, understated place, providing a warm and friendly welcome. It also has a beer garden and serves basic pub grub.

THE BALTIC

Address: 74 Blackfriars Road, SE1 8HA (☎ 020-7928 1111,
🖥 balticrestaurant.co.uk).
Opening hours: Mon-Sat, noon to midnight; Sun, noon to 10.30pm.
Transport: Southwark tube.
Go for: A wide selection of vodka and Polish food.

This sleek, minimalist Polish bar and restaurant has a great atmosphere and professional service, and is the perfect place to sample the drinking (and eating) culture of the Poles. It includes a modern bar, and a restaurant serving good value set menus.

278

They take their vodka seriously here. There are two menus dedicated to plain vodkas (premium and super premium) and three to flavoured vodkas, including traditional, new and Baltic flavours. Some are made on the premises, using fresh fruit and spices, while others include some unusual ingredients, such as wormwood. Shots start at £2.95 or you can order a carafe (10cl, 25cl or 50cl). Martinis are also a speciality and have their own section on the cocktail list.

The wine list features around 70 bins, with prices starting at £4.50 a glass, £13.50 a carafe (500ml) and £17 a bottle. Prosecco costs from £6.50 per glass and £28 a bottle, while champagne is priced from £8.50/£48.

You need something substantial to mop up the alcohol, and there's a selection of Eastern European bar food including blinis, dumplings and charcuterie, or try *zakuski* – a plate of Polish tapas to share.

THE BENUGO BAR & KITCHEN

Address: BFI Southbank Centre, Belvedere Road, SE1 8XT (☎ 020-7401 9000, ⌨ benugobarandkitchen.com).
Opening hours: Mon-Sat, 10am to 11pm; Sun, 10am to 10.30pm.
Transport: Waterloo tube/rail.
Go for: A chill-out session on the South Bank.

279

The South Bank has enjoyed a renaissance in recent years and become a major cultural and tourist attraction, driven by the opening of Tate Modern in 2000. But it's famously been short of decent places to drink and eat. The Benugo Bar & Kitchen, at the British Film Institute (BFI), bucks this trend and is widely regarded as the area's most atmospheric place to meet for a drink.

Benugo operates a number of cafes and restaurants around the capital but the South Bank outlet has its own special character, and you don't feel as if it's part of a bland brand. The restaurant serves modern British food but the main attraction for drinkers is the large bar area, called Loungeside, where the comfortable mismatched chairs and sofas invite you to kick off your shoes and flop down. It has a buzzy atmosphere generated by the cinema-goers, culture vultures and revellers who meet up here.

There's a wide choice of cocktails, wine and beer – including some interesting lagers – and if prices are a bit above average, remember that you're drinking in one of southeast London's prime destination bars.

THE BOOT & FLOGGER

Address: 10-20 Redcross Way, SE1 1TA (☎ 020-7407 1184, 🖳 davy.co.uk/bootandflogger).
Opening hours: Mon, 11am to 10pm; Tue-Fri, 11am to 11pm; closed weekends.
Transport: Borough tube.
Go for: Charm, bonhomie and exceptional fine wines.

This looks like a pub and sounds like it should be a pub, but it's actually a wine bar, owned by Davy's, wine merchants founded in 1870. The Boot & Flogger opened in 1964, but the atmosphere is redolent of a much earlier period, its wood panelling and leather armchairs suggesting the bonhomie of a gentlemen's club.

280

The wine list is shorter than you might expect, and includes around 40 bottles, some 15 available by the glass – prices start at £4.55 a glass, £16.95 a bottle, plus a fair choice of half bottles. If you're in the mood to celebrate, you can have a tankard of champagne! If you're really pushing the boat out, Davy's list of fine wines contain some serious Bordeaux and Burgundy vintages, including a Chateau Latour from 1970 (only £660!).

This is a great place to unwind and has a loyal clientele, including some of the area's movers and shakers. By contrast, it's opposite one of London's more poignant historical sites: Cross Bones

Graveyard, the resting place of more than 15,000 Londoners (mostly women, many prostitutes) buried in unmarked graves on un-consecrated ground and remembered by floral tributes on the gate.

THE BREW WHARF

Address: Brew Wharf Yard, 14-16 Stoney Street, SE1 9AD (☎ 020-7378 6601, 🖳 brewwharf.com).
Opening hours: Mon-Fri, 11am to 11pm; Sat, 10am to 11pm; closed Sun.
Transport: London Bridge tube/rail.
Go for: A chance to try beers from around the globe.

With an entrance next to the **Wine Wharf** (see page 302), the Brew Wharf is impressively situated within spacious railway arches near Borough Market. Its stated aim is to persuade us to take beer 'as seriously as wine' and it offers a 'rare opportunity to sample a wide range of beers from around the world'.

It resembles a German beer hall and has around ten beers on tap and up to 50 by the bottle. It also serves good food and can suggest beers to go with dishes, another nod to their philosophy that beer is as serious and complex as wine. There are also more than 20 wines listed, as well as spirits and a few cocktails, but most come solely for the beer.

It's quite an expensive bar (owned by Vinopolis, a visitor attraction themed around wine), but it does its thing well and has the added bonus of an attractive terrace, with good outside space – something that's at a premium in London.

281

THE BRIDGE HOUSE

Address: 218 Tower Bridge Road, SE1 2UP (☎ 020-7407 5818,
🖥 bridgehousebar.co.uk).
Opening hours: Sun-Wed, noon to 11pm; Thu-Sat, noon to midnight.
Transport: London Bridge tube/rail or Tower Hill tube.
Go for: Adnams beer and good-value food.

The Bridge House is close by the southern end of Tower Bridge, not quite a waterside location but near enough to have views across and along the Thames. It's owned by the admirable independent brewer Adnams, which is based in Southwold, Suffolk, and runs around 70 pubs and four hotels in East Anglia. Although Adnams ales are quite widely available in the capital's better hostelries, this is the brewery's only London pub.

The Bridge feels more like a bar than a pub and describes itself as Bridge House Bar and Dining. There's a first floor dining room serving good-quality gastro-level fare, and bar food is also available. The lunchtime special, priced at £5.50, is a popular draw. It's a friendly place, bright and modern, with a mixed clientele of locals, tourists and workers from the surrounding offices and businesses.

In addition to its range of Adnams ale, both permanent and seasonal selections, there are bottled beers, some German lagers and a guest beer from Purity. As befits a pub serving good food, there's also a reasonable wine list.

THE CUTTY SARK TAVERN

Address: 4-6 Ballast Quay, SE10 9PD (☎ 020-8858 3146, 🖥 cuttysarkse10.co.uk).
Opening hours: Mon-Sat, 11am to 11pm; Sun, noon to 10.30pm.
Transport: Cutty Sark DLR or Greenwich DLR/rail.
Go for: A lovely maritime pub with tremendous views.

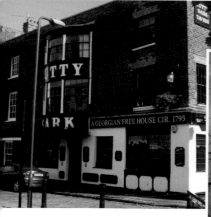

There's been a tavern on this Greenwich riverside site since at least 1743, although the current building dates from around 1795. The pub has had various names over the centuries and only became the Cutty Sark in 1953, when the eponymous ship arrived in Greenwich. You can't miss it as the name is writ large across the impressive, curving Georgian façade.

The interior has low ceilings, old floorboards, a wood-beamed bar, beer-barrel seats and maritime ephemera and decorations, and some inviting leather chairs in the old Smoke Room. One of its great attractions are the views it enjoys along and over the Thames, towards Canary Wharf, Docklands and the O2. Window tables are much sought after, as are the riverside terrace tables in good weather.

The Cutty Sark Tavern was a freehouse owned by the same family for more than 40 years, but has been a Young's outlet since 2012 and now stocks the solid range of Wells and Young's beers, as well as around 30 wines, most of which can be bought by the glass. Appetising food is served in the first floor restaurant.

THE DEAN SWIFT

Address: 10 Gainsford Street, SE1 2NE (☎ 020-7357 0748,
🖥 thedeanswift.com).
Opening hours: Sun-Thu, noon to midnight; Fri-Sat, noon to 1am.
Transport: London Bridge tube/rail or Tower Hill tube.
Go for: A brilliant choice of local ales.

This is an attractive bar in Shad Thames that calls itself a 'local beer house'. Opened in 2010, it's named after the Irish satirical writer (and later Dean of St Patrick's Cathedral in Dublin) Jonathan Swift, whose most famous character, the much travelled Lemuel Gulliver, had connections with Bermondsey.

284

The Dean Swift has a great choice of beer, many from local brewers, including four handpumps dispensing Partridge by Dark Star (the house bitter) and guests beers from the likes of Arbor Ales, Brodie's, Crouch Vale, Redemption, Roosters and Sambrook's. There are also keg offerings from BrewDog and Harviestoun, among others, while the impressive bottled choice runs to around 40, with beers from Belgium, France, Scotland, Sweden and the US, plus a wide selection from local brewery Kernel, also in SE1.

Wine drinkers can choose from around 26 wines, a number available by the glass and carafe, and there's also good food, including bar snacks, well-made burgers and a reasonable lunch menu.

THE GEORGE INN

Address: 77 Borough High Street, SE1 1NH (☎ 020-7407 2056, 🖥 gkpubs. co.uk/pubs-in-london/the-george-inn-pub and nationaltrust.org.uk/george-inn).
Opening hours: Mon-Sat, 11am to 11pm; Sun, noon to 10.30pm.
Transport: London Bridge tube/rail.
Go for: To explore London's last galleried coaching inn.

One of London's most famous pubs, the George is the city's only remaining galleried coaching inn, Grade I listed and worth visiting for its history alone. There's been a hostelry here since 1598 – probably much earlier – but the current structure is from 1676, when the inn was rebuilt after a fire destroyed much of Southwark. It's no longer complete, but enough remains to give you a good idea of what such inns were like.

Coaching inns were arranged around a courtyard, so that coaches could be loaded and unloaded in a secure environment, and provided travellers with food and accommodation. They were the forerunners of today's railway stations – it was the arrival of the railways that signalled their decline.

Shakespeare, Pepys and Johnson reputedly drank at the George, and Charles Dickens mentions it in *Little Dorrit*. These days, it's on the tourist trail and usually busy, although there are plenty of tables in the large courtyard. It's owned by the National Trust, which leases it to Greene King, so drinkers can enjoy Abbott, IPA and Old Speckled Hen, plus other beers, in historic surroundings. Good quality British food is also served.

Samuel Johnson

THE GREENWICH UNION

Address: 56 Royal Hill, SE10 8RT (☎ 020-8692 6258, 🖥 greenwichunion.com).
Opening hours: Mon-Fri, noon to 11pm; Sat, 11am to 11pm; Sun, 11.30am to 10.30pm.
Transport: Greenwich DLR/rail.
Go for: A tremendous selection of high-quality craft beer and lager.

The Meantime Brewing Company is a microbrewery based in Greenwich and this was its first bar, opened in 2001 and a forerunner of today's craft ale bars. The Union – the name comes from Meantime's Union beer – focuses on the brewery's own beers, craft lagers, rarities, specials and seasonals, although it also stocks 60 beers from around the world. If you find the choice bewildering, you can sample a flight of four Meantime draught brews on a beer paddle for £5.50.

The Union consists of a long, narrow, functional bar, with bare wood and comfortable leather chairs, a light, airy conservatory and an attractive beer garden and terrace. Wine, spirits, coffee and tea are available, and there's a concise but tasty food menu, which provides a beer recommendation for each dish (see website for kitchen times).

Staff are enthusiastic and knowledgeable, and the Union provides a friendly, relaxed environment – it even hosts live jazz. Despite competition from a more recent Meantime outlet, the **Old Brewery** (see page 293), it's still packing them in.

THE HIDE BAR

Address: 39-45 Bermondsey Street, SE1 3XF (☎ 020-7403 6655,
🖥 thehidebar.com).
Opening hours: Tue, 5pm to midnight; Wed-Thu, 5pm to 1am; Fri-Sat, 5pm
to 2am; Sun, 4-10.30pm; closed Mon.
Transport: London Bridge tube/rail.
Go for: A bar with something for everyone.

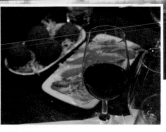

287

The Hide Bar has a simple
but effective formula: stock,
prepare and serve a wide and
well-chosen selection of drinks in a modern, clean space with warm
lighting, creating a relaxed, unpretentious environment. And stay open
late.

Cocktails are the speciality – this is primarily a cocktail bar – and
most are priced at around £9. The bar's owners are sufficiently
interested in the history of classic cocktails to have collected a small
library of books about them, dating back to the 1890s, and customers
are welcome to browse. If you prefer your drinks straighter, there are
over 500 spirits available, from mezcal to Armagnac!

The Hide Bar's wine list runs to around 150 bins and has been
carefully compiled with the help of the Wine and Spirit Education Trust,
which is located in the same building. Beer is local, too, the main tap
supplier being the lauded (Greenwich) Meantime Brewery. Snacks,
mains and sharing platters help to offset the effects of the alcohol.

This is a deservedly popular venue and booking is recommended.

HOOPERS

Address: 28 Ivanhoe Road, SE5 8DH (☎ 020-7733 4797, ⌨ hoopersbar.co.uk).
Opening hours: Mon-Tue, 5.30-11pm; Wed, 5.30-11.30pm; Thu, 5.30pm to midnight; Fri, 5pm to midnight; Sat, 12.30pm to midnight; Sun, 1-11pm.
Transport: East Dulwich rail.
Go for: A friendly, traditional local that knows about beer.

A Victorian corner freehouse, Hoopers is on a residential street in the area where Camberwell, Peckham and East Dulwich lock horns. It manages the trick of being both a destination for beer lovers and a proper, family-friendly local at the same time.

It has four handpumps, offering a changing selection of fine ale, including offerings from Adnams, Ascot, Brodie's, Dark Star, Harveys and Skinner's; the pub also has its own uniquely brewed Hoopers Ivanhoe ale. There's an interesting range of around 50 bottled beers, primarily from Belgium but also from Czechoslovakia, Germany and the UK (e.g. Meantime), including abbey/trappist, blonde, fruit, pilsner, stout and wheat beers, something to suit most tastes. Good wines are also available.

288

Hoopers hosts regular beer festivals, in spring, autumn and at Christmas, often featuring local brewers. And there are also more cerebral events, with a pub quiz on Thursdays at 8.45pm and comedy nights on the first Sunday of the month. Established comedians sometimes try out new material here, so you could be in for a treat (or not).

KATZENJAMMERS

Address: Hop Exchange, 24 Southwark Street, SE1 1TY (☎ 020-3417 0196, 🖳 katzenjammers.co.uk).
Opening hours: Mon-Thu, noon to 11pm; Fri-Sat, noon to midnight; Sun, noon to 10.30pm.
Transport: London Bridge tube/rail.
Go for: A bierkeller located in an old temple to hops.

Katzenjammers is a vaulted basement bar, dedicated to German beer and ideally located in the Hop Exchange. This graceful, curved, colonnaded building dates from 1867 and was originally London's centre for hop trading – now Grade II listed and a local landmark, it's a reminder of the central role brewing once played in Southwark.

289

The bar describes itself as a 'bierkeller and restaurant' and has up to nine draught beers on tap, with alcohol levels ranging from a gentle 4.1 per cent to a dangerous 6.8 per cent. There's also a choice of around 30 bottled beers, mostly German (plus the odd Belgian), including dark lagers, dunkels, kolsch beers, pilsners and weissbiers. To round off there's a short wine list, featuring some German bins, and a selection of schnapps.

The food is heavy on schnitzel and 'wurst, neither subtle nor distinguished but suited to the Bavarian atmosphere. The same can be said of the Oompah band on Friday nights which includes covers of Oasis and Queen songs in its repertoire – you have been warned! Katzenjammers can get rowdy, but it's fun and worth visiting for the beer alone.

THE KING'S ARMS

Address: 25 Roupell Street, SE1 8TB (☎ 020-7207 0784,
🖳 windmilltaverns.com/the-kings-arms).
Opening hours: Mon-Fri, 11am to 11pm; Sat, noon to 11pm; Sun, noon to 10.30pm.
Transport: Waterloo tube/rail.
Go for: A characterful local with good beer and Thai food.

One of Waterloo's best pubs, the King's Arms is in a street of early 19th-century cottages. Well preserved and full of atmosphere, both the pub and surrounding streets are redolent of Victorian London and resemble a film set for a prestigious period drama; indeed, it's a popular location with film and TV directors.

An award-winning pub (it's also included in *The Good Beer Guide*), the King's Arms feels rustic and old-fashioned. It has separate public and saloon bars – an increasingly rare division – and open fires in winter. Beer drinkers are well served by a constantly evolving beer list which includes nine ales on tap, including Adnams, Brakespear, Butcombe Bitter, Dark Star, Marston's, Nethergate Howler, Sambrook's and Tetley. Around 15 wines are available, most available in two glass sizes (glasses from £4.25, bottles from £15).

Thai food is the speciality in the dining room – see the website for kitchen hours – and roasts are served on alternate Sundays. News of the pub's attractions has spread and it's busy most nights.

THE MARKET PORTER

Address: 9 Stoney Street, SE1 9AA (☎ 020-7407 2495, 🖳 markettaverns.co.uk).
Opening hours: Mon-Fri, 6-8.30am and 11am to 11pm; Sat, noon to 11pm;
Sun, noon to 10.30pm.
Transport: London Bridge tube/rail.
Go for: A huge choice of great beer… for breakfast if you can manage it.

This long-established freehouse is immediately opposite Borough Market and has an early morning licence so that it can offer alcoholic sustenance to traders and buyers – and anyone else who happens by. If you think it looks familiar, it stood in for the Third-Hand Book Emporium in the film *Harry Potter and the Prisoner of Azkaban*.

It's an attractive premises with a comprehensive selection of real ale – one of London's best – and is so popular that most punters have to stand and many spill out onto the street. Don't come here if you're after a quiet drink in comfort.

The Porter has between 15 and 18 beers at any one time, with the choice constantly changing – up to 50 different cask ales can be stocked in any one week – therefore you need to study the hand pumps to see what's on, which can be tricky when the bar is crowded and the staff too busy to offer advice. But the sublime choice of ale is worth a bit of discomfort.

The (slightly) quieter restaurant upstairs serves good hearty fare, most of it sourced from Borough Market.

THE MAYFLOWER

Address: 117 Rotherhithe Street, SE16 4NF (☎ 020-7237 4088, 🖥 themayflowerrotherhithe.com).
Opening hours: Mon-Sat, 11am to 11pm; Sun, noon to 10.30pm.
Transport: Rotherhithe rail.
Go for: A waterside tavern with history and hot water bottles.

This tavern on the Thames path at Rotherhithe has had various names over the years and only became the Mayflower in 1957 (the Pilgrim Fathers set sail from a nearby mooring in 1620). The current building dates from the 18th century but there's been an inn on this spot for much longer.

292   It's a charming little pub with a black and white frontage and leaded windows, oak beams and wood panelling. There's a dining room upstairs, while simpler fare is served in the bar and there are barbecues on the jetty on summer weekends. The choice of drinks is solid rather than remarkable – four or five ales, which change every two weeks, and some 20 wines, most sold in by the glass from £4.10 (bottles from £15).

The Mayflower draws locals and tourists to enjoy the Thames views from its rear deck, which juts out over the river (and can flood during high tides!); blankets and hot water bottles are provided on cold nights. To really enjoy the atmosphere as it was in the days of the Pilgrim Fathers, visit after 6pm on a 'Blackout Sunday' when the pub is lit only by candlelight.

THE OLD BREWERY

Address: Pepys Building, Old Royal Naval College, SE10 9LW (☎ 020-3327 1280, 🖥 oldbrewerygreenwich.com).
Opening hours: Mon-Sat, 11am to 11pm; Sun, noon to 10.30pm (see website for café and restaurant hours).
Transport: Cutty Sark DLR.
Go for: A striking setting for one of London's best breweries.

Another offshoot of the innovative Greenwich Meantime Brewery (see also the **Greenwich Union** on page 286), the Old Brewery 'multitasks' as a microbrewery, pub, café and restaurant. It's favourably situated in a Grade II listed building dating from 1712 – part of the Royal Naval College – that has housed this modern, dynamic brewery since 2010.

It's a striking space, with the brewery's eight, 1,000-litre copper tanks providing an impressive backdrop, looming over the tables below in this stylish bar. The main attraction for many people is the extensive, detailed beer menu: around 50 beers are stocked, including a number of Meantime's own – some of latter are made using old recipes and ingredients such as bog myrtle and wormwood.

Excellent modern British food is served by the friendly, knowledgeable staff and there's a large courtyard terrace with around 30 shaded tables. Wine and spirits are also available, but the emphasis is very much on beer. This fine venue isn't exactly cheap, but it isn't ruinous either and is a must-visit for ale lovers.

THE OXO TOWER BAR

Address: OXO Tower Wharf, Barge House Street, SE1 9PH (☏ 020-7803 3888, 🖥 harveynichols.com/oxo-tower-london-bar).
Opening hours: Mon-Thu, 11am to 11pm; Fri-Sat, 11am to midnight; Sun, noon to 10.30pm.
Transport: Waterloo tube/rail.
Go for: A charming building, glorious views and classy cocktails.

The OXO Tower is a fascinating old building which was rebuilt in the late '20s as an Art Deco advertisement for a well-known stock cube, and refurbished in the '90s to house galleries, shops, apartments, plus a bar, brasserie and restaurant, all owned by Harvey Nichols.

The OXO Tower Bar is white and shaped like a boomerang, the design hinting at a classic cruise liner with a modern edge, while the glass frontage allows drinkers to make the most of the views of the Thames, St Paul's Cathedral and Somerset House; this is a great location to watch the sun set.

There's a cocktail list and a large, French-dominated wine list, with some wines available by the glass. There are also well-chosen bottled beers – not always the case in upmarket venues, where beer can be regarded as a poor relation – including Meantime Pale Ale from Greenwich's Meantime Brewery.

If you're hungry, the bar menu includes cheese and charcuterie platters (you must book to eat in the brasserie and restaurant).

Not a cheap destination but undoubtedly an impressive one.

THE PALMERSTON

Address: 91 Lordship Lane, SE22 8EP (☎ 020-8693 1629,
🖳 thepalmerston.net).
Opening hours: Mon-Thu, noon to 11pm; Fri-Sat, noon to 1am; Sun, noon
to 10.30pm.
Transport: East Dulwich rail.
Go for: An award-winning gastropub with good drinks as well as great food.

Another haven of drinking
civilisation in East Dulwich,
The Palmerston was a
spit and sawdust boozer
in a previous life, but was
transformed into a celebrated gastropub in 2004. It's now regarded as
one of southeast London's best places to eat and drink, as a number
of awards attest – it was voted 59th in *Restaurant* magazine's list of
the UK's 100 Best Restaurants in 2008.

It has two attractive, wood-panelled rooms, with photographs and
art on the walls. Quite a lot of the space is given over to the dining
room, but this is a traditional pub as well, as demonstrated by the
thoughtful choice of ales, including Hogs Back TEA and St Austell
Tribute. There's a comprehensive wine list of around 50 bins, many
available in two glass sizes as well as by the bottle; prices are
reasonable, from £3.75 for a glass and £14.25 a bottle.

The food is good, if rather pricey – most main courses are in the
£17-19 range – although the set lunch on weekdays is a good way to
sample the skills of the kitchen and costs a more reasonable £13 for
two courses or £16.75 for three.

THE RAKE

Address: 14A Winchester Walk, SE1 9AG (☎ 020-7407 0557, 🖥 utobeer.co.uk).
Opening hours: Mon-Fri, noon to 11pm; Sat, 10am to 11pm; Sun, noon to 8pm.
Transport: London Bridge tube/rail.
Go for: A stunning selection of beer.

Run by Utobeer, this is a beer aficionados' venue, with around 140 brews available, including seven keg, three cask and some 130 in the cooler. The range is ever changing and updates every few days, sometimes even daily. Cask ales include BrewDog, Dark Star, Hardknott, Otley and Thornbridge, while the bottled selection is too numerous to name check. Regular beer events, festivals and tastings are held in an upstairs room.

The bar is on the edge of Borough Market. It used to be a greasy spoon, but was converted in 2006 into one of the capital's great craft beer destinations. The plain, dark blue exterior makes it look like a private club, while the interior is small and plain. It gets very busy, with drinkers spilling out into the small heated courtyard – go mid-afternoon if you like things quieter.

As well as beer anoraks, regulars include market traders and foodies, making for a lively clientele. There's no room for a kitchen, however, so the 'menu' is limited to pork pies, crisps and olives.

THE RICHARD I

Address: 52-54 Royal Hill, SE10 8RT (☎ 020-8692 2996, 🖳 youngs.co.uk/pub-detail.asp?pubid=442).
Opening hours: Mon-Sat, noon to 11pm; Sun, noon to 10.30pm.
Transport: Greenwich DLR and rail.
Go for: A traditional pub near Greenwich Park.

Sitting next door to the **Greenwich Union** (see page 286), this Young's pub is in complete contrast to its esteemed neighbour. It's a traditional venue for those who don't want the choice of hundreds of beers from every corner of the globe or, for that matter, cutting-edge wining and dining (though the Richard's food is tasty enough).

297

The pub is on one of Greenwich's loveliest roads, lined with Georgian properties and close to verdant Greenwich Park. It's housed in an 18th-century building that used to house two shops, and it has separate public and saloon bars – a division which is increasingly rare. Locals know it as the Tolly, as it was once owned by the now-defunct Tollemache and Cobbold Brewery of Ipswich.

The beer list includes three Young's ales plus a guest, such as Bombardier, Courage and Doom Bar, as well as some good bottled brews, as well as wine, spirits and a fair selection of food, including sausage and cheese platters. If the weather is mild, you can drink in the pub's large, attractive back garden.

THE ROYAL OAK

Address: 44 Tabard Street, SE1 4JU (☎ 020-7357 7173,
🖥 harveys.org.uk/pubs-tenancies/find-our-beer/the-royal-oak-2).
Opening hours: Mon-Sat, 11am to 11.30pm; Sun, noon to 6pm.
Transport: Borough tube.
Go for: Fine ales from Sussex's oldest independent brewery.

Slightly off the beaten track, but close to many of Southwark's tourist attractions, this is one of only two London pubs in the stable of noted Sussex brewer Harveys (the other is **The Cat's Back** – see page 248), which is based in Lewes and has 47 pubs in total. The Royal Oak is on Tabard Street, which is itself named after a pub: the now-demolished Tabard Inn mentioned in Geoffrey Chaucer's *Canterbury Tales*.

This is a Victorian corner pub, with an understated interior which retains a number of original features, including cast-iron pillars, a carved bar and plasterwork ceilings. It is spread over two rooms – the public and saloon bars remain separate – and provides a friendly welcome. The clientele includes locals, workers and beer devotees in search of the fine ales of Sussex's oldest and highly esteemed independent brewery.

(Harveys was founded in 1790 and was a triple gold winner at 2012's International Beer Challenge.)

The Royal Oak offers the range of Harveys ales, plus a guest, as well as a wide and interesting choice of bottled beers. Stomachs can be lined with solid, plain pub grub.

THE SKYLON

Address: Royal Festival Hall, Belvedere Road, SE1 8XX (☎ 020-7654 7800, ⌨ skylon-restaurant.co.uk).
Opening hours: Mon-Sat, noon to 1am; Sun, noon to 10.30pm.
Transport: Waterloo tube/rail.
Go for: A special sundowner overlooking the river.

This bar is named after the iconic cigar-shaped structure that was built for the Festival of Britain in 1951 and once dominated the South Bank skyline. So it's appropriate that there's a hint of the '50s in the design of the Skylon bar, which is a large, airy, high-ceilinged space on the third floor of the Royal Festival Hall, with a slate bar and huge windows.

The windows provide amazing river views and this has turned the Skylon into a popular place for a sundowner, with the setting sun casting the rather sludgy river in a flattering light – booking is recommended at this time of day.

There are excellent cocktails on offer, both classics and innovative mixes such dessert cocktails and infusions, and most are priced at £11.50. There's also beer and an extensive wine list, as well as a bar food menu of fishy and Oriental sounding treats. As with many riverside venues, this is by no means a cheap destination, but neither will you pay the astral prices that some London venues demand for such a glorious view.

THE SOUTHWARK ROOMS

Address: 60 Southwark Street, SE1 1UN (☎ 020-7357 9301,
🖥 southwarkrooms.com).
Opening hours: Mon-Wed, noon to 11pm; Thu-Fri, noon to 2am; Sat-Sun,
private hire only.
Transport: London Bridge tube/rail.
Go for: Keenly-priced cocktails in a friendly atmosphere.

300

Housed in a corner building within view of the Shard, this is a stylish but unpretentious venue which generates a great party atmosphere. On the ground floor, there's a glamorous dining room with large gilt mirrors, cream leather chairs and chandeliers, while downstairs is the inviting cocktail lounge, its bare brick walls lit by the warm glow of candles.

They're passionate about cocktails here. The choice is extensive and the quality excellent, and most are priced around £8. Even better, during 'Happy Hour', from 5-7pm, there's two-for-one offer on cocktails. The wine and sparkling wine list runs to around 30 bins, a number available by the glass as well as the bottle; glasses cost from £5.20, bottles from £16. If you fancy some fizz, prosecco is priced at £7.50 per glass, while champagne starts from £40 a bottle. Food includes 'small bites', salads and mains; look out for specials such as a burger and drink for a tenner on certain days.

The Southwark Rooms gets crowded with a mixture of City suits and media types, who know a good-value, hospitable watering hole when they find one.

THE TRAFALGAR TAVERN

Address: Park Row, SE10 9NW (☎ 020-8858 2909, 🖳 trafalgartavern.co.uk).
Opening hours: Mon-Thu, noon to 11pm; Fri-Sat, noon to midnight; Sun, noon to 10.30pm.
Transport: Maze Hill rail or Cutty Sark DLR.
Go for: The riverside location, naval history and whitebait suppers.

Dating from 1837 and restored in the '60s, this handsome, Grade I listed tavern near the Royal Naval College retains its historic atmosphere. It enjoys a great location directly on the river and its original bay windows afford fine views.

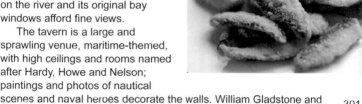

The tavern is a large and sprawling venue, maritime-themed, with high ceilings and rooms named after Hardy, Howe and Nelson; paintings and photos of nautical scenes and naval heroes decorate the walls. William Gladstone and Charles Dickens came here for the noted whitebait suppers; Dickens set the wedding feast scene in *Our Mutual Friend* in the pub.

The Trafalgar stocks a couple of good ales, e.g. Adnams and Sharp's, as well as beers by the bottle, and there are around 40 wines, some available in two glass sizes. There's a traditional menu of bar snacks and mains. If you want to eat as Dickens did, a serving of Greenwich whitebait is £7.75, although it's no longer scooped straight from the Thames.

Prices are on the high side, but this is no deterrent and the Trafalgar gets busy on fine summer days.

301

THE WINE WHARF

Address: Stoney Street, Borough Market, SE1 9AD (☎ 020-7940 8335, 🖥 winewharf.co.uk).
Opening hours: Mon-Wed, 5.30-11pm; Thu-Fri, noon to 3pm and 5.30-11pm; Sat, noon to 11pm; closed Sun.
Transport: London Bridge tube/rail.
Go for: A vast choice of wine in a chic environment.

Part of Vinopolis (a wine exhibition, education and retail centre), the Wine Wharf is housed in a redeveloped Victorian warehouse by Borough Market, in an area which has become something of a gourmand's holy grail. The bar has a chic industrial look, with high ceilings, exposed brick walls, gentle lighting and leather sofas. But it's a laid-back place – not intimidating or stuffy at all – with friendly, knowledgeable staff. It has the same ethos as Vinopolis: to make wine accessible to all.

Naturally, the wine list is tremendous with around 300 bins, over half of which are available by the glass, so you can expand your horizons and try a selection of different wines. Wine tasting 'flights' are also available, allowing you to sample a number of wines for a fixed price (see website for details). Once you get hungry, there are good bar snacks and sharing platters or you can head along to Cantina Vinopolis for a full meal.

Wine Wharf's success means that it gets busy, particularly on Thursday and Friday evenings.

THE YACHT

Address: 5-7 Crane Street, SE10 9NP (☎ 020-8858 0175, 🖥 taylor-walker. co.uk/pub/yacht-greenwich/c7591).
Opening hours: Mon-Sat, 11am to 11pm; Sun, 10am to 10.30pm.
Transport: Cutty Sark DLR.
Go for: A riverside pub which isn't packed with tourists.

The Yacht is a Taylor Walker pub situated close to the **Trafalgar Tavern** (see page 301). It's less famous than the Trafalgar and attracts locals rather than tourists, therefore it's usually less crowded. But it's still a popular choice for a drink along this stretch of river, and is a relaxed venue with friendly staff.

The Yacht looks like a traditional boozer, with dark wood, open fireplaces, and cosy nooks and crannies. The accommodation spread over two levels, and the window tables on the upper floor are especially sought after for their fine views of the Thames.

There are usually four good, well-kept beers on the hand pumps, from the likes of Fuller's, Sharps, Wells and Young's. There's also a reasonable wine list and the pub serves robust pub grub, with the fish and chips especially popular. The Yacht can become busy on sunny weekends, but during the rest of the week it's often easier to enjoy a comfortable drink here than at many of the area's other riverside venues.

303

ZEITGEIST AT THE JOLLY GARDENERS

Address: 49-51 Black Prince Road, SE11 6AB (☎ 020-7840 0426,
🖥 zeitgeist-london.com).
Opening hours: Sun-Mon, noon to 10.30pm; Tue-Thu, noon to midnight;
Fri-Sat, noon to 1am.
Transport: Vauxhall tube/rail.
Go for: German beer, food and football (and Germans).

This describes itself as a German gastropub
(if that isn't an oxymoron) and you don't
stumble across those every day. It's in a large
Victorian building near Lambeth Bridge and
its décor is a combination of traditional and
modern: black walls and banquettes, a red
ceiling and an ornate central bar.

Zeitgeist is German-owned and there are
German flags on the walls, but it's certainly no
theme bar and lederhosen are nowhere to be seen. Rather, it's a well-
conceived venue, with a fine list of German beers, many of them little
known in this country. About 40 are available; around 15 on draught
(£4.50 per pint, £2.50 per half pint, so it isn't cheap) and the rest by
bottle, including regional ales, wheat beers and ciders.

The German food on offer includes the anticipated sausages and
schnitzel, but also lesser-known dishes such as homemade noodles
and slow roast pork, and there's an all-you-can-eat buffet on Wed and
Fri between noon and 2pm (£6.95).

The bar attracts German expats, but also locals and tourists, drawn
by the good beer, convivial atmosphere and screenings of Bundesliga
(soccer) matches. There are some outdoor tables, too.

ZERO DEGREES

Address: 29-31 Montpelier Vale, SE3 0TJ (☎ 020-8852 5619,
🖥 zerodegrees-microbrewery.co.uk).
Opening hours: Mon-Sat, noon to midnight; Sun, noon to 11pm.
Transport: Blackheath rail.
Go for: Home-brewed ale and wood-fired pizza.

A shiny, stylish microbrewery in affluent Blackheath,
Zero Degrees opened in 2001 and was one of the
first British venues to ape the American craft
brewing approach; it also has outlets in Bristol,
Cardiff and Reading. The name is a reference
to the nearby Greenwich Meridian (which is,
of course, at zero degrees longitude) and the
stripped back interior has wooden floors, bare
brick, with modern designs painted on the walls
and steel staircases leading to a mezzanine
level, along with some outside tables.

305

Large copper vats contain the four house
ales – a pils, a pale ale, a black lager and a
wheat beer – while two others contain
a varying choice, include seasonal offerings and fruit
beers. Prices are reasonable: house ales cost £3.25 per pint (£1.75
per half pint).

There's also wine, a
large television and food
in the dining area, which
includes high-quality,
wood-fired pizzas (in
homage to the American
microbrewery style of
eating) and robust dishes
such as pasta, sausages
and mash, and mussels
and fries.

APPENDICES

APPENDIX A: INTERESTING WEBSITES

Adventures in Pubs (adventuresinpubs.co.uk). Excellent website dedicated to showcasing the finest pubs, bars, wines, beers and ales.

All in London (allinlondon.co.uk/clubs-bars.php). A comprehensive list of the city's pubs, bars and clubs.

Bar Chick (barchick.com/city-guides/london). Guide to London's coolest bars and cocktail lounges.

Beer and Pub (beerandpub.com). The voice of the beer and pub industry.

Beer in the Evening (beerintheevening.com/pubs/results.shtml/county/london). A searchable database of almost 4,000 London pubs, including contacts and reviews.

Belgian Beer Guide (belgianbeerguide.co.uk). Where to find pubs, bars and restaurants London serving Belgian beer.

Bon Vivant (bonvivant.co.uk/the-guide/bars.html). Good guide to London bars and gastropubs (the latter are listed under restaurants).

British Beer and Pub Association (beerandpub.com). The voice of the beer and pub industry.

Brodies Beers (brodiesbeers.co.uk). Microbrewery in East London which has produced 150 different beers in just four years.

Campaign for Real Ale/CAMRA (camra.org.uk). An independent, voluntary organisation campaigning for real ale, community pubs and consumer rights. CAMRA also maintains a register of heritage pubs.

CAMRA London (camralondon.org.uk). London branch of the real ale campaigners.

City Pubs (citypubs.co.uk). Find a pub or bar in the Square Mile.

Fancy a Pint (fancyapint.com). Excellent search engine for London pubs, listed by area, with reviews. It also covers other towns in the UK.

Fluid London (fluidlondon.co.uk/drink_home.aspx). Comprehensive guide to London's bars and restaurants with more than 8,000 listings and reviews.

Fullers (fullers.co.uk). Website of London's last major brewery, offering brewery tours and tastings. Also a major London pub owner.

Gay Cities (london.gaycities.com/bars). Guide to London's gay and lesbian bars.

The Good Pub Guide (thegoodpubguide.co.uk). Britain's oldest and only truly independent pub guide – both in print and online.

Great British Beer Festival (gbbf.org.uk). One of the UK's largest annual beer festivals, held in August at Olympia.

Heritage Pubs (www.heritagepubs.org.uk/download/realheritagepubsoflondon.pdf). CAMRA's guide to London's best preserved historic pubs.

Jancis Robinson (jancisrobinson.com/articles/a20111222.html). The doyenne of wine experts' guide to London's wine and sherry bars.

Live Sports Bars (www.livesportsbars.tv/bars/london). Where to watch live sports in London, listed by area.

London Bierfest (thelondonbierfest.com). The spirit of Oktoberfest in the City of London.

London Brewers' Alliance (londonbrewers.org). Aiming to unite the capital's beer makers with its beer drinkers.

London Online (londononline.co.uk/pubs). Guide featuring thousands of listings, including pubs (and bars).

London Pub Crawl Co (thelondonpubcrawlco.com). Download self-guided walking tours (pub crawls) taking in many of London's oldest and most interesting boozers.

London Pubs Group (londonpubsgroup.org.uk). Promoting historic pub preservation and good pub design in London.

London Tavern Trails (londontaverntrails.com). Book a guided walking tour around some of London's historic pubs.

Make Mine a Beer (makemineabeer.com). Interesting blog and guide to London pubs.

Match Pint (matchpint.co.uk/best-pubs-in-london). Helps you find the best pubs and bars to watch sport on large-screen TV.

Nicholsons Pubs (nicholsonspubs.co.uk). One of London's largest pub owners, with around 45 pubs.

Publican's Morning Advertiser (morningadvertiser.co.uk). The trade newspaper for publicans, sponsors of the annual Top 50 Gastropub Awards (top50gastropubs.co.uk).

Pubs.com (pubs.com). Excellent independent guide to traditional pubs in London and England. Great all-round site.

Qype (qype.co.uk). See what others have to say about pubs and bars on Europe's largest, user-generated local reviews site.

Random Pub Finder (randompubfinder.com/map.php). The online equivalent of sticking a pin in a map to find a pub; good information and reviews.

Real Ale Guide (realaleguide.co.uk/id27.html). Guide to real ale pubs and breweries in London.

Real Ale Pubs (realalepubs.co.uk/area.asp?aid=15). Lists real ale pubs in the capital.

Real Pubs (realpubs.co.uk). Reviews of 'real' pubs, with warm and friendly service and great food and drink.

Samuel Smith (samuelsmithsbrewery.co.uk). Celebrated Yorkshire brewery (est. 1758) and owner of many London pubs.

Shepherd Neame (shepherdneame.co.uk). Kent brewery (est. 1698) making traditional ales and owning hundreds of pubs in and around London.

Sports Pubs (sportspubs.co.uk). Find sports pubs in London and throughout the UK.

Square Meal (squaremeal.co.uk). One of London's (and the UK's) best guides to bars and restaurants, with great reviews.

Standard (standard.co.uk/goingout/bars). The London Evening Standard newspaper's recommended pubs and bars, with reviews.

Tales of the Cocktail (talesofthecocktail.com). Dedicated to the advancement of the craft of the cocktail through education, networking and promotion.

Time Out (timeout.com/london). Find reviews of pubs and bars and where to drink in London, whatever your budget or requirements.

Travels With Beer (travelswithbeer.com). One of the UK's best and most comprehensive websites, with excellent bar descriptions and information.

Urban Path (urbanpath.com/london/gastro-pubs). Guide to London's gastropubs.

Urban Spoon (urbanspoon.com/f/52/5150/london/pubs). Restaurant guide to London pubs serving food, with diners' reviews and comments.

Wikipedia (en.wikipedia.org/wiki/pub). All you ever wanted to know about British pubs and their history from Wiki.

World's Best Bars (worldsbestbars.com/united-kingdom/london). Information and reviews of London's best bars, cocktail lounges and clubs.

Young's (youngs.co.uk). London brewery – formerly located in Wandsworth, but now in Bedford – established in 1831. Young's is also one of London's (and the UK's) largest pub landlords.

SPECIALITY INDEX

Country-specific Pubs/Bars

Gastropubs

Heritage Pubs

Hotel Bars

Bars with Music

Restaurant/Brasserie

Rooftop Bars/Views

Spirit Bars/Pubs

Sports Bars

Theatre pubs

Traditional

312 Waterside Pubs

Wine Bars/Specialists

INDEX

313

£10.95

London Sketchbook

ISBN: 978-1-907339-37-0, 96 pages, hardback.

Jim Watson

London Sketchbook is a unique guide to the most celebrated landmarks of one of the world's major cities. In ten easy walks it takes you on a fascinating journey around the most famous of London's huge variety of vistas, with identification of the panoramic views and relevant historical background along the way.

Jim Watson's illustration technique is traditional line and wash, but his approach is that of a curious neighbour, seeking out the scenes which give each area its individual character – while keeping a keen eye open for the quirky and unusual.

Where to Live in London

ISBN: 978-1-907339-13-4, 464pp

David Hampshire & Graeme Chesters

Essential reading for newcomers planning to live in London, containing detailed surveys of all 33 boroughs including property prices and rental costs, schools, health services, shopping, social services, crime rates, public transport, parking, leisure facilities, local taxes, places of worship and much more. Interest in living in London and investing in property in London has never been higher, both from Britons and foreigners.

£15.95

Living and Working in London

ISBN: 978-1-907339-50-9, 6th editon, 336pp

Graeme Chesters & David Hampshire

Living and Working in London, is essential reading for anyone planning to live or work in London and the most up-to-date source of practical information available about everyday life. It's guaranteed to hasten your introduction to the British way of life, and, most importantly, will save you time, trouble and money! The best-selling and most comprehensive book about living and working in London since it was first published in 1999, containing up to twice as much information as some similar books.

£14.95

London's Secrets

LONDON'S HIDDEN SECRETS

ISBN: 978-1-907339-40-0, £10.95

Graeme Chesters

A guide to London's hidden and lesser-known sights not found in standard guidebooks. Step beyond the chaos, cliches and queues of London's tourist-clogged attractions to its quirkier side.

Discover its loveliest ancient buildings, secret gardens, strangest museums, most atmospheric pubs, cutting-edge art and design, and much more: some 140 destinations in all corners of the city.

LONDON'S HIDDEN SECRETS VOL 2

ISBN: 978-1-907339-79-0, £10.95

Graeme Chesters & David Hampshire

Hot on the heels of London's Hidden Secrets comes another volume of the city's largely undiscovered sights, many of which we were unable to include in the original book. In fact, the more research we did the more treasures we found, until eventually a second volume was inevitable.

Written by two experienced London writers, LHS 2 is for both those who already know the metropolis and newcomers wishing to learn more about its hidden and unusual charms.

LONDON'S SECRET WALKS

ISBN: 978-1-907339-51-6

Graeme Chesters

London is a great city for walking – whether for exercise or simply to get from A to B. Despite the city's extensive public transport system, walking is also often the quickest and most enjoyable way to get around – at least in the centre – and it's also free and healthy!

Many attractions are off the beaten track, away from the major thoroughfares and transport hubs. This favours walking as the best way to explore them, as does the fact that London is a very interesting city with a wealth of stimulating sights in every 'nook and cranny'.

320 PAGES, PRINTED IN COLOUR

ONDON'S SECRET
PLACES

978-1-907339-92-9, £10.95

e Chesters & David Hampshire

n is one of the world's
tourist destinations
wealth of world-class
ons: amazing museums
lleries, beautiful parks
rdens, stunning palaces
and houses, and much,
more. These are covered
erous excellent tourist
and online, and need no
ction here. Not so well
are London's numerous
attractions, most of which
lected by the throngs who
d upon the tourist-clogged
ghts. What London's
laces does is seek out
s lesser-known, but no
thy, 'hidden' attractions.

LONDON'S SECRETS:
MUSEUMS & GALLERIES

ISBN: 978-1-907339-96-7, £10.95

Robbi Atilgan & David Hampshire

London is a treasure trove for
museum fans and art lovers
and one of the world's great
art and cultural centres, with
more popular museums and
galleries than any other world
city. The art scene is a lot like
the city itself – diverse, vast,
vibrant and in a constant state of
flux – a cornucopia of traditional
and cutting-edge, majestic and
mundane, world-class and run-of-
the-mill, bizarre and brilliant.

So, whether you're an art lover,
culture vulture, history buff or just
looking for something to entertain
the family during the school
holidays, you're bound to find
inspiration in London. All you need
is a comfortable pair of shoes, an
open mind – and this book!

LONDON'S SECRETS:
PARKS & GARDENS

ISBN: 978-1-907339-95-0, £10.95

Robbi Atilgan & David Hampshire

London is one the world's
greenest capital cities, with a
wealth of places where you
can relax and recharge your
batteries. Britain is renowned
for its parks and gardens, and
nowhere has such beautiful and
varied green spaces as London:
magnificent royal parks, historic
garden cemeteries, majestic
ancient forests and woodlands,
breathtaking formal country
parks, expansive commons,
charming small gardens,
beautiful garden squares and
enchanting 'secret' gardens. Not
all are secrets, of course, but
many of London's most beguiling
green spaces are known only to
insiders and locals.

320 PAGES, PRINTED IN COLOUR

A Year in London:
Two Things to Do Every Day of the Year

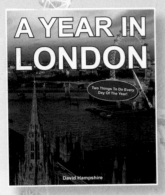

Published December 2013

ISBN: 978-1-908282-69-1, 256 pages

David Hampshire

London offers a wealth of things to do, from exuberant festivals and exciting sports events to a plethora of fascinating museums and stunning galleries, from luxury and oddball shops to first-class restaurants and historic pubs, beautiful parks and gardens to pulsating nightlife and clubs. Whatever your interests and tastes, you'll find an abundance of things to enjoy – with a copy of this book you'll never be at a loss for something to do in one of the world's greatest cities.

£12.95

London's Secrets: Bizarre & Curious

Published January 2014

ISBN: 978-1-908282-58-2, 320 pages

Graeme Chesters

London is a city with 2,000 years of history, ove which it has accumulated a wealth of odd and strange buildings, monuments, statues, street trivia and museum exhibits, to name just a few examples. This book seeks out the city's most bizarre and curious sights and tells the often fascinating story behind them, from the Highga vampire to the arrest of a dead man, a legal brothel and a former Texas embassy to Roma bikini bottoms and poetic manhole covers, fron London's hanging gardens to a restaurant whe you dine in the dark. This book is guaranteed keep you amused and fascinated for hours.

£11.95